CLICKO

CLICKO

The Wild Dancing Bushman

NEIL PARSONS

FOREWORD BY
Alexander McCall Smith

THE UNIVERSITY OF CHICAGO PRESS
CHICAGO AND LONDON

NEIL PARSONS is professor emeritus of history at the University of Botswana.

The University of Chicago Press, Chicago 60637
The University of Chicago Press, Ltd., London
Jacana Media (Pty) Ltd, Johannesburg South Africa
© Neil Parsons, 2009
First published in southern Africa by Jacana Media in 2009
All rights reserved. Published 2010
Printed in the United States of America

19 18 17 16 15 14 13 12 11 10   1 2 3 4 5

ISBN-13: 978-0-226-64741-8 (cloth)
ISBN-13: 978-0-226-64742-5 (paper)
ISBN-10: 0-226-64741-2 (cloth)
ISBN-10: 0-226-64742-0 (paper)

Library of Congress Cataloging-in-Publication Data

Parsons, Neil.
  Clicko : the wild dancing bushman / Neil Parsons ; foreword by Andrew McCall Smith.
    p. cm.
  Originally published: Auckland Park, South Africa : Jacana Media, 2009.
  Includes bibliographical references and index.
  ISBN-13: 978-0-226-64741-8 (cloth : alk. paper)
  ISBN-10: 0-226-64741-2 (cloth : alk. paper)
  ISBN-13: 978-0-226-64742-5 (pbk. : alk. paper)
  ISBN-10: 0-226-64742-0 (pbk. : alk. paper) 1. Taibosh, Franz, d. 1940. 2. Circus performers—
Biography. 3. Korana (African people)—United States—Biography. I. McCall Smith, Alexander,
1948– II. Title.
  GV1811.T33P37 2010
  791.3092—dc22
  [B]

                                                                                           2010018261

♾ The paper used in this publication meets the minimum requirements of the American National
Standard for Information Sciences—Permanence of Paper for Printed Library Materials, ANSI
Z39.48-1992.

For Annie and Semane

CONTENTS

FOREWORD

By Alexander McCall Smith

'Out of Africa there is always something new' – *ex Africa semper aliquid novi*. This hoary Latin adage is often used far too freely, but every now and then there comes an African-themed book that really is novel and thoroughly deserves this description. This fascinating study by Neil Parsons, the fruit of a long and productive scholarly engagement with southern Africa, is just such a book.

The Bushman people of southern Africa – to use the name by which they are still widely known – have long intrigued outsiders. Like many aboriginal peoples, they suffered greatly in their early contacts with colonial expansion, being progressively relegated to those inhospitable regions where people with lesser skills would simply not survive. These very skills, however, became the basis of our fascination with them – a fascination which, in some cases at least, led to a romanticising of the Bushman. As Neil Parsons points out in his introduction, even Carl Gustav Jung dreamed of a Bushman. Later in the twentieth century, Laurens van der Post's romantic and controversial writings continued to fix the Bushmen in a special place in the Western imagination.

By contrast with earlier treatments, this careful piece of historical investigation provides a vivid and well-documented account of the life of an apparent Bushman whose life followed the most extraordinary trajectory. Not only does Neil Parsons give us a glimpse into what it was to survive on the fringes of South African mining towns in the early years of the twentieth century, but he also takes us headlong into the largely vanished world of British and American vaudeville and circus. Reading these descriptions of travelling shows, one can almost smell the grease-paint – and one can distinctly smell the exploitation.

One of the most satisfying aspects of the moral progress mankind has made since the beginnings of the modern human rights movement is the recognition of the principle that it is wrong to laugh at or exhibit those who are different from ourselves. It seems astonishing to us that many people once delighted in freak shows, would find performing midgets amusing, or would in general be entertained by human oddity. Yet that happened, and there were people who lived and worked in precisely such a setting. Most of them are forgotten, their lives of no real consequence to those they amused. But sometimes we are enabled to see them as people, even if through a long historical lens, and they are restored to us as men and women of ability, humour and courage. Neil Parsons has identified such a person here, has made him live again. It is an astonishing story that illuminates the history of a talented person who represented a fragile culture to the world. It entertains and astonishes us – but it also enriches our knowledge of a hardy and resourceful people and a fascinating slice of southern African history.

INTRODUCTION

CAPE TOWN WAS A NOVEL EXPERIENCE FOR ME. I had lived and worked for many years in other African countries, but never inside South Africa. The university had advertised films that were connected somehow with Bushmen in the Kalahari, and I walked down the hill into the cavernous lecture hall where they were to be shown. Much to my surprise, the first film turned out to be an old black-and-white episode of the BBC's 'Face to face' interviews conducted by the late John Freeman, acerbic editor of the *New Statesman*. The interviewee was a jovial and relaxed Carl Jung, the great psychologist.

Once the film was over, the lights came up and a lecturer from the Carl Jung Institute in Zurich stood before us. I looked around the audience and saw a couple of hundred middle-class and middle-aged white people, nearly all wearing glasses, in woollen dresses and tweed jackets, and there were plenty of beards and bald pates. Though myself visibly white and middle-aged, I was unused to finding myself in such company in Africa. I felt as if I did not belong—as if I had stumbled into the coven of some cult, or at least into the wrong performance.

The lecturer launched into an account of one of the master's dreams, on the night of 18 December 1913. It had been a fraught year for Carl Jung, breaking away from his mentor Sigmund Freud to develop his own ideas— ideas about dreams in particular. In March and April 1913 Jung had travelled to the United States, to give a paper at the New York Academy of Sciences. In August he had gone to London to give two papers: one at the Psycho-Medical Society on 5 August, rejecting Freud's dream theory, and another—a recap of his New York paper—at the 17th International Congress of Medicine between 6 and 12 August 1913.

The break with Freud was sealed. From about October 1913, Jung felt he was alone on a journey across an ocean turning to blood. Europe was in turmoil, with industrial strife from Cracow to Cardiff and rumours of pan-continental war in the offing. May 1912 newspapers had headlined 'The coming Armageddon'. Jung's particular concern was the bellicose stance adopted by the German empire. In his Swiss refuge on the edge of Lake Zurich, not far from the German border, Jung dreamed his most significant dream that night in December 1913. 'I was with an unknown, brown-skinned man, a savage, in a lonely, rocky mountain landscape. It was before dawn; the eastern sky was already bright, and the stars were fading. Then I heard Siegfried's horn sounding over the mountains ...'

At this point Jung adds, 'and I knew that we had to kill him', later noting that 'the small, brown-skinned savage' had taken the initiative. Jung and this companion lay in wait with their rifles until Siegfried 'appeared high up on the crest of the mountain', the rays of the rising sun behind him. The great warrior was furiously driving a chariot—a sled made of dead men's bones—down the mountainside. Together Jung and 'the small, brown-skinned savage' fired their guns at Siegfried, who plunged to his death on the crags below. Fresh rain then fell, wiping out all traces of the assassination.

The resplendent Wagnerian figure of Siegfried, no doubt with shining breastplate and winged helmet, was easy enough to explain as a symbol of the aggressive Germanism that Jung realized he must kill within himself. Siegfried was drawn from the 'amplificatory material' of culture—myth and legend, art and literature. He could also have been the father figure whom Jung had just killed off—Freud.

'The small, brown-skinned savage' was more of a problem. Was he drawn from cultural symbolism or from personal experience? On reflection, Jung thought not. Psychoanalysis suggested 'infantile or other early or primitive mental and emotional processes' lying deep within the unconscious mind. Jung concluded that the small brown man was 'an embodiment of the primitive shadow' of a common human ancestry, an archetype surfacing from the collective unconscious memory of a primeval past thousands and thousands of years before.

Jung's voyage of discovery continued after the First World War with travels in North Africa, North America and East Africa, where he experienced key moments of self-realization in contact with 'primitive' peoples. But he never found anyone like his small brown man.[1]

Perhaps, the Zurich lecturer in Cape Town suggested, the small brown man—the living shadow of our primitive ancestor—had been found later in southern Africa by Laurens van der Post. (The lecturer now wanted to show us a film about Bushmen in the Kalahari.) Sitting in that lecture hall, I held my breath. I wanted to blurt out, 'But I know who the small brown man was!' Sampson-like, I would pull down the whole Jungian edifice—by exploding the ultimate archetype:

Jung was in London in August 1913 and probably passed through Paris thereafter. Likewise a small brown man from South Africa, a Bushman dancer called Franz Taibosh, who first appeared in London music halls in June, attracting attention in academic circles. Letters about Taibosh by the Cambridge anthropologist W.L.H. Duckworth were published in *The Times* newspaper in October and November 1913—at the same time as Taibosh was appearing in a Paris circus. Duckworth had been present and had given a paper at the same London conference as Jung in August.

Surely Jung could have heard or read about Taibosh and his demonstrations of simulated hunting, even if Jung—as we all do after reading Sunday newspapers—had deleted this item from conscious memory, only to dredge it up some months later in a dream.

But I could not speak: my heart was beating too fast and I hesitated and lost the right moment. I could now see in my mind's eye, not astonishment on the faces turned towards me, but bemusement as I stumbled through an explanation. The lecturer would have mercifully cut me short, telling me to come and see him afterwards. So I kept the drama in my skull to myself. Needing fresh air, I got up and left the hall. Later a member of the audience asked me why I had walked out so abruptly. Was it a protest, or had I felt ill? I found it difficult to explain.

A few months later, I took the overnight train from Kimberley to Cape Town and booked myself into a second-class sleeping compartment. My fellow passengers were five men who were self-identified as Coloured (people of colour including Khoe and San), black (Bantu-speaking African), and white (of European ancestry).[2] The middle-aged white Afrikaner disappeared after tipping the ticket inspector to find him a private couchette. A black youth, rather naïve, I mentally dubbed the Mother's Boy. He told us that he had spent virtually his whole life closeted inside an affluent Soweto cantonment. Two of the Coloured men were tall and chubby, possibly schoolteachers or small businessmen, with bellies beginning to burst out of cheap three-piece suits. The third Coloured man was very short and slight and rather wizened, but evidently not more than thirty-five years old.

The short man sat on the edge of his bunk and prattled on and on, in lilting Cape Afrikaans, to the continual amusement of all except the Mother's

Boy and myself who could not follow what he was saying. He occasionally turned to the two of us, and translated his jokes and stories into an English touched with the same singsong cadences.

He told us that he was on his way home to Cape Town, after three or four years in the notorious Barberton jail of the eastern Transvaal. He had been jailed for smashing shop windows when drunk, and regretted that he had not given the magistrate a political excuse for doing so—as that would have got him released two years earlier under the amnesty for political crimes. Now, he was simply glad to be going home. Today was the first time in years that he had not been kicked around and continually disparaged as a 'stupid Bushman'.

He was obviously a man of intelligence and sensitivity, roughened but not defeated by the prison experience: a wounded man who found consolation in spontaneous humour. For the rest of the evening he kept us amused with a stream of jokes and comments on the pretentiousness of the New South Africa, shouted above the rattle of the train and punctuated by sips from a bottle of brandy—about blacks who thought they were whites, whites who pretended they were blacks, and Coloureds who were caught between. After a few hours of sleep, the commentary and the drinking resumed as the train slid and wound its way down from the escarpment mountains on to the plains of the Western Cape. I cannot recall now what he talked about; it was certainly of no great moment. But as I looked at this short brown man in the light of dawn, I knew that I had met someone like Franz Taibosh.

A note on the term 'Bushman'

Franz Taibosh fitted the Western stereotype of a Southern African Bushman in being short and brown-skinned, with a muscular body and wrinkled face. The word Bushman is actually extremely vague but has long been applied to people speaking Khoe and San languages whose recent ancestors lived by hunting and gathering. The English appear to have picked up the word Bushman (Bosman, Bosjeman, etc.) from Dutch people in South Africa.[3] The word is not intrinsically insulting, but it can become so—like the words peasant and pagan for a country-person (from the French 'paysan'), boor meaning small farmer in Dutch, heathen (i.e. heath people), and yokel being the name of a green woodpecker. Today, on the contrary, identity as Bushmen has been re-adopted as a badge of pride by some Khoe and San people in Namibia.

Most Bushmen in Angola and northern Namibia speak Northern San languages, such as !Kung or Ju/'hoansi. Most Bushmen in Botswana and central Namibia speak Khoe languages, such as G/wi and Nharo. Bushmen within the present borders of the Republic of South Africa, such as the !Ko and Xam, used to speak Southern San languages. (The word Khoe means a person in Khoe languages; the word 'San' being given by Khoe-speakers to other people. Southern San people actually use the terms !Ui or Taa to refer to themselves as a person.)

One or two thousand years ago some Khoe-speakers migrated southwards from the Kalahari, herding sheep and cattle as far as the Cape of Good Hope. They called themselves Khoekhoe (i.e. super-Khoe) to distinguish themselves from surrounding Southern San people. Early Dutch settlers gave Khoekhoe the insulting epithet of 'Hottentots', probably meaning stutterers. Franz Taibosh's father was descended from the Korana clans of these Khoekhoe, but his mother was quite likely of San ancestry.

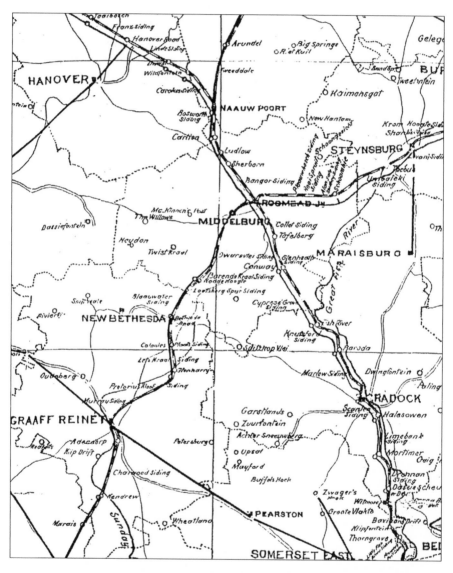

Middelburg district, Cape Colony, c.1902. Heydon and The Willows are to the west of Middelburg town, Collett Siding and Tafelberg to the south-east; Taaibosch and Franz Siding are north of Hanover. (British War Office map of Cape Colony)

1

GROWING UP IN THE SNOW MOUNTAINS

FRANZ TAIBOSH WAS IN FACT KORANA, not Bushman (San), by paternal ancestry. The clicking language spoken by him has been identified as Korana by, for instance, the word *koo-rang*. It was applied by Franz to a pretty young woman in Paris in 1913, and means a girl ('diminutive-feminine singular').[1]

Franz's Korana ancestral identity is confirmed by the notes on the back of a 1931 museum photograph of him: 'He ... is said to be a direct descendant of a tribal king.' This establishes that Franz Taibosh (Taaibosch) was a descendant of Matsatedi Taaibosch, who succeeded his brother as leader of the Korana group of Khoekhoe around the Orange and Vaal rivers in the middle of the eighteenth century. (*Taaibosch* or *taibos* is Dutch-Afrikaans for a 'tough bush' found near rivers.) Matsatedi Taaibosch and his brother were themselves the direct descendants of the Korana clan's founder, a man named !Kora or Gora who had resided in the area of later Cape Town in the early part of the seventeenth century.[2]

Prominent members of the Taaibosch family, like a son and a grandson giving evidence to colonial commissions in 1837 and 1869, prided themselves that 'they could with tolerable correctness trace the line of [their] ancestors to that remote period when they held possession of the country about Cape Town'.[3] !Kora or Gora, recorded in English written documents as 'Corey', was kidnapped from Table Bay in 1613 by an English sea captain named Gabriel Towerson, who took him to England to train as a *comprador* or trading agent for the English East India Company. Living in the London house of Sir Thomas Smythe, governor of both the East India Company and of one of the Virginia companies, 'Corey' pined for home.

On his return to the Cape in June 1614, Corey 'threw away all his Clothes, his Linnen, with all his Covering, and got his sheeps skins upon his back [again]'. A year later, English sailors in Table Bay found him settled with his followers in a village of a hundred houses on the Liesbeek River, trading in livestock with visiting ships. But Corey now knew the true value of European goods, and drove increasingly hard bargains. In the words of a Welsh visitor of 1627, on the people of Table Bay: 'They hate the dutchmen since they hanged one of the blackes called Cary who was in England & upon refusall of fresh victuals they put him to death.'[4]

By 1658, settlers of the Dutch East India Company—'unjust and often cruel to them, thus provoking reprisals'—had taken over the pastures of the Liesbeek valley from the original Korana (recorded in documents as Gorachoqua). The Korana retreated to the hills across the plains—after they had been expelled by the Dutch.

The Korana trekked hundreds of kilometres north with their sheep and cattle in two major groupings. The Links (or Left-hand) Korana migrated north-west up the Atlantic coast as far as the Orange River. The Great (or Right-hand) Korana under Corey's grandson Eiyakomo migrated north-east to the Camdeboo plains, south of the Sneeubergen (Snow Mountains). Camdeboo was a local Khoekhoe (Inqua) word for a 'green pool in a river' with fat hippos ready for the taking.[7] Eiyakomo was subsequently killed hunting elephants, and was succeeded as chief of the Great Korana by his son !Kunansoop. Dutch hunters followed the Great Korana, and !Kunansoop abandoned the Camdeboo to them sometime before 1760. He led his people again northwards to rejoin the Links Korana on the Orange River.[5]

On the Orange River !Kunansoop faced the aggressive competition of King Tau (the Lion) of the Rolong clan of the Tswana, who murdered !Kunansoop after tricking him into unarmed negotiations. The Korana chose Eiyakomo's younger son Matsatedi Taaibosch to be their chief, and used their poisoned arrows against the spears and battle-axes of the Rolong. Tau was killed, and lost his capital, known as Taung, to Matsatedi Taaibosch.[6]

The Korana under Matsatedi Taaibosch dominated the Orange River valley for the last half of the eighteenth century. The nation was organized in numerous clans: Bag People, Black Chins, Cats, Mud People, Narrow-Cheeks, Reds, Seacows, Scorpions, Side People, Sorcerers, Springboks. There was extensive intermarriage with local San women, and with Tswana men and women. Trade with the Boers of the Cape in ivory, cattle and furs brought in firearms and gunpowder, horses, wagons, clothing and coffee— and also attracted 'rogues, rebels and runaways'. Oorlam people of mixed Khoekhoe and Dutch ancestry began to raid San Bushmen and Korana for cattle and child slaves to supply to the farms of their Boer relatives in the south. There was also a renegade Prussian sailor, Jan Blüm (Bloem), who fled from the Cape and married into the Springbok clan of the Korana. He died in 1798, but his sons continued to lead Springbok-Korana bandits who raided as far south as the spring named Bloemfontein after them.[7]

By 1785 there were so many Boers in the Camdeboo that a Dutch *landdrost* (magistrate) was posted at a spot thereafter known as Graaff-Reinet. However, the local San Bushmen of the Sneeubergen, the Sun'ei (known to the Dutch as 'Chinese' Bushmen on account of their narrow eyes), fiercely resisted Boer encroachment during the 1770s–1790s. Boer men and their Khoekhoe servants were organized into mounted troops known as commandos, which radically depleted Sun'ei numbers by genocidal raiding. Adult men were systematically killed as vermin, while captured women and children were given to the Boer settlers and to their Khoekhoe (Inqua and Korana) servants.

For the first half of the nineteenth century, the South African interior can be described as a whirling cockpit of bandits and settlers, mounted on horses and wielding firearms. Springbok-Korana horsemen under the Bloem brothers on the highveld 'rounded up the cattle when they were at pasture, killing the herdsmen and keeping any pursuers at bay with their guns ... [or] they were bolder still, and entered a village just before sunrise, opened the kraals, and drove the animals away under the very eyes of their astonished and terrified owners. But these attacks were not conducted without risk to themselves, for their numbers were few and their discipline poor.'

Korana brigandage was effectively subdued by a combination of conquest by King Moshoeshoe of Lesotho, Boer trekkers and British Wesleyan Methodist missionaries. Some Taaibosch-Korana from Taung were persuaded by the Wesleyans to settle on the Lesotho frontier. Gert Taaibosch, a famous horseman and warrior, made common cause with incoming Boer settlers in 1840–1, and was eventually killed in battle with Moshoeshoe in 1853.[8] By the early 1850s, Boer settlers in the interior came together in republics— the Transvaal (South African Republic) and Orange Free State (around Bloemfontein)—which were embroiled in endemic warfare with their African neighbours.[9]

The main body of Taaibosch-Korana moved from Taung to settle at nearby Mamusa on the Harts River on the Transvaal border. Matsatedi Taaibosch's grandson David Massouw Taaibosch became their chief, until he was killed and his people were dispersed by Transvaal Boers in December 1884. Mamusa was in future marked on maps under the name of Schweizer-

Reneke. Henceforward the Korana were a forgotten people who had apparently disappeared from history. But his remarks about an ancestor, recorded in 1931, show that Franz Taibosh knew his heritage. It is equally likely, though, that Franz was descended from those Korana left behind in the Camdeboo or the Sneeubergen during the eighteenth century, in Boer service, rather than from those Korana who ranged north over the highveld.[10]

◎

In 1937 Frances Cook Sullivan, whose family had taken in Franz Taibosh, told a US district court that his earliest memories were of working for 'English planters in South Africa', the last of whom was named Roberts, who also employed his three brothers. Evelyn Cook and her daughter Barbara Cook later added that Roberts was Christian Roberts (or Roberts Christian) and that his farm was on the road to Kimberley or Johannesburg. The Taibosh family worked for him herding sheep, while Franz himself worked as a household servant and as a post-rider.[11]

It is now clear that Christiaan Willem Roberts, an Afrikaner of British ancestry, was sole tenant from 1899 through 1907 on one of the farms around Heydon Hill in the Middelburg district of the Cape Colony, on the south side of the road from Richmond to Middelburg. Heydon Hill lay on the most northerly wagon pass through the Sneeubergen, through which the headwaters of the Little Seacow River flowed. The pass carried an old wagon road that ran from Graaff-Reinet in the Camdeboo towards Kimberley, or to Johannesburg via Bloemfontein.

The small hill-farm devoted to sheep-raising leased by Christiaan Willem Roberts at Heydon from 1899 was almost certainly Boschman's Hoek (Bushman's Glen or Bend), which was actually owned by an Englishman called John Herbert Staples. Staples was a land magnate who owned many other farms in the vicinity. Franz Taibosh and his family probably came to Willem Roberts with the farm tenancy. Alternatively, they came as personal retainers with Roberts from the Bethesda district, a few days' walk to the south, where Roberts was born.

Heydon Kop (Heydon Hill) had first appeared on a map in 1805, as the northernmost point of the Cape Colony surveyed by British army engineers. No doubt an engineer-surveyor was nostalgic for one of the villages in England named Heydon. Heydon Kop stood next to the pass of the Little Seacow River known as Cephanje's Poort—one of four possible wagon routes through the Sneeubergen.

The first white farm at Cephanje's Poort was a colonial 'loan place'—a farm area around a watering point ceded free of charge by the Dutch East India Company to a Boer trekker in 1772. But it could not be occupied until the end of the wars between Boers and Bushmen around 1800, when a small farmhouse made of rocks and clay was built for summer occupation. 'Wild' Bushmen were persuaded to stop raiding farms by gifts of meat and beads, and were induced to join other Khoekhoe and San employees herding Boer sheep and cattle.[12]

Franz Taibosh was born most probably around the later 1860s or early 1870s. A full-body photograph taken in 1912 suggests a man in his thirties or forties. At the time of his death in 1940 he looked to be in his seventies.

The later 1860s saw bitter winter chills in the Sneeubergen. In mid-1869, snowstorms buried flocks of sheep: shepherds walked through the mountains looking for telltale wisps of steamy breath rising from the snowdrifts. Young Franz must have remembered the great drought of 1877–8, when the hippo pools were parched dry, after less than one inch of rain. Larks, twittering high above the land, fell dead from the sky.[13]

In 1959 Evelyn Cook recalled that Franz had 'told us his father had also been a shepherd, but he didn't recall his mother'. Franz's death certificate listed his father's name as Hans Taibosh, while his mother's name was unknown. We know that he had at least three brothers, and that one of his older brothers was also named Hans. We may speculate that Franz's mother died not long after giving birth to him, and that she was of San ancestry—which would account for Franz's short and slight stature.

As a small child, Franz joined his father and three brothers herding sheep. But he was subsequently chosen to be a household servant and gardener ('He worked as a houseboy ... he knew how to dust, wash dishes, prepare vegetables, and work in a garden'). In later years he showed particular delight and skill in growing roses. As the diminutive 'runt' of his family, no doubt Franz was petted one moment and bullied the next—which may help to account for his fatalistic acceptance of life's vagaries, and his self-defence of becoming a jester and entertainer. Franz's cavorting and good humour help to explain the 'mascot' status he developed in later years with white patrons.

The 1870s and 1880s saw an industrial and farming revolution in the interior of South Africa. Diamond mines opened at Kimberley, followed by gold mines around Johannesburg. The wagon routes into the interior were progressively replaced by railway lines. African peoples lost their independence, to become a labour force under new racial controls. Mining was the magnet for people of many new ethnicities from Africa and beyond, but the dominant culture of the new capitalists was English. Capitalized English farmers came to settle among the Boer or Afrikaner farmers of the north-eastern parts of the Cape Colony, as farms rose in value with the opening by the railways of new urban-industrial markets for farm produce.

Around 1878–9, the Boschman's Hoek farm was acquired by an English land speculator called James Collett. Within a few years Collett in turn sold Boschman's Hoek as well as the neighbouring Cephanje's Poort to John Herbert Staples, and another Heydon farm, Klein Cephanje's Poort, to Maurice James Hall, a Cambridge graduate originally from Nottinghamshire, who renamed his farm The Willows. (Like his friend Herbert Rhodes, Cecil Rhodes's ne'er-do-well older brother, Hall had failed to strike it lucky in diamonds or gold.)

Hall turned The Willows into a conspicuous centre of progressive agriculture. He drained the hippo pool in the Little Seacow River on his farm, and controlled the clover (poisonous to sheep) around it by stocking the area with ostriches—it was boom time for ostrich feathers exported overseas to adorn fashionable ladies' hats. Hall planted hundreds of willow and poplar trees as windbreaks around the house and garden—a splash of green in the otherwise perennially brown landscape. He scorned the farming practices of his Boer neighbours, who only raised sheep and cultivated a few fruit trees, by bringing in four hundred European shorthorn cattle. By 1887 Hall had enough capital to invest in a cream separator for his cows' milk, a mechanical mower that could be hitched to oxen, steel wire fencing to protect land and livestock against flocks of grazing springbok and predatory jackals, and the first farm windmill (a wooden one, for pumping underground water) seen in the district. During the 1890s the Halls invested in a small sanatorium, which brought in tuberculosis sufferers from Britain who could afford the fares and the fees.[14]

It was J.H. Staples who leased out the sheep runs of hilly Boschman's Hoek to Christiaan Willem Roberts between 1899 and 1907, while the Staples family remained in the valley on the main Cephanje's Poort farm. The Taibosh family would have had long experience of English farm owners, but their everyday contacts would have been with Boer farm managers and their wives. Afrikaans was the lingua franca of all farming. Franz seems never to have learnt any English as a child. The Staples and Hall families must have been the 'well respected and well to do' English planters recorded by Evelyn Cook in 1959 as being among Franz Taibosh's 'earliest memories'. On the other hand, his learning of 'Father Abraham' as he grew up, 'so they must have been religious people', could refer to a Boer family—an Old Testament kind of Christianity being implied. Franz Taibosh would have had such formative experiences long before C.W. Roberts arrived.[15]

It is possible that Franz as a boy underwent the *doro* initiation ceremony of the (Khoekhoe-speaking) Korana. Male adolescents, with their faces painted, were taught step-dancing to the trilling music of reed-pipes. But it was the mark of (Bantu-speaking) Xhosa initiation into manhood, namely circumcision of the penis, that Franz was to bear for the rest of his life.

Xhosa people had come from the Eastern Cape in considerable numbers as farm workers to the Camdeboo and Sneeubergen, after the great 'Cattle-Killing' and famine of the late 1850s. Travelling specialists went from farm to farm to hold circumcision camps for young males. Boys were painted white, ate only watery vegetables, no meat, no salt, and waited for their wound to heal—looking from a distance 'like bright white statues among the small grey bushes'. After weeks in seclusion, the boys emerged as confident young men, returning home with new clothes and new blankets—everything old had been discarded.[16]

It was by no means unusual for a Korana boy to undergo Xhosa circumcision. All farm workers' adolescent sons went to the same circumcision camp, regardless of ethnic origin. Khoekhoe and San and even white boys were initiated into Xhosa age-grades. Secret knowledge learnt by heart bound the young men together for life as age-mates. Circumcision would have given Franz Taibosh a respect among Xhosa men that would have served him well in adult years as a farm worker and later as a Kimberley resident.

A cave a mere thirty kilometres from Heydon, on Tafelberg Hall farm south of Middelburg, bears witness to such circumcision camps and to more ancient history which Franz may have been taught. The walls of the cave are covered in paintings, some old and faded, others newer and brighter, of wild animals and sheep, cattle, horses and humans. Older paintings include sheep and cattle; newer paintings of men on horses are said to be of Korana. Men in the classic 'aggressive-possessive' posture of bent arms on hips suggest Boer invaders. The walls are also covered with an extraordinary number of finger-mark dots in parallel lines and in different colours. White dots, found together with circles and spirals and stripes, are typical of those made by circumcision initiates.[17]

If Franz was born around 1870, we may calculate that he was circumcised in the 1880s. There was also another event around this time that impressed Franz, as reported by the Johannesburg *Star* newspaper in October 1913: his memory of the arrival of British troops 'out of the sea'. The Warren expedition of 1884–5 was fresh out from England to disarm the Boer 'filibusters' of Stellaland. It boasted the latest equipment, including observation balloons, and it was the first time that British forces in Africa wore khaki uniforms: significantly there is no mention of red coats in the 1913 source. Young Franz could have seen General Warren himself in December 1884, meeting with local white farmers to reassure them about his military intentions. Most likely it was at The Willows, on the main road between Richmond and Middelburg, which was owned by the leading English farmer in the district.[18]

The 1890s were remembered in the Middelburg district as years of good rainfall, starting with twenty inches (twice the norm) in 1891, and covering the Karoo with greenery and wild flowers.[19] For Franz, no doubt the big event was the arrival of Christiaan Willem Roberts at Boschman's Hoek at the end of the decade. He was a relatively young man, born in December 1872 in the neighbouring Bethesda (Nieu-Bethesda) district, on the south side of the Sneeubergen. He was descended from one of the three or four Robertses from England and Scotland among 1820s immigrants to the Eastern Cape. His first names suggest Afrikaans maternal ancestry, and he himself married an Afrikaner, Maria Dorothea Viljoen. She was from a large clan of Viljoens that could be traced back to old Jan Viljoen, who lived in defiant poverty in the Sneeubergen at the beginning of the nineteenth century. Franz Taibosh may have thought of Willem Roberts as an Englishman, but it is likely that Roberts confined himself to speaking Afrikaans.

The 1899 Cape Voters' List (limited to adult males with sufficient property) records Willem Roberts (Farmer) as one of five householders giving a Heydon residential address: the other four being John Herbert Staples (Farmer) and Abraham Diedrik Koekemoer, Peter Gabriel Pretorius and Frederick Vrij (Agriculturalists). Cephanje's Poort was a valley bottom farm, suitable for irrigation and subdivision among the three Boer 'agriculturalists'. Willem Roberts was almost certainly the tenant of Boschman's Hoek, on a ten-year lease, running sheep and renting the farm and farmhouse from Staples.[20]

When the Anglo-Boer War broke out in 1899, most white farmers in this part of the Cape Colony, being of Afrikaner descent, sympathized with the

Boer republics. Willem Roberts joined the army of the Orange Free State together with his Viljoen in-laws. Thereby they were regarded as rebels in the Cape Colony, where they had their farms and had left their families and servants. On the other hand, eighteen-year-old Charlie Hall, son of Maurice Hall at The Willows, opted for 'weeks of boredom punctuated by intense periods of fear' with a British column, culminating in sentry duty with the Middelburg town guard.

After the collapse of the Boer republics, the guerrilla phase of the war ensued. Boer general Kritzinger led his commando to the Camdeboo and back, aided by local Boer farmers lighting fires 'on every hill [to give] warning of every British movement'. In what has been described as a 'kaleidoscopic field of operations', British columns were harassed into mid-1902 around the Sneeubergen and other escarpment mountains by Messrs Kritzinger, W.D. Fouché, Gideon Scheepers and Wynand Malan—despite later First World War heroes Douglas Haig and John French taking charge of British troops based at Middelburg.

There were two skirmishes around Heydon. The first was in August 1901 when D. Smit, escaping northwards from Nieu-Bethesda, joined one Lotter and C.J. Botha at The Willows, where they were intercepted by a British detachment under B. Doran. The second skirmish was on 3 May 1902, when Wynand Malan and W.D. Fouché, escaping north from a British 'game drive' across the Camdeboo, attacked British troops billeted at The Willows.

A Captain Hicks was in charge of a group of men fighting for the British Army, consisting mostly of 'poor whites' who were in it mainly for the money and so inefficient that they were nick-named the DMTs (Delirium Military Tremens). When Hicks was stationed at The Willows homestead he was shot dead outside the front of the house by a Boer sharpshooter. His ghost is said to frequent the spot. Wynand Malan was captured by a famous Scottish unit, the Lovat Scouts, at the end of May 1902, just before the war ended.[21]

Franz recalled having been a post-rider during the war of 1899–1902, riding the mules that carried the mails between Middelburg and the Heydon post office, which was located on The Willows farm. Franz also said, in 1930, that he had been 'an orderly for a British officer in the Boer war'.

British troops were stationed on the railways around Middelburg. When the British army mounted its advance northwards towards the Orange Free State in late 1899, the Midland railway through the Sneeubergen was its main supply route. The farm Grootfontein, next to Middelburg, became a major depot for the Army Ordnance Department and a remount station for the Army Service Corps. The remount station housed horses bought from local horse-dealers like Abel Seligman, as well as mules brought in enormous numbers from South America—imported together with alien 'khaki weeds' in their fodder. Middelburg was also the site of a large army hospital. Registered voters at Grootfontein camp listed in 1903 included many officers of the Royal Engineers, plus musketry instructors, farriers, armourers and a lieutenant of the Royal (Navy) Fleet Artillery.

Franz Taibosh's career as an entertainer began with his dancing for British troops. His small stature also made him an obvious choice to be a jockey in horse racing. Military garrisons, full of troops with money to spend, attracted crowds of hangers-on, young men and boys as well as hawkers and entertainers. Photographs taken during the siege of Mafeking show British troops entertaining each other with a blackface minstrel show. The minstrels grin as a local African boy, aged about twelve, joins them on stage to do a vigorous dance. Such fraternization with Africans was frowned upon in white settler circles. In the words of an editorial in *The Friend* (Bloemfontein), dated 9 March 1903: 'Now that the war is over, and the necessity for officers and privates of the British Army chumming with Negroes and—I regret to say—with Negresses, has passed, it is time for us to place the native back to the status he was placed in before the war.'[22]

Willem Roberts and his Viljoen brothers-in-law were captured by the British. They did not return home until after the end of the war, but by 1903 were registered on the Cape Voters' Roll for Heydon. Willem Roberts and Abraham Diedrik Koekemoer were registered as sole tenants at Heydon (i.e. the two Staples farms of Cephanje's Poort and Boschman's Hoek), with Matheous Roberts (presumably a relative) as a salaried employee of Edwin Staples at next-door Sunnydell farm; and four Viljoens as joint tenants further away at Dwaarsvley farm. Willem Roberts continued to be registered as householder, sole tenant and voter at Heydon in 1905, 1907 and 1909. In 1908 Cephanje's Poort and Boschman's Hoek were subdivided and sold off to Phillip Segall and Leopold Lurie, both of them Jewish traders from Middelburg.[23]

Severe drought set in after 1902–3: an average three inches less than the annual norm of ten inches on the south side of the Sneeubergen. The north side was probably even drier. It was a time of depression among white farmers, undercut by African peasant production of meat and grain or by cheap bulk imports from overseas. The only white farmers who stood to benefit were those who lived off share-cropping with African peasant tenants, and the few better-capitalized white farmers investing in fencing and dams and earthworks, and in the mechanization of pumping, planting, harvesting, and processing and transport of crops. Agricultural depression was blamed for 'religious mania' among Boers in the Graaff-Reinet and Middelburg districts during 1911. White men and women calling themselves Weder Doopers (The re-baptized), with long hair and flowing white robes, prophesied in 'tongues' and were baptized by total immersion by a prophet called Schoeman. Other people pelted them with eggs, but they were happy to be martyrs.[24]

According to his son, interviewed in the 1990s, Willem Roberts found sheep farming unprofitable, and looked around for other ways to make a living. He and his family moved from Heydon to Middelburg town. By 1910 the town boasted a population of 6,137 (3,373 being not white). Willem Roberts and one of his wife's Viljoen brothers, who was a blacksmith, made their living instead as wandering mechanics installing and maintaining new-fangled metal (rather than wooden) windmills on farms. The Willows farm at Heydon had been a pioneer in installing windmills. After metal windmills from the US began to be manufactured locally, Middelburg became known as the windmill capital of South Africa.[25]

We cannot know for sure when houseboy-gardener Franz Taibosh left the employ of Willem Roberts. Sources are contradictory. Franz's later manager claimed that he had 'captured' the Bushman in the Kalahari in or about 1907. Barbara Cook believed Franz was first spotted by his future manager in a troupe of dancers entertaining British troops. Frances Cook Sullivan's legal deposition in 1937 stated that 'From Roberts this Bushman went to work in Kimberly [*sic*] and it was there he was found by a captain of the British army at about the time the Boer War ended.' Probably the most reliable source, a *Rand Daily Mail* report of 1913, suggests that Franz was recruited from a farmer visiting Kimberley around the beginning of 1912.

The story about capture in the Kalahari is obvious nonsense, though the date around 1907 is suggestive of the approximate date that the Roberts family left Boschman's Hoek for Middelburg. Barbara Cook supports the idea of Franz moving into part-time entertainment for troops at the nearby Grootfontein camp, making a little money for Willem Roberts. Grootfontein's South African Garrison Institute embraced blacksmithing, laundries, stores and canteens, but was closed as a military camp in 1909–10. (It was re-opened two years later as a Cape provincial agricultural college.)[26]

The 1913 newspaper supports the idea that Franz Taibosh probably remained in Willem Roberts's employ until early 1912, accompanying Roberts on his travels. There is no suggestion in any source that their relationship was anything but good. Indeed this was probably the period in which Franz honed his skills as a humorous sidekick across barriers of caste, class and race, with a fluent stream of jokes and japes in Afrikaans.

We do not know enough about exactly how Franz Taibosch danced, but all observers agreed that he danced with considerable panache and incredible energy. He combined elements of traditional dance with fashionable steps performed to gramophone music. The early years of industrialization in South Africa resulted in the growth of different ethnic styles of dancing through Sunday competitions between men on the Kimberley and Witwatersrand mines. Franz appears to have developed his own dancing style out of Korana or Khoekhoe traditions.

Korana or Khoekhoe dancing was traditionally accompanied by men blowing reed-flutes and women clapping their hands—sometimes amplified by clacking pieces of hinged wood. The Korana also had a form of drum, typically a wooden milk-jug covered by a skin, played by women accompanying male dancers. The Portuguese voyager Vasco da Gama was greeted by a Khoekhoe pipe-band of four or five players when he landed near Mossel Bay in 1497; and pipe-bands of thirty or more players were recorded. The male players stood in a circle, each man shuffling sideways as he tooted his note at a different pitch, surrounded by a larger circle of women rhythmically clapping. Miniature dramas, usually about hunting of wild animals or the 'sex play' of courtship between man and woman, were played out by individual men inside the circle. The German anthropologist Schultze added in 1907:

> The dance movements of the men consist of small jumps, close to the ground, both legs being bent weakly at the knees, and the feet placed one before the other. The dancer moves forwards and backwards in this manner, bent forward, his head bowed over his chest, and his lips on the reed. The women 'chassez' forward with small, and often most graceful steps, swaying about, protruding their posteriors, and rolling their buttocks from the haunches, clapping their hands loudly before their faces, while they sing with an expression of the greatest excitement. There is no fixed number of dancers.

The major exotic influences on Korana music by 1900 were the cadences of mission church music and the 'breathing' and 'trilling' of the portable concertina (invented in England in 1829), which was also influential in Boer trekker and North American cowboy music. A mouth organ or harmonica might substitute for a concertina.

The other major influence on Franz's solo dancing was undoubtedly American in origin. Jim Crow or 'coon' dancing was a jig or frolic: hopping up and down and turning round in a confined space, with much heeling and toeing and slapping of hands on the thighs. This dancing tradition had taken hold among Coloured people at the Cape after the 1862 tour of the Christy Minstrels from America. It was reinforced by the amateur blackface efforts of visiting British soldiers and sailors (some of them being of West African or Caribbean origin), and by the cakewalking of Orpheus McAdoo's Virginia Jubilee Singers touring South Africa in the 1890s—which were incorporated into the annual Coloured 'coon' New Year carnival at Cape Town during the twentieth century.

Franz was a great mimic with facial expressions to match, and was able to switch from step-dancing and cakewalk to wild ragtime, from stamping with jangling metal rings round his ankles to dancing in heavy wooden clogs, and from the imitation of wild animals being hunted to parody of the walk and manners of some prominent person. Many Southern San dances were based on parody of wild animals or imaginary monsters: imitating frogs, bees, birds and baboons. Southern San dancing was typically accompanied by the rhythm of rattles, cutely called 'Bushman bells', consisting of strings of rattling seedpods tied round the upper arm or shoulder, or round ankles. Franz somersaulted and cavorted gymnastically as he sped around the dancing arena, letting out ungodly 'wild' yells of incredible pitch, and he could keep on dancing for hours at a stretch.

Franz may have indulged in stimulants: early nineteenth-century Korana bandits had taken a hallucinogenic herb to help them fight, and Franz certainly enjoyed alcohol and probably smoked cannabis (*dagga*) as well as tobacco when he could. But he was genuinely urged on by audience participation, seemingly as happy to accept derisive laughs and shouts as to accept genuine applause. Persistent dancing may also on occasion have put him in contact with a spirit world—as dancing did for Northern San trance-dancers of the Kalahari, and for Siberian and Native American shamans, Christian Shakers or whirling Sufi. The rhythmic encouragement of women chanting and clapping round a night-time fire, encouraging San trance-dancers, may be compared with the intoxicating applause of a theatre audience sitting in darkness beyond the lights. Some Northern San (Ju/'hoansi) men and women in the Kalahari

Bosjemans performing in London, 1847. (Prof. Bernth Lindfors)

dance for hours till the *n/um* ('boiling energy') in their stomachs rose painfully up the spine, during a great sweat, to explode in their brains—reaching the state of trance known as *!kia*.[27] But there is no evidence that Franz Taibosh ever pretended to be a shaman or healer for other people.

Franz's theatrical performances can be seen as part of a long-standing tradition that Bernth Lindfors has called 'ethnological show business'.[28] European fascination with the 'Hottentots' and 'Bushmen' of Southern Africa resulted in the semi-nude exhibition of a Khoekhoe woman named Sara (Saartje) Baartman for private viewing in London and Paris in 1810–16. A 'genuine' live Bushman was exhibited at a holiday fair in Elberfeld, Germany, in 1826. In England, a boy aged about 13 and a girl aged about 6, from the Limpopo in the northern Transvaal, were displayed with audience approval between 1845 and 1847, and appear then to have been returned home. They were followed by a competing exhibition known as the Bosjemans, two men and two women and a baby from the Cape, who were first shown in Liverpool in November 1846. The Bosjemans were regarded with almost universal opprobrium. *The Times* called them a 'stunted family of African dwarfs, in appearance little above the monkey tribe … continually crouching, warming themselves by the fire, chattering or growling, smoking &c. They are sullen, silent, and savage.' (The Bosjemans might have seen their tormentors in a similar light.)

Two of Farini's Earthmen. (Prof. Bernth Lindfors)

The Bosjemans travelled about Britain, France and Ireland for nine years, displaying 'horrid screeches' and 'marvellous imitation of the pursuit of the lion'. Their subsequent fate is unknown, but adverse public reaction to them accounts for the next Khoesan performers, imported to England from the Limpopo in 1852, being promoted as admirable 'Earthmen' rather than as despised Bushmen. Flora, aged about 16, and Martinus, aged about 14, were bright and affectionate, and were presented before Queen Victoria and Prince Albert for royal endorsement.[29]

Martinus died a few years later, and Flora became one of P.T. Barnum's Little People at New York's American Museum in 1860, advertised as a 'missing link' between apes and people, before returning to England and dying there in 1864. Barnum recruited six more 'Earthmen' in 1884–5 from Guillermo A. Farini (William Hunt, 1839–1929), who had obtained them indirectly from Lehututu in the Kalahari Desert of Botswana in 1883–4. (Farini himself tried recruiting more from Lehututu in 1885, but returned with only one or two after the rest escaped on the road to Cape Town.) Farini's Earthmen were taken to France in 1886 to appear at the Folies Bergère, and passed on to Germany in early 1887. Their fate also remains unknown.

Pejorative and mendacious images of Bushmen as vagabonds and vermin lived on in the West. Sir Godfrey Lagden's *The Native Races of the Empire* (1924) referred to them as 'very low down on the social scale ... polygamists and cannibals ... almost without intelligence'.[30]

2

RECRUITED AT KIMBERLEY

AFTER FRANZ TAIBOSH first appeared in England as the Wild Dancing Bushman, the question of his origins was addressed by Kimberley and Witwatersrand newspapers. To quote the *Rand Daily Mail* of 6 October 1913:

HOW HE CAME TO KIMBERLEY

Here is the story of the Kimberley 'dancing Bushman'. About eighteen months ago a farmer, who had been on a visit to the Kalahari desert, came into Kimberley with a Bushman and put up at a certain hotel. The antics of the Bushman were often a source of amusement to those stopping at the hotel. The boy could dance; and during his executions he executed some weird steps, accompanied with uncanny noises produced by the jangling of iron and copper rings which he wore on his arms. He was of small stature and of a bronze yellow colour, but fairly well proportioned. His features were repulsive, and during the dancing he made startling grimaces.

Now the hotel-keeper had staying with him a brother who had been for some years connected with Leonard Rayne's dramatic company, and who had also toured South Africa with his own sketch company. The actor saw the possibility of a new and original 'turn' in the Bushman, so he persuaded his brother to employ the boy at the hotel stables for a while. The actor then proceeded to complete his engagements, after which he disbanded his company and returned to Kimberley.[1]

The supposition that he came from the Kalahari can be ignored, but the suggestion that Franz Taibosh arrived in Kimberley around (or before) the beginning of 1912 can be pursued, once the hotelier and his actor brother are identified. The hotelier in question, though maybe more a clerk than a manager, must be Paddy Hepston, who is to feature so heavily in the story of Franz Taibosh over the next few years. Paddy had a vaudeville-theatre performer brother, variously calling himself Ronald Steyne and Randolph Epsteyne. Ronald or Randolph was a member of the Merry Mascots concert party that toured South Africa. The Merry Mascots appeared on the Kimberley stage for the fourth time at the beginning of July 1911, and for their fifth and penultimate season in February 1912. Franz Taibosh could have been spotted by the Hepston brothers on either occasion.

When did Christiaan Willem Roberts bring Franz Taibosh to Kimberley? It could have been as early as June 1911, when Kimberley, in common with the rest of the British Empire, was celebrating the coronation of King George V. The celebrations were marked by Zulu war-dancing by miners, firework displays, and a demonstration by Mr Weston's flying-machine—a Bristol biplane which thrilled twenty thousand people at the racetrack. Street processions and the Big Wheel at the funfair were filmed by a Mr Savage, and were projected in mid-July at the local Theatre Royal.

The coronation fair was set up, with its mechanical rides and sideshows and its Ferris wheel, in Beaconsfield market square on the south-eastern side of the city. The funfair was so successful that the municipality agreed to buy it, to be opened to the public each Wednesday and Saturday afternoon. This would have been the sort of opportunity that could have been exploited by the exhibition of a 'Wild Dancing Bushman'.

Roberts could have put up at any one of a number of hotels and hostelries in Beaconsfield, with Taibosh parked in the servants' quarters. In Market Square there was the Victoria Hotel, and Latooy's private boarding house and restaurant, which boasted electric light and hot baths; also in Beaconsfield were the Phoenix and Derwent hotels. Maybe it was at one of these that Paddy Hepston was working while his brother was also in town. He is not mentioned in the Kimberley press advertisements as the proprietor or manager of a major hotel, but he could well have been an assistant manager or the keeper of a minor hotel.

At this juncture, we may be forgiven for a little speculation on what Franz thought about his transfer from Willem Roberts to the Hepston brothers. Franz had been together with Willem Roberts for many years as performer, comic servant and travel companion. Now, as economic depression began to bite even harder, Roberts no doubt justified the 'sale' of his little friend as sending Franz off to a better life overseas. Did they pine for each other thereafter? Certainly in later years Franz remembered Roberts without rancour.

Christiaan Willem's grandson, who shares the same names as his grandfather but was only five when his grandfather died, has no recollection of the family ever talking about a dancing Bushman. Maybe Willem Roberts had a nagging conscience that kept him quiet. After a lifetime in the windmill business at Middelburg in the Cape, Willem Roberts went to live with his youngest son in Pretoria, where he died after an automobile accident, on 11 September 1943.[2]

The Merry Mascots were one of the Adeler & Sutton groups of singers and sketch players that had come out to South Africa from England since 1909—variously described as concert parties, 'vaudeville comedy parties' or New Pierrots. The first to come were the Musical Madcaps, led by Edwin Adeler himself—appearing on stage in evening dress for the second half of the performance, after performing in whiteface like old-fashioned Pierrots. The Madcaps were followed over the next two years by the Merry Mascots and the Smart Set Entertainers. Their shows were described as full of mirth and merriment, and their songs clean, clever and catchy. The Adeler & Sutton concert parties hit a boom time in South African popular entertainment and fashion between 1909 and 1913. Glamorous white women 'went shopping in cart-wheel hats, with long flippant quills poking out from towering bows; pencil slim skirts going down to the heels'.[3]

Press profiles tell us that Randolph Epsteyne was already in South Africa when the Merry Mascots arrived from England in October 1910. He had previously been an actor (rather than a singer) with Leonard Rayne's famous company of light but 'legitimate' players in South Africa. Epsteyne gained 'wonderful popularity' as 'one of the youngest tenors on the [South African] stage'.[4] This suggests that Randolph Epsteyne was a younger brother who had come out from Ireland to join Paddy Hepston and his wife some time before 1910, staying with them at Green Street in Kimberley when his concert party periodically hit the city.

During the week of Monday, 3 July 1911, the Merry Mascots arrived at Kimberley from Johannesburg, where they are said to have packed the Coliseum Theatre for seven weeks. Curiously, the publicity for Kimberley's Theatre Royal now referred to Randolph Epsteyne as 'Ronald Steyne' (possibly a subterfuge to escape legal or criminal action?).

THEATRE ROYAL
Proprietors: Kimberley Theatre Co. Ltd.
Lessee: E.F. PASCOT
TO – NIGHT
And Every Evening at 8

Messrs. Adeler & Sutton's Latest
and Strongest London Company.
The Famous
MERRY MASCOTS

SEVEN SELECTED ARTISTS:
Miss HARRIE FAWN,
Mr. STEVE BUCKINGHAM,
Miss EDITH THORNE,
Mr. RONALD STEYNE,
Miss DOROTHY SUTTON,
Miss MAUD WILSON,
and
Mr. CHARLES CARDLE

Merry Bright and Humorous

PRICES: Stalls, 3/-; Dress Circle, 2/-;
Family Circle, 1/6; Gallery, 1/-;
Boxes, 1/1/- and 15/-

The *Diamond Fields Advertiser* reviewed the show as 'splendid' and poured clichés and superlatives on the entertainers, starting with Steve Buckingham's rollicking songs with many 'funniosities', and ending with:

Last, but not least, Mr. Steyne, a tenor vocalist of first-rate quality, sang a generous number of well-chosen songs in a manner that left his hearers longing for still more. In 'Nirvana' he demonstrated the charm of a fine voice splendidly controlled, and he followed a most efficient rendition by an equally pleasing interpretation of the 'Aristo ["Vesti la giubba"?] from Pagliacci'. He was prevailed upon to favour the audience with still another number, for which he chose 'Garden of Roses'. He rendered that song most effectively, and at its conclusion was accorded applause in ever increased measure.

Seven months later, the *Diamond Fields Advertiser* for Monday, 12 February 1912 announced the appearance again of Adeler & Sutton's Merry Mascots, at Kimberley's Olympia Garden Theatre that night in their New Pierrot review. 'The Mascots have established a South African record in the number of towns [in which they have played] since they landed on these shores.' The only rival show in town was Willison's Circus with its Laughing Lilliputians and Wee Waratahs. Next day's paper mentioned the Merry Mascots' excellent tenor Randolph Epsteyne (no longer Ronald Steyne) as 'one of the best ballad singers in the Union'.[4]

If the *Rand Daily Mail* is correct, Paddy Hepston employed Franz as a hotel stable-hand until Paddy's brother returned for final performances at Kimberley in May 1912. It intrigued people in later years to observe how close Franz Taibosh was to horses, though he declined to ride them, and how accurately he could mimic jockeys running hell-for-leather at the races. This is no mystery when we consider that he had been a wartime 'post-rider' as well as a stable-hand, mucking out and no doubt chattering to the horses. His refusal to ride sounds as if he had been badly thrown by a horse at some time.

While he was still in Kimberley, Franz would have had plenty of opportunity to speak with people in his native Afrikaans at the hotel stables. A later newspaper source tells us that he socialized at the quarry and brickfields on the Schmidtsdrift Road, which were a short walk away at the end of Green Street, where the Hepstons lived. He made friends and drank liquor with Coloured workers there. Though Korana featured in the long list of 'native races' for whom alcohol was prohibited by Kimberley by-laws ('Hottentot, Attaqua, Cenaqua, Namaqua, Outeniqua, Bushman, Koranna, and Damara …'), it was freely available through such people as Griqua and others who were not specifically listed.

A year later, an employer of workers at the brickfields on the Schmidtsdrift Road recalled: 'The so-called Bushman is known personally to several of the Cape boys [i.e. Coloured men] who are now working for me. They said that he spake the Taal [Afrikaans] as well as they do. They, in fact, have been associated with him, and have often seen him dance on his head under certain influences.'[5]

Barbara Cook imagines that at this stage Paddy Hepston had to speak to Franz Taibosh in a persuasive manner about the idea of going overseas:

He painted a tantalizing picture of the world beyond Kimberley and the veld, enticing the little Bushman with tales of a place where the most luscious food was plentiful, beer flowed in perpetual cascade and cigars were smoked in chain … a world populated by endless 'white dollies', who would be his for the taking. It was easy to enlist the services of the naive little Bushman.

We can surely dismiss what Paddy Hepston later told a British newspaper about Franz: 'He did not know he could dance until one day, a few months before he left for Europe, he [Hepston] started a gramophone, and to his surprise the savage began doing his steps.'[6]

The Merry Mascots reappeared in Kimberley on Friday, 31 May 1912, on their fourth tour of South Africa and their sixth engagement at Kimberley, culminating in their one thousandth performance—which seems also to have been their last in South Africa. Echoing earlier publicity, Randolph Epsteyne was described as 'too well known in South Africa to need any introduction', and as one of the youngest tenors on the stage who had 'gained wonderful popularity'.[7]

On 25 July 1912, according to US court proceedings eight years later, Franz Taibosh 'was placed in the care and custody of the plaintiff [Hepston] as his servant in accordance with the legal requirements of British South Africa'. 'The agreement … wherein the plaintiff was allowed to leave British South Africa with said Bushman under the agreement that the plaintiff would return said Bushman to said country, was in writing, signed by the plaintiff, and delivered by him, but he received no copy of said agreement; therefore, is unable to produce same.'[8]

In the absence of a copy, it is not clear what form the document took. But it appears to have referred to Franz Taibosh not by his real name, but under the cognomen of 'Bushman, W.D.'—the initials standing for Wild Dancing. Under the impression that Hepston had been an army captain, Evelyn and Barbara Cook referred to Hepston's declaration before 'the military authorities' that Franz Taibosh was his 'batman'. The declaration is more likely to have been before a magistrate in terms of the Masters and Servants Act, or in the form of a 'pass' issued by the police. In either case, Hepston is bound to have been given a copy but might have surrendered it on boarding ship at a South African port. (Passports were not yet in vogue but the authorities would have demanded some kind of pass for Hepston to export a 'native' overseas as his servant.)

On the day after Hepston received permission to take Taibosh overseas, the leading Adeler & Sutton group, namely the Musical Madcaps (rather than the Merry Mascots), presented themselves on the stage of the Vaudette Theatre in Kimberley. Both Adeler and Sutton appeared in person: Edwin Adeler as 'raconteur and vocalist', and W.G. Sutton as 'portly as ever' singing a song titled 'Sunny South Africa'. Maybe Paddy Hepston and his brother Randolph were in the audience on this big occasion before they took their train to the coast. Franz Taibosh, not permitted to sit in the audience, might have had some sight of the performance from the wings backstage.[9]

◎

In thinking that a Bushman from South Africa would be a sensation on the London stage, Paddy and Randolph were undoubtedly hoping to exploit current anthropological interest. The Cape Town linguist and anthropologist Dorothea Bleek, daughter of the great Dr Wilhelm Bleek, gave a public lecture on the languages of the Bushmen at Kimberley in December 1911. Maria Willman, curator of the new McGregor Memorial Museum in the centre of Kimberley, was avidly building up a collection of Bushman artefacts and physiological remains, by touring in the Kalahari—and corresponding with the likes of the Pitt Rivers Museum at Oxford. In March 1912 she described a 'pleasing addition to our collection' in the form of a skeleton of 'a Cape Bushwoman', donated to her museum by Dr Borcherds of Upington.

Maria Willman's willing collaborator in accumulating exhibits was old George Lennox, better known as the retired bandit Scotty Smith. In the tradition of Burke and Hare, he confessed to having personally killed some of the Bushmen whose skeletons he sold. However, he justified himself as having shot and buried them many years earlier, when they had been employed as police trackers against him as a horse thief.[10]

One other Taaibosch got into the news at Kimberley around this time. In July 1911 a certain Daniel Tyebosh, described as 'Koranna labourer', appeared before Mr Justice C.J. Schermbrucker at the Beaconsfield court. Daniel Tyebosh was accused of swearing, opening a clasp-knife, and stabbing a guard at Wesselton labour compound in the hand after uttering the words 'I will show you what a Bushman can do'. He had been resisting the order of the guard, who had then called him a Bushman. He was sentenced to a fine of £3, or one month's hard labour. Such cases were not extraordinary: two years later, a plea in mitigation on a charge of murder argued that the killer had been provoked after being called a Bushman by the 'Hottentot' whom he murdered.[11]

3

Enter
Paddy Hepston

In these early days, Paddy Hepston may have been just as companionable to Franz Taibosh as Willem Roberts had presumably been. The iron and copper leg-rings in which Franz danced at Kimberley imply that he was able to keep some personal possessions. But any such camaraderie was to turn sour over the next year or two. In the eyes of the Cooks who later took in Franz Taibosh as a member of their family, Paddy Hepston was a cruel villain. But he appears to have been a complex character caught in conflicting situations, taking out his frustrations on Franz when there was no woman present.

Paddy Hepston had been born in Ireland in 1877—officially registered as Morris Hepston, and in the records of the Dublin Jewish congregation as Morris Epstein. The name Patrick or 'Paddy' was added by the time he was living in South Africa, indicating a strong Irish identity.[1] He thus had a double identity, both Irish and Jewish, usually calling himself Paddy Hepston rather than Morris Epstein, except in show business management where a Jewish surname had some cachet.

Todd Engelman's *Radical Assimilation in English Jewish History 1656–1945* argues that Jews were more easily assimilated in the British Isles than Jewish Americans in the United States. Old-established Jews in London kept their religion, but many were 'Cockneyfied' even to the extent of eating pork and jellied eels and drinking beer in pubs. Other writers have remarked on the fact that, in Europe as well as in North America, a significant number of Jews and other individuals from marginalized communities found niche employment sheltered from the cruel gentile world in popular entertainment, as well as in the clothing industry.[2]

◎

Paddy Hepston's passport application of April 1916 gave his full name as Morris Patrick Hepston, plus his date and place of birth, which enable us to trace his origins. The child born on 5 February 1877, at 14 Upper Mercer Street in Dublin, was officially registered by the state under the name of Morris Hepston. His parents were recorded as being Isaac Hepston and Anne Hepston, née Davis, of the same address. The birth was witnessed by an illiterate midwife who made her mark on the birth certificate. The birth was also registered with the Dublin Hebrew Congregation on 8 February 1877, the child's name being given as Morris Epstein, and his father's name as Isaac Epstein.[3]

Morris Hepston's mother Anne Davis came from a large and important Dublin Jewish family. Many Davises, including at least one rabbi, appear in synagogue records that go back to 1820. Morris Hepston's father's origins are unknown. There were at least two other Epstein families in Dublin by the late 1880s. A previous Epstein, Moses Epstein Margoliouth, had entered Trinity College at Dublin in 1840, becoming a Protestant Episcopalian clergyman in 1844. (In 1846 his wife, no longer living with him, defiantly registered a daughter with the synagogue in Hebrew script, rather than in Latin script like most other entries.)

Within four years of Morris Hepston's birth, the Hepston/Epstein family had moved to the city of Cork in the south of Ireland, at the head of the estuary that ran down through Queenstown (Cobh) to the sea. Transatlantic liners stopped at Queenstown on their way to and from Liverpool and New York, taking with them the Irish immigrants who flowed east to Great Britain and west to America in the later nineteenth century. Many men, Jewish as well as Irish, migrated overseas, leaving their wives and children destitute at home.[4]

The Jewish population of Ireland is estimated to have increased from 450 in 1881 to 3,769 in 1901, mostly in Dublin. Jewish emigration westwards out of the Baltic peaked around the time of the Russian empire's notorious May Laws of 1881. Cork received refugees from three Lithuanian villages in 1881, and the foundation of a synagogue was authorized there that year by the Chief Rabbi of the British Empire. Paddy Hepston's father 'Isaac Epstein, formerly of Dublin' was appointed the first president of the Jewish congregation at Cork, while 'The arrival of east European Jews made something of a stir among townsfolk, to whom for the most part the sight of a Jew was a rarity. The people flocked to the neighbourhood of the Hibernian Building, where the Jews found lodging, and clamoured to be allowed to see what Jews looked like.'

The immigrants, most of them penniless and without particular skills, became 'struggling peddlers' in town and countryside, hawking bundles or trays of goods through the streets ... and outlying districts, usually allowing their customers to pay by weekly instalments'—like the Jewish *smouse* of South Africa. Those who did not lodge in the gaunt structure of the Hibernian Building found lodgings in the slums of Cork. (The Cork slums stood in for the slums of Limerick for the 1999 film *Angela's Ashes*.)

Tension between Yiddish-speaking immigrants and the already established 'English' (i.e. English-speaking) Jews soon came to a head, as immigrants formed a new tabernacle that broke away from the official synagogue at Cork. By contrast, established Irish Jews—such as Simon Spiro who succeeded Isaac Epstein as president of the Cork synagogue congregation—climbed towards local respectability as magistrates and college professors. In Dublin the split between 'English' and Lithuanian Jews was widened by the refusal of the official synagogue to accept as a member anyone who lent money to the poor on usury.

The Jewish community at Cork was welcomed by a local Presbyterian minister, an 'ardent Home Ruler' and Irish nationalist, who organized the purchase of a Jewish burial ground. When Irish trades unions raised a rumpus in 1888 about cheap foreign labour and cheap imports brought into Cork by German Jewish businessmen, the unions were brought into line by no less than Charles Stuart Parnell, leader of the Irish Party in the Westminster parliament, with the words 'Irishmen are proud of the fact that theirs is the only country in Europe in which Jews have never been persecuted'.

Jews and Protestants were sometimes conflated in the popular imagination of the Catholic majority. In 1894 a Catholic crowd, infuriated by the fiery preaching of evangelical Protestants on the Cork marina, attacked a newly arrived Lithuanian Jew, mistaking his sombre attire for that of a Protestant preacher. When it was discovered that he was in fact Jewish, the mob stoned the Hibernian Building, breaking many windows and chasing Jews along the streets.[5]

The young Morris Hepston missed the events of 1894 at Cork, because his father had moved back to Dublin by 1890. But as a boy he would have experienced the 'sudden antipathy to the Jewish community' in Cork that was evident in the 1880s. His Cork years, between the ages of four and thirteen, were vital years for character building. It is likely that he went to a local school, probably a Protestant school, since no Jewish denominational school was set up at Cork until 1896. There he would have acquired the cultural camouflage that enabled him to be seen in adult life as an Irishman rather than as a Jew.

It was possibly for school purposes that Morris appropriated the extra name of Patrick, Ireland's patron saint, giving him the concomitant nickname of 'Paddy'. Harassment at school may also help to explain why Paddy Hepston was a bully later in life: victims all too often become victimizers.

Back in Dublin, Paddy's father Isaac Epstein (no longer Hepston) was recorded in the annual commercial publication, *Thom's Irish Almanac and Official Directory*, as living at 28 Lombard Street West in every year between 1890 and 1904. The same address, 28–29 Lombard Street West, near the corner with St Kevin's Parade in South Dublin, was also registered as the premises of Messrs Sayers & Golding, general drapers. The Epstein/Hepston family thus lived above or behind a fabric store, and it is possible that members of the family were employed there. Immediate neighbours as of 1897 were of both Irish and Jewish origin: families headed by William O'Brien, L.J. O'Reilly, Samuel Isaacson and James O'Meara.

Dublin's small but significant Jewish community was concentrated in the area of South Dublin, enclosed between the south bank of the Liffey River and the South Circular Road. Many such families lived in rooms in single-storeyed houses, rather than the multi-storey tenement buildings, one-third of which were said to be unfit for habitation, that characterized North Dublin. 'Dirty Dublin' was, like dirty London and Glasgow, blackened with layers of coal soot from domestic and industrial chimneys, but in 1899 its mortality per thousand was thirty-four people a year in the city area, compared with London's twenty and Glasgow's twenty-two. By 1915–16 slum clearance and new sanitation reduced mortality from above to below the levels of Prague, Budapest, Moscow, Cairo and Madras. However, Dublin still had ten years to go before long-drop privies gave way to water closets, and a very long way to go before it could be anything like a garden city.[6]

Thanks to scholarship following up the writings of James Joyce, we have a rich knowledge of the Jewish community of South Dublin in the early years of the twentieth century. Joyce's heroine Molly Bloom is said to have been based on a woman called Sarah Bloom née Levy, who had been abandoned by her husband Joseph Bloom in about the year 1900 when he left for South Africa. (By 1922, when *Ulysses* was published obscurely in Paris, Sarah had disappeared to America and was assumed to be out of libel range.)

The Bloom/Levy and Hepston/Epstein families must have known each other well in Cork and Dublin. Joseph Bloom came from a well-established

German immigrant family; Sarah was the beautiful daughter of Joseph Levy, a Lithuanian immigrant. When Sarah Levy married Joseph Bloom at Cork in 1889, her parents were still living with other immigrants in the Hibernian Building, though they became more 'respectable' thereafter. Her father Joseph Levy was appointed beadle of the Cork synagogue. He was known as a great wit, while his children were known as talented musicians. Joseph and Sarah lived in Cork until 1893, when they moved to Dublin to stay with Joseph Bloom's father, Jonah (Yonah), at 38 Lombard Street West, a few doors down from the Hepston/Epstein family.

Old Jonah Bloom appears to have been an ineffective ne'er-do-well, his daughter Bella slightly crazy, and his son Joseph feckless. Joseph's escape to South Africa around 1900 could have been inspired by the example of Paddy Hepston, their near neighbour. Joseph left Sarah in the lurch with two daughters and three sons to support. The spirited Sarah took in lodgers but was rejected by her own parents after she became pregnant by a lodger. She was reduced to selling drapery outside Jacob's Biscuit factory and probably finally resorted, with her eldest daughter, to prostitution.[7]

A number of Dublin Jews besides Joseph Bloom and Paddy Hepston sought their fortunes around this time in the gold and diamond fields of South Africa. Philip Moise, son of a greengrocer and poultry dealer in Arbutus Place off Lombard Street West, left his wife (the daughter of an Episcopalian clergyman) in the late 1890s and ran off to South Africa, where he died in 1903. Benny Bloom (no relation to Jonah or Joseph) volunteered for military service in the Anglo–Boer War in 1901; after working overseas as a waiter and a bookmaker's runner, he returned home in 1916 to eke out a living selling religious pictures on Dublin streets. Pesach Bloom's son Solomon—'nicknamed "Pat" because of his pronounced brogue'—emigrated to Johannesburg in 1905, followed by another son called Nathan Bloom, who emigrated there via Seattle and Alaska.

Paddy Hepston was five or more years younger than Sarah Levy and Joseph Bloom. Exactly why and when he left for South Africa is unknown. South Africa was already famous in the 1890s for its Jewish and other millionaires, such as Barney Barnato. The war of 1899–1902 put the country on the front pages and the British army actively sought recruits in Ireland for service in South Africa. Enquiries made about Hepston in the 1920s produced the improbable type-story that he had been a 'remittance man' from the upper classes, paid by his family to escape the British Isles under a massive cloud of debt. But Paddy had had no rich daddy; he had been young and poor.[8]

◎

The arrival of Paddy Hepston in South Africa could have been as early as 1894 (at the age of seventeen) or as late as 1906 when he was twenty-nine—or, most likely, at some date in-between. The year 1894 is suggested by the claim in a 1919–20 circus publication that he arrived in Johannesburg to fight in the Malaboch (Mmalebogo) war of that year. But his name does not appear in the record of foreign volunteers who fought in that war in order to gain Transvaal citizenship. Hepston himself said that he had reached South Africa in time to fight on the British side in the 1899–1902 war. But his claim to have been an army captain, tantamount to assuming membership of the Irish gentry, can be discounted for a Jewish townsman of modest origins.[9]

Paddy Hepston's acquisition of a white South African accent, such that people in Britain were to mistake him for a Boer, indicates long-term residence in South Africa since youth. His command of Afrikaans was enough to communicate with Franz Taibosh, who appears to have had very limited command of English at first. Clicko's pamphlet biography of 1919–20 indirectly suggests that Hepston had been in South Africa at least since 1900, by telling us that he had much admired the sculpture of a Bushman in Pretoria. This sculpture, actually a bronze frieze on the side of Anton van Wouw's Paul Kruger statue, was removed by British soldiers in 1900 and not restored to this place until after Hepston left South Africa.[10]

The earliest published record of Paddy Hepston in South Africa is clear but indirect. The *Kimberley Year Book and Directory* for 1906–7, printed in June 1906, records a Mrs Epstein living at 24 Selby Street in the Malay Camp area of Kimberley. The same address (actually 24a Selby Street) is given for Maurice [*sic*] Patrick Epstein, registered as a voter in 1909. His occupation is given as 'clerk', his 'race distinction' as European, and he is recorded as occupant and joint tenant at the address. (M.P. Epstein does not appear on earlier or later electoral rolls.) This suggests that Mrs Epstein was his wife, and that Paddy was based at the same address for at least four years, but that he was away for a period of time around 1906. The economic slump at Kimberley between 1906 and 1909 threw thousands of men out of employment, to seek an alternative living.

Selby Street lay in the heart of the Malay Camp, a lively multiracial area in the heart of the city—demolished in the 1940s and since replaced by grass lawns and municipal offices. 'Malay' referred to Muslim Coloured people of Indonesian origin, and the streets bore names like Canton, Mosque and Malay, or Irish names like Shannon and Coghlan. It was a bustling commercial and residential area, crowded with Malay, Indian and Chinese stores and houses, as well as a smattering of Eastern European Jews and Irish, and better-off black families such as that of the journalist and novelist Sol Plaatje. (His house escaped the demolition of later years, and is today a museum.)

There were plenty of Jews at Kimberley, in all walks of life, including (though Unitarian in religion) the Mayor of Kimberley from 1912, Ernest Oppenheimer—future millionaire boss of the Anglo American Corporation. This may help to explain why at this stage of his career Hepston was happy to go under the name of Epstein.[11]

The last recorded mention of Hepston in South Africa is as 'M.P. Epstein, insurance agent', living at an unspecified house number in Green Street in the West End district. (The source is the *Kimberley Year Book* published in January 1914, but its information was probably a couple of years out of date, given the fact that the *Year Book* appeared once every few years.)

Green Street was in a new suburb on a new road leading to excavation pits and a burial ground, with good lower-middle-class houses on relatively small plots, in the West End district lying to the northwest of the Big Hole (Kimberley Mine). The street seems to have drawn its residents from more prosperous former occupants of the Malay Camp, such as I. Joshua, a Coloured businessman and African People's Organisation politician, and a Chinese entrepreneur named Lai Kwon. As an insurance agent, Paddy Hepston may have been living hand-to-mouth on commission, but he must have had sufficient nous, plus sales-talk experience, to support a modest suburban lifestyle.[12]

After he left South Africa, the Johannesburg *Star* newspaper referred to Paddy Hepston as formerly a diamond buyer at Kimberley. However, the diamond trade was strictly controlled, and illicit diamond buying (IDB) was considered the most heinous of crimes in South Africa, and there is no known record of Hepston registered as a diamond buyer. He could have been engaged in the underworld of diamond smuggling. The scar from a bullet wound in his right cheek, officially noted as a distinguishing mark in 1917, also suggests—if it was not an old war wound—a criminal background.[13]

4

DISAPPEARANCE TO AUSTRALASIA OR THE FAR EAST?

THE BIGGEST GAP in the known biography of Franz Taibosh is the eleven months between July 1912, when Paddy Hepston was given official permission at Kimberley to take on 'Bushman, W.D.' as his servant, and June 1913, when the Wild Dancing Bushman made his first appearance in a London theatre. There are three distinct possibilities. First, that the two brothers and the Bushman stayed on in South Africa, employed in entertainment or some other business. Second, that the trio went first across the Indian Ocean, maybe to Australasia, to get theatrical exposure and managerial experience in another colonial setting. And third, that Franz was taken to Europe more or less immediately but lived for months in obscurity before getting a booking on the London stage.

Enquiries made in the small world of variety theatre in South Africa in 1919 elicited no memory of a Wild Dancing Bushman. Franz could have been brought on stage as an act between movies at the Orpheum bioscope-vaudeville theatre in Johannesburg, as that theatre was managed at one stage by G. Holderness, who had also managed the Merry Mascots. But it is unlikely that a 'native' would have been welcome or permitted on a commercial stage, given the rough, hard-drinking, all-white male nature of audiences in mining areas. At Benoni near Johannesburg, for example, all Africans had to be off the streets by 9 pm and by law were not even allowed to enter theatres.

Entertainment business in South Africa was also suffering from depression in 1912–13, after a 1910–11 mushrooming of bioscope-vaudevilles and 'picture palaces'. Show business bankruptcies resulted in amalgamations and near monopoly by the Schlesinger theatre corporation (ancestor of today's Ster-Kinekor).

South African circuses were in even more desperate straits. The only effective circus left was that of William Pagel, a German Pomeranian strong man and lion-trainer, who had come to South Africa via Australia in 1905. Frank Fillis's circus was closed for ever in 1913: he had previously gone off to seek better pastures in South-east Asia, leaving his circus under the management of his wife Lazel. (The Cattel brothers, two former Fillis employees, later set up their own Boswell circus, taking the name from their mother's illustrious circus ancestry in Britain.) It is just possible that the Hepston/Epsteyne brothers could have attached Franz Taibosh and themselves to a humble travelling carnival show—such as the Marvellous Midgets exhibited at 'Tiny Town' on the De Beers Road at Kimberley in March 1913. But, given their grand pretensions to enter variety theatre overseas, that is unlikely.[1]

Randolph Epsteyne, who had the necessary theatrical contacts and expertise, must have set the initial career pattern of the Wild Dancing Bushman. Randolph is unlikely to have abandoned his own career as a song and dance man; Franz and Paddy probably followed wherever Randolph went. Randolph could have continued with the Merry Mascots, but their whereabouts are unknown between June 1912, when they left Kimberley, and May 1913, when they appeared at Gravesend on England's Kent coast.

The South African film and theatre historian Thelma Gutsche tells us that the Merry Mascots' manager G. Holderness married one of the Mascots, the comedienne Miss Gertie Lanner—*on the eve of their departure for Australia*—but she gives no date for this event.[2] This suggests that the Wild Dancing Bushman could have made his theatrical début over the 1912–13 summer season in Australia. Variety artists from Britain who stopped in South Africa frequently went on to Australia and New Zealand, as well as playing in British India and Ceylon, Malaya and Singapore, and even French Indo-China, Dutch Indonesia and the American (ex-Spanish) Philippines.

Franz Taibosh's later billing in Ireland and America as an 'Australian Bushman' may not have been completely off the mark. Ships sailed from Cape Town and Durban via India and Singapore, or direct across the Southern Ocean to landfall at Fremantle. The gold fields of Western Australia almost rivalled Johannesburg's, and were an obvious draw for light entertainers. So too were the older gold-mining towns (Ballarat, Bendigo, etc.) inland from Melbourne. Australia was experiencing a great growth in popular entertainment, along with urbanization and industrialization, improved workers' pay, drinking and gambling. The Australian Tivoli theatre circuit was established in 1912, but brought in more acts from the US than from London. Among American imports in 1912 was the play *Get-Rich-Quick-Wallingford*, starring actor-manager Fred Niblo—said to be formerly of Zululand—who ten years hence was to direct the epic film *Ben-Hur*. By October 1913, reportedly 'dozens of vaudeville artists from the United States' were touring Australia.[3]

However, searches for the Merry Mascots and the Wild Dancing (African) Bushman in the Australian press have so far been unsuccessful—and they do not appear in the data for 1912 circuses compiled by the Australian circus expert Mark St Leon. The only 'bushmen' on entertainment pages were mounted stockmen cavorting on their horses in a Wild Australia show, and a touring melodrama called *The Bushwoman*—with a white woman tough enough to fell a tree across a stream to meet her lover, and the only 'blackfellow' or aboriginal Australian in the plot shot dead. The Melbourne weekly *Table Talk* noted Adeler & Sutton's Smart Set Entertainers as being imported by the Tait brothers from South Africa, but made no mention of an Epsteyne or Steyne being among them.[4]

Fifteen years later, African Bushmen touring Australia were dubbed Pygmies. Dave Meekin's Pygmies (later also known confusingly as Meekin's Ubangi) toured Australia for thirty-five years, even venturing back on tour to South Africa in July 1951. These 'fine little people ... [so] civilized' were presented to the public as 'strange and fascinating jungle folk ... tiny little killers from the Congo'. They were led by Maria Peters, a Coloured woman of Khoesan ancestry. Jimmy Robert Thomas claimed to be of mixed Khoekhoe and Native American ancestry, the child of a Pawnee performer from Texas Jack's Wild West show stranded in South Africa. Edward Hill, otherwise known as Shonna or Zegri, was said to be 'a tiny bearded Kalahari Bushman' from Bechuanaland (Botswana). He played the Wild Man by 'a mad rush at the audience with his assegai, supposedly tipped with poison'. Most other members of the troupe seem to have been short-statured Zulu-speakers from Natal. When not touring, Meekin's Pygmies lived in the urban jungle of King's Cross in Sydney.[5]

It is possible that the Wild Dancing Bushman act was being tried out in provincial resorts of the British Isles during 1912–13, in company with one of Adeler & Sutton's many concert parties besides the Merry Mascots. The impresarios Edwin Adeler and W.G. Sutton were already running twenty whiteface Pierrot concert parties in British and Irish seaside resorts in 1900, with tours of South Africa and Australia following by 1909. Pierrot singers appeared as clowns with faces powdered white or greased with zinc and lard, in baggy white and spotted suits, with extravagant ruffs round their necks and cornet hats decorated with pom-pons.

The Merry Mascots were one of the New Pierrots that evolved after 1908, when Henry Gabriel Pelissier's Pierrots began to present their French-style 'Follies' adult revues (with 'potted plays' burlesquing serious drama) in London's West End. New Pierrot concert parties appeared on stage—at least for the second half of the performance—without whiteface makeup, in evening dress with top hats, or in striped blazers and straw boaters. The Merry Mascots themselves were immortalized by the tune 'Dance of the Merry Mascots' composed by Albert Ketelbey, the musical director at the Vaudeville Theatre in London's Strand and composer of 'In a Persian market' and 'In a monastery garden'.[6]

Yet another possibility for the whereabouts of the Wild Dancing Bushman during 1912–13 is that he was being exhibited in continental Europe. As we will see, he was to dance in France in the latter part of 1913 and there are suggestions that he later went to Germany and to Spain. But the true beginning of Franz Taibosh's career in show business was in London in June 1913.

5

ᴛʜᴇ ᴅᴀɴᴄɪɴɢ ʙᴜꜱʜᴍᴀɴ
ɪɴ ʟᴏɴᴅᴏɴ

AFTER RELATING ITS VERSION of the origins of the Wild Dancing Bushman in South Africa, the *Rand Daily Mail* of 6 October 1913 continued:

> **AT THE HALLS**
>
> The next move was to take the Bushman to London. This was done, and a trial show was given at the Hippodrome, the chief hall of the Stoll and Moss tour. The management, however, did not take kindly to the 'turn', but the Bushman has since been exploited in the Provinces with the aid of a Press agent.

Wild Men were evidently out of fashion, as were circuses, by the time that Franz Taibosh reached Britain—but new dances were all the rage. 'Wild' was dropped from his billing when he first danced on a London stage in the week beginning Monday, 23 June 1913. He was simply presented as the Dancing Bushman. His first appearance was at the Putney Hippodrome, an inner-suburban variety hall within the London Theatre of Varieties (LTV or Moss Empires) circuit. The Dancing Bushman appeared together with song and dance acts—the Wedgwood Classics, the New Macs, and the popular piano-entertainer Elsie Roby.[1]

Paddy Hepston, schooled by his theatrical brother, introduced the act standing beside a cinema screen. Against the projection of a short silent movie—probably made in the African bush by Mr Savage of Kimberley—he told the tale of how as a colonial farmer he had 'discovered' the Bushman in the wilds. No doubt he was dressed appropriately, with a *sjambok* or rhino-hide whip in his hand. One of the movie images was probably the photo postcard that was on sale after the performance: a youthful Franz sitting crouched on the branches of a thorn tree, with 'Yours faithfully, The Wild Dancing Bushman' scrawled across the bottom.

Publicity postcard of the Wild Dancing Bushman distributed
in England in 1913, probably photographed at Kimberley a
year earlier. (Prof. Bernth Lindfors)

We may imagine that Franz appeared from the wings after a rolling of drums and clashing of cymbals from the pit orchestra. He danced on to the stage, scantily dressed, letting out great wild whoops and chattering excitedly in his own incomprehensible language as he vigorously step-danced and cavorted to the music.

The Dancing Bushman was engaged on the LTV circuit for an initial six weeks. The claim by the *Rand Daily Mail* that he was given a trial show at the London Hippodrome ('the chief hall of the Stoll and Moss tour') must refer to an audition rather than an evening performance. The London 'Hipp' (above one of the Leicester Square tube exits at 39 Charing Cross Road) was the headquarters of Moss Empires and its LTV circuit, built by 'the Scottish Barnum,' Edward Moss, a decade earlier for aquarium and horse shows, before reverting to playing variety.

The 'Hipp' was currently taken up with *Hullo! Rag-time*, a plotless but melodious dance revue with music by Louis A. Hirsch. It had opened in December 1912, and was to run for 451 consecutive performances, going through a number of editions. The famous comedian Harry Tate appeared with a 'beauty chorus' of forty dancing girls, while Leslie Owen impersonated the—then not altogether popular—politician Winston Churchill. In June 1913 English dancers were replaced by American girls who 'can dance rag-time better'—with rapid ragging, described as flopping arms picking up a pin from the floor, first with the left hand and then with the right. The core of the show was the hit songs of 24-year-old Irving Berlin: not only 'Alexander's Ragtime Band', but also 'Everybody's doing it', 'Oh, you beautiful doll', 'There's a girl in Havana', and 'Rum tum tiddle'. For the first week of the show's third edition in July 1913, Irving Berlin himself crossed 'the herring pond' from New York to demonstrate his prowess as a performer.[2]

The dance craze was now in full spate. *Hullo! Rag-time* was to be followed at the 'Hipp' by *Hullo! Tango* in December 1913, running for 485 performances. Imitation dance revues in London and provincial theatres included *What Ho! Rag-time* set at Atlanta Beach with characters such as Rasmus B. Washington and Miss Issipi; *Hello, London!*; *The Seven Ragged Rag-time Gypsy Girls*; *Hello! Exchange!*; and Jack Hulbert's *Cheer-Oh Cambridge!* Even British army bands resorted to ragtime, using tunes such as 'Hitchy koo' for recruiting purposes. The Real Rag-Timers, a group of black American entertainers, danced the grizzly bear and other ragtime dances in London and the provinces, with comic cakewalks and eccentric high-stepping, but could not out-rag Irving Berlin in the show market.[3]

By 1913 black Americans were increasingly appearing on the London stage, and Africans were by no means an unusual sight in the city. A.B.C. Merriman-Labor, a schoolmaster from The Gambia living in the still-fashionable southern suburb of Brixton, published his own guide to London for African visitors. He starts an imaginary tour from Threadneedle Street in the old city, noting the proliferation of poor street-vendors, proceeding along the Thames embankment and through Westminster Abbey to Piccadilly, where 'gay' fashionable women flock to expensive shops in the day and 'overgay'

prostitutes populate the area at night: the appropriate motto being 'Take no lady thereto: bring no woman therefrom'.

There are Scotsmen, Irishmen, Jews and Yorkshiremen in the street— and Japanese, who are given new respect since their country's naval victory over Russia. A man taps you on the shoulder, as you cross the street, to say 'Kind friend, beware ... motor-car coming'—as he fleeces your pockets. The only people who talk to an African on the streets of 'lonesome London' are beggars, confidence tricksters, loan-seekers or chancers testing a black man's command of the language. But no one exceeds the rudeness of visiting 'Euro-Americans', who visibly object to the presence of black people. Merriman-Labor also advises his companion to avoid working-class areas where schoolboys might assault him with stones or rotten eggs, shouting 'Go wash your face, guv'nor', or 'Nigger! nigger! nigger!'

Merriman-Labor jokes with his dark companion: 'we seldom see the sun—as it is often very foggy—so thick and black, that if you stretch your hand it will be impossible for you to see it.' The two men are shocked by couples lying on the grass and 'spooning' (cuddling) in Hyde Park at five o'clock on a steamy summer's afternoon. That evening they visit a variety theatre for its 'music, singing, cake-walk ... sand-dance, shows of trained animals, acrobatic and aquatic performances' and, once in a while, 'songs composed or sung by Negroes'. The ballet girls at the London Pavilion are alluring but not plump enough for their tastes. One wears a flesh-coloured costume that 'fits her more than a glove'. Merriman-Labor adds that it is a hundred times more pleasant to gaze at such living beings than to inspect all the stone maidens who reside in museums and art galleries.

In England as in Africa, according to Merriman-Labor, men exhibit 'proprietary ownership in women ... I see in their history and present position, in more respects than ten, a parallel with those of the Negro.' The author concludes his tour of the sooty metropolis with observations on 'rampant poverty in the midst of superfluous plenty ... more than a submerged tenth of men and women' living a life of immorality and crime on the streets.[4]

The London Theatre of Varieties circuit or 'tour' shuffled the pack of their performers, never putting on quite the same combination in a different theatre each week. Artists had to appear for rehearsals at half past twelve or one o'clock on the Monday before starting each week's engagement. Moss Empires instructed them 'to clearly understand that their business must be free from all vulgarity'.[5]

Theatre bill of the Grand Palace, Clapham, July 1913,
with Dancing Bushman at the bottom. (Prof. Bernth Lindfors)

The Dancing Bushman's second week on the LTV circuit began on Monday, 30 June, at the Croydon Empire, in rather more distinguished theatrical company. The bill was topped by Jack and Evelyn, celebrity dancers 'stopping the programme', and included Leo Stormont & Company, Lily and Ida Hallé, and Queenie Leighton.[6] Jack and Evelyn were an American celebrity dancing couple, paid $4,000 a week, consisting of foxtrot instructor Jack Clifford (Virgil Montani) and showgirl Evelyn Nesbit. She had earned notoriety in New York in 1906 as 'the girl on the red velvet swing', on which she had reputedly swung naked. Her millionaire husband Harry Thaw had shot her architect ex-lover dead during a rooftop stage performance at Madison

Square Garden. Dancing couples like Jack and Evelyn engaged in 'topical cross-talking' or witty social backchat while demonstrating the Argentinian tango, the bunny-hug and the turkey-trot—the three dances described by the theatrical weekly *The Encore* in June 1913 as the 'great stir of late'. After being shown on stage, the new dances were spread by instructors in the dance schools that were springing up in Kensington and elsewhere.[7]

Franz Taibosh probably incorporated elements of these new dances so far as he could as a solitary dancer, but he was essentially an acrobatic step-dancer who on occasion appeared in wooden clogs. Step-dancing had been quite the vogue in the 1890s but was now generally considered 'disappointingly dull' on the variety stage. However, the massed dancers of 'Henley Sports and Revels' at the London Hippodrome in 1912 had embraced the 'novel idea' of dancing with the drop curtain concealing everything but their leaping feet.

Franz Taibosh would have been more than a match for the aptly named F. Fedia Stepanoff, a perennial favourite on the London variety stage and supposedly 'the champion top-boot dancer of Russia', or for Pep of 'Mart and Pep', advertised in Scotland as 'the best acrobatic wooden shoe dancer in the business bar none'. The great days of clog-dancing in music halls had been the 1880s, when even Americans had been wild about it. There had been a world clog-dancing championship competition at the Empire Theatre in Bow, East London, in 1898. But the era had more or less ended in 1904 with the suicide of Dan Leno, unofficial world clog-dancing champion and *de facto* court jester to Edward VII. By 1913, one of the leading Northern English clog-dancers, simply known as 'Jimmy', died forgotten and alone in the cellar where he lived below street level in the centre of Stockton, Lancashire.[8]

For his third week on the LTV circuit, the Dancing Bushman became a variety 'turn', appearing at more than one theatre nightly. This involved rushing hell-for-leather through city streets, usually by motor car, from one theatre performance to another some miles away. The LTV managing director, Charles Gulliver, stipulated that artists must do this for midday Monday rehearsals as well—in default of which contracts would be cancelled. (The Variety Artistes' Federation vigorously opposed the 'split week' of three days in one theatre and three days in another theatre, which had been widely adopted in America, as a clever management ploy to reduce performance-related earnings.)[9]

Hence for the week beginning Monday, 7 July, the Dancing Bushman appeared at both Balham Hippodrome, ninth of eleven acts on the bill, and—for the first time north of the Thames—fifth on the bill at the Hammersmith

Palace. There were no other artists appearing at both theatres with Hepston and Taibosh, so they must have hired a motor taxi or found their way by public transport—by a combination of trains and electric trams via Clapham Junction or across Putney bridge. At the Hammersmith Palace (not to be confused with the later Hammersmith 'Palais de Dance'), the Dancing Bushman appeared again with the Stormont company, Lily and Ida Hallé, and the New Macs. The presence on the bill of a concert party called the Ten Merry Sparks raises the question whether Hepston's brother Randolph Epsteyne was also performing on the LTV circuit.[10]

Monday, 14 July saw the start of the Dancing Bushman's fourth week on the circuit. He was fifth out of ten on the bill (though bottom on an extant poster) at the Grand Palace at Clapham Junction (21 St John's Hill), and second on the bill at the Kilburn Empire seven or eight miles north. The Clapham Grand was one of South London's two premier entertainment spots—the other being the South London Palace of Varieties at the Elephant and Castle.[11]

The arrival of the Dancing Bushman at the Clapham Grand, next to the busiest rail junction in the world, was marked by a short review of his act in one of the theatrical trade newspapers, *The Encore, with which is incorporated the Music Hall and Theatre Review*:

> A turn that is an actual novelty to be seen—is the wild South African Dancing Bushman. His manager introduces him in a short speech illustrated by cinematograph pictures, and then the Bushman appears—a diminutive figure in a skin loincloth. But he can dance! Whether or not he is over 90 years of age as claimed and can speak no human language, matters not. He is quite original, and is endowed with tireless energy.[12]

Hepston's introductory spiel was not at this stage written down but must have approximated to the text delivered by him to a journalist in Paris a couple of months later:

> Mr. Epstein is a big game hunter. He has been for 25 years in South Africa, where he has a farm near Kimberley. About seven years ago, while he was hunting for monkeys for the industry of karass [*kaross*], an African term for monkey skins, he decided one day to go with his friends on an ostrich shooting expedition in the Kalahari Desert, near the new [*sic*] German South-West Territory, where there are hardly any human beings.
>
> One day, at a distance, he noticed a strange form among a group of ostriches.

He galloped in its direction, at the same time firing his revolver. As he got near, the strange form, which he now made out to be a human being with a bow and arrow in his hand, tried to escape, but the horse came on top of him and knocked him down.

The account continued in Paddy Hepston's own words:

> In a second I was down from the saddle. I captured the creature, and, after binding him with cords, placed him on the saddle and returned with him to our camp. It was on examining the savage that we realised it was the last of the tribe of Bushmen. For some time he had to be kept tied to a wagon to prevent him from escaping.
>
> When he had been on the farm some six months Franz, as I called him, was already tamer. He showed no desire to run away, and I employed him in the farm looking after the fowls. It was only last year that, on the advice of some friends who saw my Bushman, I decided to come over to Europe to exhibit him.[13]

No doubt the short film that introduced the act showed Franz in the guise of an ostrich, in order to hunt unobtrusively on the open veld. The idea was not really novel. It had been pictured in Robert Moffat's 1842 *Missionary Labours and Scenes in South Africa*, and was part of the performance of Farini's Earthmen in London and New York in 1884.

During the week of Monday, 21 July, the Dancing Bushman appeared at no less than three theatres nightly. He was high on the bill at both Woolwich Hippodrome and Poplar Hippodrome, and low on the bill at the Holborn Empire—the nearest that Franz Taibosh got to a West End theatre. The Poplar Hippodrome (51–55 East India Dock Road, destroyed by bombs in 1940) showed mixed bills of variety and films. Its patrons were dockyard workers known for their militancy and for brooking no nonsense. The Woolwich Hippodrome, on the south bank of the Thames beyond Greenwich, the location of large munitions factories, was sometimes counted as a provincial rather than metropolitan 'hall' in the trade press.

During his sixth week on the LTV circuit, beginning Monday, 28 July, the Dancing Bushman reverted to dancing in two theatres nightly: the Islington Empire and the Shoreditch Olympia. Jack and Evelyn once again topped the bill at Islington. The bill at Shoreditch by contrast was curiously depleted, with only five items listed, of which the Dancing Bushman was fourth in line.[14]

Shoreditch on the evening of Saturday, 2 August 1913 was probably the last time that Franz Taibosh appeared on a London stage. The Dancing Bushman act had been put through the mill by the Stoll–Moss management: starting mildly with single evening appearances in the more genteel western and southern suburbs of Putney and Croydon; continuing with double evening 'turns' in less genteel Balham and Hammersmith, and less suburban Clapham and Kilburn; and progressing into proletarian inner-urban East End territory through triple 'turns' at Woolwich, Poplar and Holborn, into a last double 'turn' at Islington and Shoreditch. But, as the *Rand Daily Mail* said, the Stoll–Moss management did not 'take kindly' to extending the Dancing Bushman's contract any further.

◎

The last two or three weeks of the London tour in July–August 1912 must have been particularly stressful for the Dancing Bushman, because of vocal working-class audiences and the strenuous 'turns' travelling between theatres. Hepston's fanciful colonial-ethnological introduction to the act was unlikely to have gone down well with East End dockyard and munitions workers, or Eastern European immigrants. Franz may have danced superbly, parodying the latest dance steps, but London audiences expected more than physical expertise from a performer. They expected verbal humour with topical chitchat, and a dour colonial with a strange accent was ill equipped to supply that.

The act may also have fallen foul of 'the gallery boys'—professional applauders who booed if they were not paid off. (Music-hall star Ada Reeve recalled that at Shoreditch she was asked for money in advance by this East End version of the French *claque*, who would 'give her the bird' if she did not pay up.) Or maybe it was simply a matter of Paddy Hepston failing to get on with the Stoll–Moss management: he had a violent temper and was not the most competent or amenable of men.

Our *Rand Daily Mail* source tells us that the Dancing Bushman act broke with the Stoll–Moss management and was instead 'exploited in the Provinces with the aid of a Press agent'. Moss Empires had a provincial variety circuit or 'tour' of thirty-six theatres in England, Scotland, Ireland and Wales, which was advertised in advance in weekly variety newspapers. But the Bushman act did not appear on any provincial circuit advertised in the trade press.

After early August 1913, the Dancing Bushman appears to have been employed in the seaside resorts of East Anglia. The sole memoir of this period is a delightful portrait, preserved in a Cambridge college, of the Wild

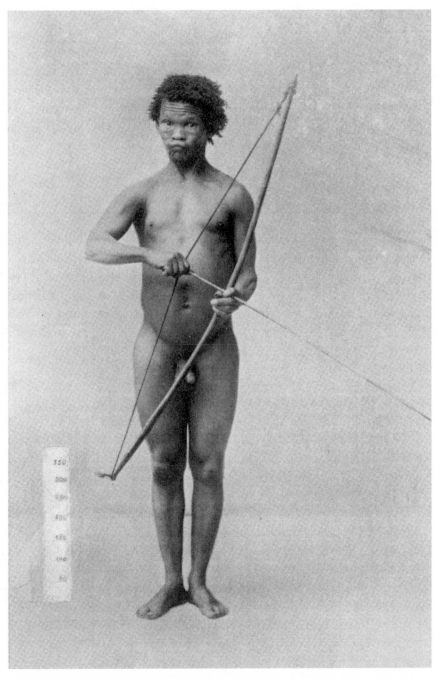

The Wild Dancing Bushman in war paint at Great Yarmouth in August–
September 1913, when he was first spotted by Dr W.L.H. Duckworth.
(Duckworth Laboratory, Cambridge)

Dancing Bushman photographed at Great Yarmouth. Slim and remarkably youthful, with war-paint daubed on his cheeks, he holds a bow and arrow. His lips are puckered in a kiss; or maybe he was stifling the running of a cold in the nose. Great Yarmouth boasted two theatres, four picture palaces, two piers with pleasure-gardens, a number of variety pavilions, and a revolving tower. Harry Tate appeared on the Wellington pier with his 'Motoring' and 'Fishing' sketches during August bank-holiday week. The big attraction on 11 September was Jack Johnson's boxing exhibition at the Yarmouth Hippodrome.[15]

The new agent must have deduced that the value of the Wild Dancing Bushman lay in his wildness or 'savagery', rather than in just his expertise as a dancer. The agent also seems to have exploited a wide range of non-theatrical contacts. During the latter part of September 1913 the Wild Dancing Bushman was being exhibited as an ethnological curiosity for academics at the University of Cambridge, across the East Anglian fens from Yarmouth. At the end of that month, Franz Taibosh was to be taken across the Channel and exhibited at the leading circus in Paris as *l'homme sauvage*.

6

Dancing in Cambridge and Paris

On Thursday, 2 October 1913, a letter to the editor was printed on the imperial and foreign intelligence page of *The Times* from Dr W.L.H. Duckworth, of the Anthropological Laboratory at Cambridge. Duckworth referred to the recent visit to this country of 'an aboriginal Bushman from South Africa', accompanied by Mr M.P. Epstein, 'on whose farm near Kimberley he has lived for seven years past'.

Duckworth stated that he was preparing for publication a detailed report on this 'genuine' Bushman's physical characteristics, and ended his letter with 'two remarkable and distinctive points'—relating to the Bushman's language and to his dancing. Duckworth cited his son-in-law, Captain W.E. Ironside, as the authority for the Bushman speaking neither a Bantu dialect nor a click (Khoesan) language nor the 'taal' (Afrikaans), adding: 'Not that he is dumb; his frequent indulgence in a sustained cry or yell of the "View-halloa" order and his animated orations to his audience leave no doubt on that score.'

Duckworth then waxed lyrical on the dancing ability of the Bushman. 'It is of the nature of "step-dancing". To me it appears to be of an extremely high artistic standard, and indeed of an order approaching perfection ... I am confident that if the Bushman returns to this country his performance will attract connoisseurs of dancing no less than expert anthropologists.'

Duckworth, who would have seen or known about the ethnological exhibition of Ituri pygmies in England a few years previously, claimed that Epstein's Bushman had 'an appreciative sense of rhythm far in advance of that shown by such comparable examples as the Pygmies of Central Africa'.

It is almost incredible that without any instruction this Bushman should have devised these dances and attained such proficiency in their performance. Yet Mr. Epstein denies that any extraneous aid was devised.

But I must not anticipate discussions which will be raised (it is to be hoped) in Paris, where the Bushman now is, or in this country at a later date. In regard to animal portraiture, the artistic talents of the Bush race have long been recognized. It may be that we shall be led to credit these primitive people [with] yet another artistic sense, and to believe that in them it is developed to a degree previously unsuspected.

I am yours faithfully,
W.L.H. Duckworth[1]

Franz Taibosh had been examined a week or so earlier in the Anthropological Laboratory at Cambridge. W.L.H. Duckworth was a lecturer in physical anthropology and later became University Reader in that subject and Master of Jesus College. His written report was not published until three years later, and then only in Italian, but declared the Bushman to be physically 'genuine'.

Duckworth was already well known as author of the popular booklet *Prehistoric Man*. Anthropology was a current intellectual craze: Piltdown Man (a hoax combination of ancient human and modern ape bones, proved to be a fake only in 1953) had supposedly been uncovered on a Sussex hillside in 1908–11, and had been announced to the world in 1912. A mere five days after Duckworth's first letter was published in *The Times*, Professor Arthur Keith, conservator of the Royal College of Surgeons' museum, rubbished theories of primeval separation of human races (polygenesis etc.) in a lecture at Birmingham University on 'The antiquity of modern races'. Anticipating later orthodoxy, he suggested instead that all mankind had 'spread from a centre and occupied the whole earth in the space of a few thousand years'.[2]

The declaration by Duckworth's son-in-law, Captain Ironside, that the Bushman spoke an unknown language without clicks can be described as peculiarly ignorant and unobservant—but not untypical of white people who posed as experts on the 'natives'. No doubt he was also deceived by Franz Taibosh speaking gibberish on the orders of Paddy Hepston. Captain William Edmund Ironside was married to the daughter of Duckworth's wife by a previous marriage. He was soon to achieve fame as the model for the dashing secret agent Richard Hannay of *The Thirty-nine Steps*. John Buchan's novel was published in 1914, and sold 25,000 copies in its first six months. Hannay was a clean-living hero, adept at disguise, and fighting sinister foreign villains. Ironside had worked for British military intelligence in South Africa during the war of 1899–1902, posing as a railway employee, and later spied in German South West Africa. Ironside lasted out the 1914–18 Great War as a staff officer in England, and then commanded the post-war invasion of Soviet Russia through Archangel. By 1939 he had risen to the highest rank in the British army, but favoured peace with Germany, and is believed to have been—without his knowledge—Hitler's choice for Lord Protector of Great Britain, heading a Nazi puppet government like Marshal Pétain or Vidkun Quisling. In 1940 the new prime minister, Winston Churchill, shunted Ironside off to become commander of the Home Guard defence force better known as 'Dad's Army'.[3]

Duckworth's letter to *The Times* was picked up by Reuters and the South African Press Agency (SAPA) and passed on to the South African press. The Johannesburg *Star* carried the Reuters report on Thursday, 2 October as 'Dancing Bushman. Found in the Kalahari'. The *Pretoria News*, edited by Vere Stent, carried the story on the same day as 'A Bushman in London. His artistic dancing'. On Friday, 3 October 1913, the Kimberley *Diamond Fields Advertiser* had the headline 'Scientist and Bushman. Farmer's interesting find in the Kalahari'.

The story printed in the *DFA* was extended into an interview with Sir Charles Mitchell, refuting the contention of a recent biographer (Gordon Le Sueur) that Cecil Rhodes had been a heavy drinker of 'sundowners', and denying that a man (Peter Kushana) calling himself Prince Lobengula in Manchester could possibly be a real son of the Ndebele king. Vere Stent responded the next day that he had been witness to Cecil Rhodes's partiality for stout, Benedictine brandy in his morning coffee, and champagne at dinner served by his faithful Coloured servant, Tony.[4]

The *Cape Times* referred to the 'dancing Bushman' as an 'interesting anthropological problem', and said it had consulted a 'well known Cape Town anthropological authority' who had pooh-poohed the idea that a Bushman could speak no known language. On the next Monday, the *Cape Times* carried a full report of its interview with that authority, Dorothea Bleek. She concerned herself mostly with the idea that the Bushman in question had come from the Kalahari:

There are a great many Bushmen in the Kalahari. It is a very large place and personally, while in Bechuanaland Protectorate, I have found four different kinds speaking different dialects or languages, I do not know which ... All the

Bushmen in the Kalahari seem to be more or less of Bantu blood. Some of them have the small figure and old face of the regular type of Bushman, and some are of distinctly tall stature and dark colour. The [Reuters/SAPA] cable does not say which part of the Kalahari the man came from ...

The newspaper added: 'All the Kalahari Bushmen she has met were not so pure as old [Cape] Colonial Bushmen who have now almost died out.'[5] The Johannesburg *Rand Daily Mail* on the same Monday, 6 October 1913 reported on its own researches:

The [Reuters] message has caused a certain amount of amusement among some of the residents of Kimberley, and also among a number of people in Johannesburg, who know the history of one 'dancing Bushman'. If the Bushman referred to is the same individual, then the Professor has been to a certain extent 'spoofed' and a very enterprising Press agent has probably secured a big 'scoop' ... It is possible that the 'dancing Bushman' referred in the cable is the one that was employed at Kimberley, and that the Professor has had his 'leg severely pulled'.

After detailing how it thought that the Bushman had been recruited, the *Mail* asserted: 'So far as can be ascertained there are no pure Bushmen left in South Africa now.' It claimed that the 'last known pure Bushman ... splendidly proportioned and bronze in colour' was employed at the Pietermaritzburg jail in Natal and had died ten years before.[6] The *Mail* report was repeated in another Johannesburg newspaper, the *Transvaal Leader*, the next day, Tuesday, under the headline 'Exported Bushman'. The Johannesburg *Star* on Wednesday, 8 October reported its own 'enquiries made locally' at Kimberley: 'it is said [this Bushman] is wonderfully adept in imitating the characteristic movements of animals. Though possessing no education, and speaking no known language, he has evidently been a close observer of nature, and his dancing represents, as already stated, the movements of denizens of the Desert.'

The *DFA* story in Kimberley on the same day recounted the *Rand Daily Mail*'s findings: 'The dancing Bushman. Has the professor been spoofed?' This led to a letter to the editor from A.T. Adams of the Brickfields, Schmidtsdrift Road, Kimberley, published on Friday, 10 October. Adams confirmed that the 'so-called Bushman' was well known to his workers and 'that he spoke the Taal as well as they do'. He concluded: 'The Yankees say a crop of fools are bred into the world every couple of years. Alas, for the poor Cambridge professor'—definitely, he had had his 'eye wiped'.[7]

The London weekly magazine *South Africa* published an editorial on

Saturday, 4 October, titled 'The Bushman and the bunny-hug', pouring scorn on Duckworth's letter to *The Times*. The magazine mocked Duckworth as 'thrice a doctor, once of medicine, once of science, and now of dancing, upon which he had written to *The Times* a most learned thesis'. The Bushman had shown London a dance that was no more novel than the step-dancing of Cockney coster-kings or 'the primitive prancing' of an African beer party. As for the Bushman speaking no known language, that was plainly ridiculous if he had really survived for seven years working on a South African farm. But 'Gone is the gaby-glide, bust is the bunny-hug, and tattered is the tango!' In Paris, he was now 'trying to substitute his dance for the obsolete can-can ... Perhaps while exercising his own legs he is pulling those of the Frenchmen.'[8]

From 29 September up to 25 or 26 October 1913, Franz Taibosh performed at the Nouveau Cirque in Paris, billed simply as *l'homme sauvage*. But we learn that it was in Paris that Franz Taibosh was first given the stage name Clicquot or Cliquot, later modified to Klikko in England and to Clico and Clicko in America—because of the *clics* or clicks in the way he spoke. Any connection was purely coincidental with Veuve Clicquot, *la grande dame de la champagne*, or with Count and Countess Cliquot in Johann Strauss's opera *Die Fledermaus* (the flying mouse or bat that stays out all night).

The Nouveau Cirque was described as 'perhaps the finest circus in Europe'. French circuses operated on a higher plane than circuses in England or America, with superior equestrian performances: they were as fashionable as operas. As the English showman Charles Cochran pointed out: 'In Paris the circus is not child's entertainment but a high form of art.' Hence there was 'no menagerie or congress of freaks'. The stars of the Nouveau Cirque had been the great French clown Footit and the Englishman Little Tich (Harry Relph)—a dwarfish talking clown who spoke in execrable Birmingham-accented French, keeping audiences in hysterics while he danced and did acrobatics in extremely long-toed boots.

A rich syndicate owned the circus, which was housed in an octagonal building with seats facing three sides of a single ring. Along the ringbank were plush red boxes ... Behind us were the arena seats and a gallery which extended to the roof. In the foyer a promenade led to a buffet where patrons preened and drank during the intermission ... A forty-piece string and woodwind orchestra occupied a platform above the performers' entrance.

But by 1913 the Nouveau Cirque was past its greatest days as 'the aristocrat of entertainment'. It organized a popular annual wrestling contest during its summer season, with raucous crowds of supporters pelting wrestlers they disliked. In the year following Franz Taibosh's performance, the contest degenerated into a riot when a Swiss wrestler among French, Turkish and Scots finalists refused to fight on until he was paid up front.[9]

And so it was in Paris that Franz Taibosh probably first experienced the 'scent of sawdust ... and the sound of the hoofs padding softly round the magic ring'. But if his manager or the manager's agent hoped that some of Little Tich's magic would rub off on Taibosh's number in Paris, they were to be disappointed. The publicity for *l'homme sauvage* in Paris appears to have been rudimentary. The theatrical columnist 'La Herse', writing on *spectacles divers* for the evening in the newspaper *Le Petit Parisien* on Wednesday, 8 October, alluded very briefly, below notices for the Folies-Bergère and the Moulin Rouge, to the *numéros sensationnels* being staged by Monsieur Charles Debray at the Nouveau Cirque with a Wednesday matinée at 2.30 pm. The Australian strongman Harold Evelyn was a veritable Hercules, lifting a dozen people with his feet. As for *l'homme sauvage*, he was simply a fantastic being (*un être fantastique*).

The London *Daily Chronicle*, alerted by the correspondence in *The Times*, sent its Paris correspondent to the Bushman's circus dressing-room. Presumably referring to an interview on the 1st or 2nd, the *Chronicle* published its account on Friday, 3 October: 'I went to the circus this evening to see the Bushman. I found him dressed in an ordinary English suit and overcoat, with nothing of the wild look I expected. Smilingly, he shook my hand warmly, and after some inarticulate words kissed it three times.' We are told, for the first time in print, that his name is Franz, while Paddy Hepston now goes under the name of Epstein. Franz is described as being 'of dwarf stature', with a face like a Negro African ('Flat nose, big lips, with very small moustache, and a few hairs at the tip of his chin that might pass for whiskers'), except that his skin is copper-coloured. He has 'a fine body but slender legs'. His wrists are 'relatively small compared with his fingers, which are quite long', and his hair looks like 'black cotton waste rag'. Epstein told the *Chronicle*: 'He has some grey hairs, and you can see from his face that he is very old. Professor Duckworth, who has seen him, believes that he is at least 100 years old—perhaps 110.'[10]

For the first time in any contemporary account, Franz Taibosh comes to life in this interview. Eighty years later, Barbara Cook was intensely moved when reading this item recovered from a newspaper library: it was something like the Franz she remembered from childhood.

He watched me with evident interest, but the little fellow also let his eyes wander constantly to the door, which opened into a corridor along which artists of the circus passed from time to time.

Every now and then he would recognise someone, and would give quite a civilised smile and wave his hand. To the fair sex he was very gallant, blowing them kisses, laying his hand on his heart, and doing the Don Juan to perfection. When one of the young ladies spoke to him the Bushman jumped from his seat, seized her hand, and kissed it respectfully.

His ears, too, appear to be sharp. Mr. Epstein was telling me of the copious drafts of edgwala [*tshwala*]— 'whisky'—which he gives the little man on certain occasions, and immediately his curious yellow face [was] wreathed in smiles, and then he began to laugh heartily, as at the recollection of a good dose. Yet Mr. Epstein declares that the Bushman has no mind. I put two coins on the table before him, a silver one and a copper one of ten centimes. I made him understand that he could have one of them. He showed no hesitation, but took the silver 50-cent one.

'He has no mind,' said Hepston. 'If I tell him to look out of the window he will do so and continue to look until I rouse him again.' No sooner had Hepston said this, than Franz deftly saved his master from embarrassment: 'While Mr. Epstein was showing me a number of photographs the little chap noticed that his master was bothered by another packet. He quickly stepped up to him and relieved him of it. Taking off his overcoat, he hung it across a chair very neatly.' Most likely the packet contained 'filthy' photographic postcards that were notoriously available in Paris. The *Daily Chronicle* added that 'In scores of other ways this Bushman showed that he possessed ordinary intelligence'. Over Hepston's assertions that Franz communicated mainly through sign language, the newspaper established that he spoke a 'taal' that was 'curious on account of the click which punctuates nearly every other word. Otherwise it is by no means disagreeable.'

Franz had already picked up a few words of French, and was able to interpret French words into his own language: '*Koo-rang* seems to be the equivalent of *joli*.' (It was actually the Korana word for 'girl' rather than for 'pretty'.) Hearing Franz speak so coherently prompted the correspondent to ask Hepston 'how he accounted for his wild man possessing a language when, according to him ... Franz is the only survivor of an extinct tribe, and had, therefore, probably lived in solitude'. Hepston proved to be 'at a loss to explain this', so the interviewer went on to comment: 'It would probably occur to the ordinary observer that to speak so fluently as Franz does—not a matter of savage cries, but a distinct speech—he must have lived with others of his kind able to converse together in the same tongue.'

Hepston admitted to the *Daily Chronicle* that he gave Franz 'very little food', just chocolate or beef-tea (i.e. Liebig's Fluid Beef Brand, Oxo, Bovril, etc.) in the morning and 'nothing else all day'. Franz slept during the day and thus slept only a few hours at night, when, Hepston claimed, 'he often gets up and shrieks wildly'. Obviously anxious to re-establish Franz's credentials as a Wild Man, Hepston claimed that Franz jumped rather than walked in the streets 'and often yells fearfully'. If this was not all theatrical artifice, it suggests that Franz had been traumatized by some horrific circumstance.

The *Daily Chronicle* article of 4 October was picked up as far away as Singapore, where the *Straits Times* republished it on 31 October as 'African Bushman. Savage who may be 110 years old. Now dancing in Paris circus'. Other press responses were more immediate. The 11 October edition of *South Africa* used the *Chronicle* report as further ammunition. Aimed at expatriate colonial readers in Britain, the magazine was not known for its sympathy towards blacks but felt obliged to protest at Hepston's boast of having tamed Franz bound with cords and tied to a wagon: 'If a Bushman had done all this we wonder if he would not have tried to escape. One need not be a negrophilist to feel that a Bushman … is deserving of better treatment, and is even entitled to it under the laws of South Africa and of every civilised country.'

South African newspapers ignored the *Chronicle* interview but picked up *The Times* letter of 2 October by cable, and made their comments—as we have seen—during the week of Monday, 6 October.[11]

On Friday, 7 November 1913, Franz Taibosh was taken to Cambridge again by Hepston at the invitation of Dr Duckworth. In the words of *South Africa*, the Bushman was now back from Paris 'full of frog's legs and French culture'. Once more he was 'under the microscope, the stethoscope, the horoscope and all the other instruments of the Cambridge Anthropological Laboratory'. Franz was examined in Duckworth's laboratory by 'leading Cambridge ethnologists', before being displayed before more people in the New Examinations Hall. The great anthropologist Alfred Court Haddon ('Headhunter Haddon') of Australasian fame, Duckworth's major competitor in Cambridge circles, was present. But only Duckworth's personal opinion was recorded:

I expressly invited discussion on the problem of his race, pointing out some features in which he is to be contrasted with the Hottentots, and again others distinguishing him from the pure 'Bush' type. As a result ... on the whole the current description (Bushman) is the most appropriate. But I should like to take this opportunity of suggesting that we may be dealing with a type of Bushman unrecognized hitherto.

'In that case', suggested *South Africa*, which was sure that the Bushman must be able to speak Afrikaans, 'the funny little fellow should at once be labelled with a scientific name. What about Homo supercaltans, or Homo gurgitans? We suspect, however, that he will go down in history, or whatever may be his destiny, as Little Legpuller ...' (Right from the start many suspected that Piltdown Man was a forgery.) [12]

Present also on that day, the ethnologist Alice Werner employed her wide knowledge of African peoples to lead a discussion in the examinations hall on what language the Bushman spoke. Because Franz had been instructed or terrified by Hepston into not speaking any Afrikaans-Dutch, no one present could understand what Taibosh was saying in his 'click' language. It was clear to Alice Werner that what Franz spoke was neither a Bantu language nor Dutch. Duckworth was forced to concede that the Bushman 'clearly ... employs "clicks" spontaneously, and not as I thought previously by way of repeating words in which these occur'. 'Finally, the Bushman gave an exhibition of dancing to a large audience in the New Examinations Hall of the University. The performance was received with much enthusiasm, and the general opinion seems to be that the power of mimicry, aided by a remarkable natural appreciation of time and rhythm, is accountable for its highly specialized character.'

Next day's London *Daily News* reported that Franz had lunched at Jesus College and 'drank afternoon tea with the ladies', which prompted *South Africa* magazine to add: 'After this it would be a short step to eating his dinners in hall and taking his degree. At the very least, in return for all the entertainment which "Franz" provided, with the assistance of a "rag-time orchestra," he should get the D.D. (Dinky Dance) honoris causa.'

The interest that Franz Taibosh stirred at Cambridge among university anthropologists can be compared with the contemporaneous exhibition at San Francisco of Ishi, billed as the 'last Californian Indian'. Both Franz and Ishi were inaccurately referred to as 'the last of their kind'. Such academic claptrap got short shrift from *South Africa*, which referred ironically to the high-browed fraternity standing around rubbing their hands with glee while the little man revolved in his highly original dances like a Catherine wheel, and fired off his clicking speech like an interminable string of crackers ... With the tango all the rage, why not establish a Chair of Dancing at the University, and install this already distinguished South African? There should be no difficulty about his refusal to speak any language but that which in such a special degree is his own; for the lectures would obviously take the form of physical demonstrations.[13]

Duckworth wrote a second letter to *The Times*, dated Saturday, 8 November 1913, giving his account of what had happened in Cambridge the previous evening. He indicated that he would be pursuing his researches further, 'as the Bushman will remain in England for some time longer'.[14]

Franz Taibosh's performance in the New Examinations Hall was not noticed in the Cambridge newspapers until after it was commented upon by the *South Africa* journal. Saturday's *Cambridge Daily News* just noted that 'London is now in the grip of the Tango craze, almost as strongly as Paris has been for many weeks past'. On the Monday the *News* remarked on an airship crossing the countryside, advertising Bovril, and on a meeting at Newnham College on Friday evening at which Dr Jane Harrison had opined that 'the difference between man and woman lay in the insularity of man and the resonance of woman'. (Hence the only private room in a middle-class house was the husband's study.) Meanwhile, it was reported that an Egyptian student, a relative of the Khedive, had been fined for using obscene language on Saturday night when he was told a Cambridge theatre was full and that no more tickets were to be sold.[15]

The trail of Franz Taibosh and Paddy Hepston over the next three winters is difficult to reconstruct. But one thing is certain in the years 1913–14 and 1914–15: continued interest in Franz in Cambridge circles. In April 1914 Franz was to reappear on stage in Cambridge, and during 1915 another Cambridge man, a dentist, was to intervene in Franz's life. Meanwhile W.L.H. Duckworth was preparing his study of Franz Taibosh, eventually published in Rome during 1916 as *Descrizione di un Boscimano del Sud Africa* in the series *Revista di Anthropologia*, volume 20 (in honour of Guiseppe Sergi), published by the Società Romana di Anthropologia.

Wherever Paddy Hepston and Franz Taibosh spent the winter of 1913–14, they were unlikely to pass up on employment during the Christmas entertainment season, whether as a main act on stage or in a sideshow. The Wild Dancing Bushman could easily have been incorporated into one of the Christmas pantomimes put on for children in many British theatres. Another possibility was as a sideshow act in a Christmas circus. In London's Olympia arena, the theatrical impresario Charles B. Cochran presented Hagenbeck's Wonder Zoo and Big Circus, direct from Hamburg, from 26 December 1913. Sideshows included the showing of Kinemacolor film of wild animals in the wild.

Cochran was credited with having modernized English circus by introducing Continental European animal training, lady riders and silent clowns—superseding the native English circus tradition of Wombwell and the Sangers. But circus in England in 1913 was 'an entertainment which seems to have gone out of fashion for the time being'. People no longer laughed at the clowns and midgets 'we laughed at 20 years ago', and attitudes towards the training of animals were changing. A November 1913 London circus audience protested at the acts of uncomfortable-looking bears and a horse terrified by the flaming torches of jugglers, but were delighted when lions skipped to one of the latest fad dances.[16]

It is possible that the Wild Dancing Bushman was taken, maybe once again, to the European continent over 1913–14. It would have been the last chance for Franz Taibosh and Paddy Hepston to travel in Central Europe before the Great War set in. There are later indications in Franz's life that he had indeed spent some time in Germany. In 1937, it was asserted in a court of law that Hepston had exhibited Taibosh 'in England, France and Germany, finally coming to the United States'. It is said that by 1931 Franz Taibosh spoke 'a smattering of Dutch, German, and English'—though this could simply reflect the fact that he had picked up a knowledge of German as the lingua franca of so many circus artists.[17] Given popular interest in Bushmen and 'Hottentots' from German South West Africa, there would certainly have been a market for a Wild Dancing Bushman act in the *völkerschauen* (live ethnic exhibits) and blackface minstrel *Shimmyshauen* (Jim Crow shows) of Germany, attached to travelling carnivals of the type immortalized in *The Cabinet of Dr Caligari* film of 1919.[18]

7

HIDING FROM HUMANITARIANS

COVERAGE OF THE WILD DANCING BUSHMAN in the local press at Cambridge in April 1914 shows that a press agent had been hard at work with advance publicity and press releases. For the first time, Paddy Hepston was credited with army officer rank as Captain Epstein. The *Cambridge Daily News* of Saturday, 25 April 1914 carried the following advertisement for the Empire Theatre in Mill Road on the following Monday:

CAPT. EPSTEIN presents
THE WILD
Dancing BUSHMAN
Captured in the wilds of South Africa
First specimen of THE MOST
PRIMITIVE RACE ever brought
before the public. His hair
stretches like elastic. A natural
Ragtime Dancer. Wild, Weird and
Wonderful. Danced for eight hours
continuously, a feat which has
never been equalled. The Bushman
is nearly 100 Years of Age. Don't
fail to see this unique specimen
of human nature. EXAMINED
BY THE UNIVERSITY
AUTHORITIES OF CAMBRIDGE,
and pronounced to be genuine.

The Wild Dancing Bushman duly appeared at the Empire Palace of Varieties in Mill Road, Cambridge, during the week of Monday, 27 April.[1] The *Cambridge Daily News* reviewed his performance on the Tuesday, under a faded publicity photograph of him standing bare-chested and holding a bone and a knife:

'Klikko' (for such he was nicknamed by the Parisians, from a peculiar clicking sound he makes with his tongue) is not black, like the Kaffirs, but chocolate-coloured; he is 4 ft. 1 in. high, and weighs 5 st. [70 pounds]; his hair is jet black, and of a soft, elastic texture, that is, if one single hair is taken hold of it can be stretched out nearly an inch. The bushman has no language as we understand it, simply a series of long calls, guttural sounds, and the peculiar clicking with his tongue already mentioned. From close questioning, from those who understand him [*sic*], he appears to remember the Great Boer Trek in 1835, and he is thought to be nearly one hundred years of age, though he does not look it.

Hepston claimed that the only previous Bushman brought to civilization had 'a monument erected to him in South Africa by the Boers, who evidently thought he was the last of the lot', and invited members of the university to examine the Bushman in private:

Those who accept the Captain's invitation will find 'Klikko' a most inoffensive fellow with a tremendous pair of lungs. Of course it is impossible to carry on any conversation with him, but he readily lends himself to examination. He has few wants, and is happy. We offered him a cigarette which he tore up and stuffed into the bowl of an old briar pipe. We then offered him a pipeful of Navy Cut and he seemed delighted. Evidently he is no victim of the cigarette habit.[2]

As for his performance at the Mill Road Empire:

The band has instructions to play what music they like, and the bushman dances to it precisely and without hesitation. It is said he never dances the same steps twice; they are purely extemporary, and vary according to the music provided. He danced for 15 or 20 minutes last evening, until he was bodily carried off the stage, for he will not stop of his own accord.

One member who took up the offer to see the Bushman backstage was an older university student from Emmanuel College named Robert Douglass Vernon. The son of a mining contractor in Newstead, Nottinghamshire,

Vernon held a previous degree from Nottingham University and had been granted an additional BA degree from Cambridge in 1911, thereafter remaining as a postgraduate student until 1914. His discipline is not known, but he appears to have been of a scholarly bent since he rejoined Emmanuel College in 1921 in order to take advantage of its facilities such as the library. On that Monday night in 1913, Vernon was in the wings at the Mill Road Empire, and was appalled by what he saw.

According to Vernon, the Bushman, wearing heavy wooden clogs for dancing shoes, was 'made to dance, gesticulate and yell ... until the man is ready to drop with fatigue ... he seems to lose all self-control and the shouting is automatic—only to be stopped by forcibly gagging the man'. When the stage was blacked out and the curtain came down, 'one man uses a pocket flash-light to see the Bushman while the second man forcibly gags him with a rag and wraps a heavy rug around him. The Bushman is then carried off by force while he tries to scream, bite, kick and fight.' Vernon was told that this was a nightly occurrence, and 'there had been some bloodshed at the man's lodging the night before'.

Vernon was appalled by the idea that the Bushman 'cannot speak nor in any way understand the language of his keepers (one is an Englishman, the other a Boer) nor can they speak his language; the Bushman is absolutely in their power'. Hepston was undoubtedly the Boer referred to by Vernon—possibly because he was swearing at Franz in Afrikaans. The Englishman could have been either the press agent or Hepston's brother Randolph, who no doubt had a cultivated theatrical voice. Vernon's account suggests that Franz might have been having a fit, but there is no mention of epilepsy later in his life. Franz had the will and energy to work himself up into ecstatic dancing that could last for hours, and on this occasion was resisting interruption of an act lasting less than ten minutes.

Next day, R.D. Vernon wrote a letter to the Aborigines' Protection Society (APS) in London. 'I wish to draw your attention to what I consider to be a case of great cruelty regarding a native South African Bushman ... It does not seem right that a member of a nearly extinct race should be exploited on the music halls for gain by men who treat him exactly as they would a performing animal.'[3]

The APS, in its offices at Denison House on the south end of Vauxhall Bridge, was run under the nominal direction of Sir Thomas Foxwell Travers Buxton. Its energetic and opinionated organizing secretary, Rev. John H. Harris, formerly a Baptist missionary in the Congo, was really in charge. Harris and Buxton shared the Colonial Office's concern about exotic 'native' entertainers being dumped on the streets when they ceased to have novelty value. The APS also specialized in the repatriation of stranded colonial subjects: recent recipients of its charity had included the politician Marcus Garvey, who was repatriated to Jamaica.[4]

The provincial tour continued. During the week beginning Monday, 4 May 1914, Franz Taibosh appeared at the Palace Theatre at Maidstone, in Kent, as 'Frantz, the Dancing Wild Bushman'.

> **PALACE THEATRE**
> MAIDSTONE
> MONDAY, MAY 4th, and DURING WEEK
> 7 AND 9. TWICE NIGHTLY. 7 AND 9
> SENSATION! SENSATION!
> **YUMA THE MYSTERY YUMA**
> **YUMA THE MYSTERY YUMA**
> WHAT IS YUMA? HE OR IT?
> VIOLET WALLACE, Comedienne
> ROUSBY AND RENE in their Comedy Sketch,
> 'FINE FEATHERS.'
> RED YOUNG CHAS. RUSSELL
> Comedian. in Song Scena
> THE LIFE SAVER assisted by
> on the Palacescope LITTLE ELSIE
> **FRANTZ THE DANCING FRANTZ**
> **FRANTZ WILD BUSHMAN FRANTZ**
> Captured in the Wilds of South Africa
> (Nearly 100 Years of Age).
> Don't fail to see this unique specimen of
> Human Nature
> Box Office open daily 10.30 till 4. Tele. 229·

Yuma was actually a person imitating a mechanical automaton (what later generations would call a robot). As for 'Frantz', who for the first time in his show-business career was given his proper Christian name, the weekly *South Eastern Gazette* reported that he 'aroused much curiosity, and is undoubtedly a unique specimen of humanity ... judging by his extreme activity and his almost boyish enthusiasm, it is quite possible he will live for another hundred years.'[5]

The man 'calling himself Captain Epstein' told the Maidstone theatre staff to keep at a distance because the Bushman was 'absolutely wild'. The stage manager at the Palace, Mr L. Norley, was appalled at what he saw backstage. After dancing so energetically for ten minutes, Franz was carried off screaming, in a hot sweat, to be locked up shivering in a bare dressing-room. When Hepston went out drinking with a friend on the Saturday night, and had not returned well after midnight, the stage manager took pity on Franz. He found him to be 'quite rational but unable to speak to me': the Bushman evidently had absolutely no knowledge of English (or we may assume that Franz was too intimidated by Hepston's violence to display any such knowledge).

Norley instructed an employee to take Franz back to his lodgings. Later Norley was confronted in the street by Hepston (together with another man, referred to as a manager). According to Norley, 'when I asked him what he intended to do with the Bushman he became abusive & enquired what business it was of mine'. Norley should have left Franz alone in the cold and dark dressing-room. 'When I mentioned that this would be a callous thing to do, he became violent & struck me.'

Hence Norley became the second person to write about the Wild Dancing Bushman to the Aborigines' Protection Society in London. He recounted his tale and asserted: 'I consider Epstein not a proper person to have charge of such a being, who is treated like an animal & is powerless to defend himself.' Harris replied on behalf of the APS, and in a later letter Norley added that the Bushman 'is absolutely at the mercy of Epstein, who himself told me that he had punished him times out of number'.[6]

For the week beginning Monday, 11 May 1914, the act moved on to the Grand Theatre of Varieties at Gravesend, where the Merry Mascots had played a year earlier. Gravesend benefited from holidaymakers who arrived on the steamers that plied the Thames estuary and the north Kent coast from London. During the first day Hepston and Franz toured the streets of Gravesend in a horse-drawn carriage to give publicity to the evening's show. Franz was in character as a Wild Man, speaking in an incomprehensible language and no doubt cavorting and letting out piercing yells from the carriage. But this week he was called neither Klikko nor Frantz, but once again simply the Wild Dancing Bushman.

The *Gravesend and Dartford Reporter* at the end of the week obviously had a little help from pre-prepared publicity:

An excitement not often seen at the Grand Theatre pervaded the whole of the performance this week for the principal item of the bill of fare is one that stands alone in its kind throughout theatre land.

When 'The wild dancing Bushman'—he has no other name—came to English shores six months ago the London Press described this little man as 'the wonder of the age' and certainly he fully lives up to the description. This specimen of a practically extinct race, is one of the little people that Mr. H.M. Stanley discovered living in the bush on his expedition in central Africa. This little Bushman is the closest resemblance of the monkey in features and physique although he was, previous to being 'discovered', a keen hunter of game and the denizens of the forest.

It is said that no white man can understand his language. His exhibition of it on Monday, when he made a tour of the town in a brougham [carriage], accompanied by his keeper, was certainly beyond the comprehension of Gravesend inhabitants.

Of the performance given by him little can be said beyond the fact it is a series of weird, wild, native dances, and although, it is stated, he is over 100 years old, he is quite willing to dance as long as the music lasts. His energy and enthusiasm are apparently limitless.[7]

Coming to England 'six months ago' could have referred to the length of time that the press agent had been representing the Wild Dancing Bushman act. This press story also shows that the agent was building on popular racial prejudices equating exotic people with monkeys, and on public memory of the ethnographic showbiz tours by Ituri pygmies or 'little people' from Central Africa a few years earlier.

In June 1914, the Aborigines' Protection Society opened a new file marked 'Bushman, Ill-treatment of Wild Dancing'. Travers Buxton and John Harris alerted the Colonial Office, the Variety Artistes' Federation (VAF), the commissioner of London's Metropolitan Police, the High Commissioner (ambassador) of the Union of South Africa, and the anthropologist A.C. Haddon at Christ's College, Cambridge. Buxton and Harris drew attention to the 'degrading character' of a performance that involved such 'cruelty to the performer'. Their aim was to release the Bushman dancer from the Svengali-type grip of his manager-master, Captain Epstein.

'Headhunter' Haddon was packing for a conference in Australia but reportedly felt strongly about the 'poor little Bushman'. His wife Fanny wrote to the APS on 23 June, suggesting that that society contact Baron G. von Hügel at Cambridge's anthropological museum and 'Dr. Duckworth of Jesus Coll.', who had arranged the private showing of the Bushman for fellow academics. The VAF, representing vaudeville performers, considered the matter at its executive committee meeting on 25 June. The meeting resolved that it 'deprecates exhibitions of this kind', and would contact the police. The VAF was particularly strict on both members and employers in its attempts to free the profession from all taint of tawdriness, and published an annual handbook of VAF-barred artistes and theatres.

The London police tracked the Bushman and his manager in mid-June 1914 to lodgings at No. 69 Kimberley Avenue, in the newly built suburb of East Ham in the fields beyond the East End of London. Kimberley Avenue consisted of lines of modest red-brick terraces, next to better-appointed Mafeking Avenue on the south side of the Barking Road. The presence of Irish immigrants in the area was reflected by Catholic investment in a fine new church building, next to the towering Boleyn public house on the corner of Barking Road and Green Street.

The police established that Hepston and the Bushman would soon be going across the sea to Dublin's World's Fair variety theatre in the third week of June, to play there until the end of August 1914. The Colonial Office therefore referred 'the matter … to the Irish Government'. Dublin's Metropolitan Police commissioner, Sir John Ross, was also alerted by the VAF and by an MP friendly to the APS.

Dr Duckworth reported indignantly to the APS that he could 'hardly believe' Mr Vernon's observations on the Bushman's act in Cambridge. 'What I did see was neither degrading, nor did it involve cruelty of the kind described.' He begged to interview Travers Buxton in person.[8]

Meanwhile the trail went cold as Paddy Hepston and Franz Taibosh ducked out of sight. Dublin police were unable to locate them at the (Sprengel Brothers') World's Fair theatre. The blacklisting of the act by the VAF had evidently taken effect.

Perhaps the Royal Irish Constabulary looked elsewhere in Dublin; certainly they should have done. There were numerous other entertainments, concerts and thrills such as switchback rides going on at the time around the Civic Exhibition at the Linenhall Buildings between 15 July and 31 August

1914. The Constabulary had better work to do rather than chase a missing African. Ireland was in turmoil after the Irish Home Rule bill had been stuck in the Westminster parliament for three years—turned down twice by the Conservative and Unionist majority in the House of Lords, after being passed by the Liberal-dominated House of Commons.

Events were moving ever faster and more furiously on the continent of Europe. Germany declared war against Russia on Saturday, 1 August, and invaded France on Sunday, the 2nd. Britain declared war on Germany at midnight on 4–5 August. Though war had been anticipated among the well-informed for at least a year, an editorial in an entertainment journal on 8 August 1914 remarked: 'The rapid move of events during the past week has come as a great surprise!' Irish Home Rule was rapidly passed into law at Westminster on Saturday, 19 September, hailed as 'Ireland's day of triumph'. But its implementation was suspended for the duration of the war. Hundreds of thousands of Irishmen flocked to join the British army in the trenches of Flanders, while some others began to see Germany as potential ally rather than enemy.[9]

It is hardly surprising that we lose sight of the Wild Dancing Bushman again at this time. But maybe a glimpse of the act, in disguise from police surveillance, is to be had in a variety theatre notice that appeared in the Dublin *Daily Express* on Tuesday, 11 August 1914. It reviewed the previous evening's programme at the Empire Theatre, when the comedienne Kitty Clinton (otherwise Kate Clinton, 'the only female Irishman') was followed by 'Taree, the Australian musical bushman, [who] quickly established himself a favourite, and was heartily applauded for his efforts'.[10] Could Taree have been Taibosh? If so, it would by no means be the last time that he was billed as an Australian.

Margate
Rendezvous

Eight or nine months after disappearing from view in Ireland in August 1914, Franz Taibosh reappeared in the guise of 'Klikko, Wild Man of Borneo' in south-east England. Where was he in the meantime? It is likely that he spent some time with Paddy Hepston in or near the Jewish community of South Dublin, probably being passed off as a manservant. It is also likely that the act toured either Ireland or across the Irish Sea in north-west England.

In Ireland, Hepston could have exhibited Taibosh in a tented threepenny-gaff, within a travelling fair or as a sideshow within a circus. Country fairs were brought into the village meadows of Britain and Ireland in trailers tugged behind heavy steam-rollers. Historian Willson Disher fondly recalled the sounds of 'rifle-shots cracking, blaring organ pipes, bells' and of people shying coconuts, and the tastes of golden barley-sugar, gingerbread, meat pies, sweet puddings and bright yellow lemonade. The evening was lit by naphtha flares. The 'rides' were mostly old swing-boats, but steam drove the merry-go-round (carousel) and the great calliope organ. Disher explained the appeal of annual fairs to country folk: 'Each emotion that is starved in real life finds a stimulus at the fair'—notably the emotion of curiosity, which made pennies flow for the showmen.

The largest touring show in Ireland at the outbreak of the First World War was Buff Bill's circus and menagerie. It included one or two black performers, probably African Americans. Thanks to a good advance agent, the show made lots of money with its lions on the west coast in Galway during the 1914 season. This was contrary to experience elsewhere in Ireland. Eliza Barker abandoned her Irish circus in December 1914 after travelling with it for seven years. She told a bankruptcy court in Scarborough, England, that 'people took no interest in circuses, and the takings fell off very much. Home Rule and strikes caused her to leave the country.'

When Ireland became cold as well as wet during winter, the best prospects for show business were the covered winter-gardens of seaside towns on either side of the Irish Sea. Blackpool, England's equivalent of Coney Island next to the port of Liverpool, prospered during the Great War as it was packed out with recreating soldiers and civilians. It featured a miniature Eiffel Tower and boardwalks and piers, night-time illumination by millions of electric light bulbs, amusement parks and rides, and the Tower Circus. These catered for working-class masses in the summer high season and for 'better class' patronage during the rest of the year. There were also numerous fairgrounds and amusement parks further inland, as well as major variety theatres doing well in the Manchester area, Leeds and Bradford. (The 1901 census suggests that Paddy had a sister-in-law called Dora Hepston living in Leeds, with three Cork-born and four Dublin-born children.) Coastal resorts on the east coast of Northern England, facing the German (North) Sea, were depleted of trippers after the good people of Hartlepool were startled by German naval shelling at the beginning of the war.[1]

By May 1915 Hepston had the confidence and the contacts to risk engaging the Wild Dancing Bushman again in lucrative south-east England. The new stage name, 'Klikko, the Wild Man of Borneo', was no doubt adopted to avoid any VAF blacklisting. Klikko appeared daily at the Fun City sideshow in the Rendezvous amusement park next to Margate pier. Margate, next to Ramsgate, lay well to the east of Gravesend on the north Kent coast. 'Merry Margate' had been a seaside resort since Regency days, and was described as breezy and invigorating, without 'blatant' brass bands. Vulgarity 'may be found anywhere, but there is less of it at Margate than is to be found in most places'.[2]

Margate had the distinction of being the first place in England to hear the sounds of war in August 1914—a 'tremendous cannonade' between British and German ships way out at sea on the very first day.[3] Thereafter people living on the north Kent coast and the Straits of Dover sometimes heard, and on fair days even saw, the explosions of trench warfare in Flanders. They also, in 1915, began to experience air raids by Zeppelin airships. Twenty German bombs fell on Ramsgate on the morning of Monday, 17 May 1915, destroying the old Bull and George inn near the harbour. Periodic air raids continued on east-coast holiday resorts as far north as Yorkshire over the summer. Up to 8 September, when twenty more people were killed in London, total deaths from Zeppelin raids numbered fifty-seven—minimal by the standards of later wars, but at the time an entirely new kind of terror, coming from the sky.[4]

War or no war, Margate was determined to make a go of the holiday season beginning with the Whitsun bank holiday in late May 1915. Tourist numbers at Margate were restricted by the wartime ban on pleasure-steamers plying the north Kent coast, but visitors came from London by train or omnibus to keep the summer season going. Entertainment spots included the Hippodrome and Pavilion theatres, Margate's Winter Gardens, Lord George Sanger's Hall-by-the Sea (later renamed Dreamland), and the new pleasure park called the Rendezvous, on the old Marine Palace site next to Margate's pier or jetty.

The Rendezvous was advertised as having 'all the fun and amusements one associates with the great Continental fairs'. Its principal attraction was to be a circus, with its 'customary accompaniments and accessories'.[5] A feature advert appeared on the front page of the *Margate, Ramsgate and Isle of Thanet and East Kent Advertiser* for Whit Saturday 1915, with Franz Taibosh billed as the Wild Man of Borneo.

THE RENDEZVOUS

MARGATE

(ADJOINING THE PIER)

GRAND OPENING Sat. 22 May 1915 with RENDEZVOUS GRAND
CIRCUS under dir. of Mr. Whimsical Walker (Drury Lane's Famous
Clown) x 3 perfs. daily

A Galaxy of Talent. Witty Clowns. Performing Animals. Lady and
Gentlemen Riders, Gymnasts, etc. Entire Change Weekly. Grand
Orchestra. Prices of Admission—6d., 9d., 1s. Children half-price.—La
Belle de Paris; La [*sic*] Tableaux Vivantes; The Indian Fakir; The Water
Nymphs; The Wild Man of Borneo;

William Wilson's Famous Fun City (direct from Agricultural Hall,
London). The Big Wheel. Motor Cars. Motor Boats. The Sensational
Alpine Slide (direct from Crystal Palace, London).

Open from 10.30 to 10.30 (Free of Charge)[6]

The *Thanet Times* rejoiced at the successful opening of the 1915 Margate season at Whitsuntide, with flags and bunting flying from the jetty and hotels, blue skies and multi-coloured sunsets. The town was full of motorbuses and charabancs in full glorious sunshine on Whit Monday, when 'The Rendezvous opened its attractions at ten in the morning, and there was an open air circus programme at eleven o'clock ... repeated three or four times during the day ... The Rendezvous also provided all the "fun of the Fair," which was well patronised all the day.'[7]

By Saturday, 5 June 'The Wild Man of Borneo' had reverted to his previous title and risen to top billing at the Rendezvous:

THE TALK OF MARGATE

The Wild Dancing Bushman

(A Genuine Specimen of an almost extinct race,

and over 100 years of age.)

The Rendezvous, and especially its Bushman, were said to be attracting large crowds during a week of fine weather. Other sideshows at the Rendezvous included expert lady swimmers and divers, a rifle range, an Olde English Village, and all the swings and roundabouts and rides of Wilson's Fun City. As evenings grew shorter, outdoor evening performances were restricted by wartime prohibition on burning lights at night. Seaside entertainment is said to have been 'a hard life but very rewarding'. Bad weather could make a hell of it. When the waves were lashing against the seafront or the pier, 'the sound of the show was sometimes difficult to hear above the noise of the sea and wind'.[8]

The August bank holiday at Margate apparently went relatively well, despite restrictions on rail travel limiting the number of excursion trippers. More than a thousand armament workers from the Woolwich arsenal, so-called 'canaries' with explosive-stained yellow hair, whooped it up for four days in town, 'sunning themselves on Margate's breezy promenades'. Charlie Chaplin's film *The Tramp*, making him an international star, was playing at both the Parade Cinema opposite the pier and at the Cinema de Luxe in the High Street. Horatio Bottomley, swaggering editor of the ultra-patriotic magazine *John Bull*, came to Margate that bank holiday to deliver a lecture on 'The present situation' at the Pavilion and in the Winter Gardens, at two to five shillings a seat. An unfortunate elderly German woman from London, visiting her daughters in Margate, was arrested for entering the town as an enemy alien without a permit.[9] Meanwhile, one of the greatest and most futile battles of the war was under way at Gallipoli in Turkey, where on 6 August 'Australians rushed forward to the assault with the fury of fanatics'.

The official spirit of the day was caught and recast by a big local newspaper advertisement for Sunlight Soap, featuring smiling sailors. 'Cheerfulness opposed to Frightfulness—Cheerfulness will overcome Frightfulness—

Cheerfulness at sea—Cheerfulness on the land—Cheerfulness in trenches—Cheerfulness in factory—Cheerfulness at war—Cheerfulness at WORK.'[10] A history of the times claimed that during the Great War leisure and entertainment were 'if anything, intensified ... war did not interfere with the night-life of the towns ... All street-lights were alight at night, [but] with their glasses painted dark-blue, so that each street seemed full of police stations. Buses and cabs ... [with lights] just slightly dimmed ... Shop-blinds and house-blinds had to be drawn ... Dress rules were in general relaxed, and in theatres and restaurants lounge suits and uniforms were more numerous than dinner-jackets.'[11]

The 1915 summer entertainment season at Margate eventually ended on Saturday, 25 September, when by tradition variety artists presented 'topsy-turvy' programmes, singing each other's songs and burlesquing them.[12]

The Wild Dancing Bushman had not gone unnoticed by humanitarians in Margate. On 12 July 1915, Jane Goddard of The Bungalow, Grotto Hill, Margate, wrote indignantly to E.D. Morel, who had made his name exposing the Red Rubber atrocities in King Leopold's Congo. (Morel's Congo Reform Association, with Sir Roger Casement, Sir Harry Johnston and Rev. John H. Harris, had been wound up in June 1913.) Morel and Sydney Olivier—uncle of the young Laurence Olivier—had got back into the news in October 1913, calling for the removal of 'all theory of race discrimination from public policy', and predicting the coming challenge of Asian nationalism to white supremacy.[13]

Miss Goddard said she was haunted by the 'piteous look and evident terror [of] an aged Bushman, said to be a hundred years old, who is being exploited by some white people' at Margate. 'He looks very old and wretched and dances until the perspiration streams off him.' Morel passed on the letter to the Aborigines' Protection Society (APS), which set investigations going again, fearful that 'no sooner do we begin to take action in one place than [the Bushman] appears to be "spirited away" in another'.

Notwithstanding Miss Goddard's lack of confidence in her local police force, Margate police were pressed to investigate. Detective Constable Frank Ashbee and Police Constable Thorpe found the Bushman dancing in a ten-by-six-foot wooden pit, to the sound of a wind-up gramophone. A man—it is not clear if it was Hepston—sat beating time with a stick on the edge of the pit. The stick was not a folded whip, as previously reported. Though he was advertised as dancing for up to eight hours at a stretch, and the wooden auditorium was open between 10 am and 9 pm every day except Sunday, the Bushman was dancing for only as long as the public threw coins into the ring. Ashbee and Thorpe reported back to their superiors:

> re. Wild Bushman, showing at the Rendevous [*sic*], Margate ... We remained in the show 16 minutes and the Bushman danced three times during that period and the rest of the time was taken up by the man in charge describing how the Bushman came to be captured ... He is supposed to have been examined by Professor Cunningham [*sic*] of Cambridge, who estimates his age as over 100 years, and states the Bushman is the nearest approach to the Ape species he has ever seen ...

After noting that the Bushman lived on raw potatoes, washed down by Bovril beef-tea, and that he drank four or five pints of dark stout ale per day, the police report continued:

> When the audience applaud the Bushman shouts and always finishes up with a laugh. He has on no occasion ever shown any signs of fear ...
>
> During the intervals when he is not dancing he sells postcards of himself (one attached) and laughs to the purchaser and kisses his hand. He then stands on his head and turns somersaults apparently of his own accord. Frequently when the man in charge is describing the Bushman, he throws a kiss to a lady or child in the audience and generally appears to like the attention he creates.

The policemen went on to interview the landlady of the lodgings 'where Captain Epstein *and his wife* [author's italics]' were staying. 'She informs me that the Bushman has a small room to himself and has a warm bath every morning and behaves in the house as an ordinary individual. The Captain takes him up his food.'[14]

As well as contacting the Home Office, which ordered the Margate police investigation, John Harris of the APS contacted the High Commissioner for the Union of South Africa in London. The High Commissioner was W.P. Schreiner, scion of a famous missionary family, brother of the novelist Olive Schreiner, and previous advocate of native political rights. He might have been expected to respond sympathetically, but his response to the Margate police report on the Wild Dancing Bushman was dismissive. If correct, he said, it showed the Bushman as 'having rather a good time, and to be kindly treated'.

While tut-tutting about 'such performances by units [*sic*] of the less civilised races', Schreiner refused to have anything more to do with the case—on the grounds that a Kalahari Bushman must come from Bechuanaland Protectorate (later Botswana), which was not part of the Union of South Africa but Great Britain's direct responsibility. Three years before, his office had been equally dismissive in the case of George Ngweni Wilson from King William's Town in the Eastern Cape of South Africa, when it had disingenuously disclaimed responsibility for him on the grounds that he was Sesotho-speaking and must therefore hail from the British protectorate of Basutoland.[15]

John Harris continued to put pressure on the Home Office. He remained convinced that 'The whole thing is part of the wicked exploitation of defenceless natives against which we are always working'. Travers Buxton agreed: 'What is the old man but a slave?', he wrote to the society's solicitor and legal adviser, W. Carey Morgan. Could the APS not obtain a writ of habeas corpus served on Epstein to produce the Bushman in court? Four years earlier, the society had acted successfully in achieving the repatriation of the 'Kaffir Boys' singing quintet of 'healthy, dark-skinned lads' (Xhosa, Mfengu and Khoe) from the Eastern Cape, brought in to tour Congregational churches in Blackpool by one J.H. Balmer, a Liverpool pastor's son.

Solicitor Morgan's reply to Buxton on 5 August 1915 was not encouraging. He said that there was nothing in anti-slavery legislation that would cover the Dancing Bushman. The legal precedent of the 'Hottentot Venus' (Sara Baartman) in 1810–11 had been inadequately recorded—and anyway the writ for habeas corpus applied for then by Zachary Macaulay of the African Institution (an antecedent of the APS) had been turned down by the court, on the ground that she was under legal contract to her 'owners'.

Harris also turned for advice to ex-colonial administrator Sir Harry Johnston, an eccentric liberal now retired to his home in the Sussex village of Poling between Littlehampton and Arundel. Johnston was engrossed in writing his *Comparative Bantu Grammar*, covering hundreds of closely related languages, which he complained was an 'awful' task because it 'grows and grows'. Harry Johnston responded to Harris with fury at the callousness of 'the Agent General of the Union of South Africa', and was equally scathing about the 'careless indifference of our Colonial Office to the welfare of our coloured fellow-subjects'. If the Colonial Office wouldn't act, he wrote in capital latters, '*THEN WE WILL APPEAL TO THE PRESS*'.

Referring to Franz as 'the negro in question', Harry Johnston poured cold water on Epstein's story of capturing him hunting ostriches in the desert, while remarking that 'Epstein has given the whole show away' by calling the Bushman his captive. He could not himself go and interview 'the supposed Kalahari Bushman' at Margate: he was not well, he suffered from high blood pressure, he might get very angry indeed, and he was not rich. The man he had in mind for that job was Solomon Tshekisho Plaatje, the brilliant native South African linguist currently resident at Leyton in Essex:

> Sol Plaatje is probably the only man in Great Britain or Europe able to converse with this Bushman. The Bushman may actually be a Mokalahari, and thus speak a debased form of Sechuana. Plaatje can size him up ... A pound or two in Plaatje's pocket at this moment might be a well-placed kindness.
>
> Don't let Epstein slip through our fingers, carrying off the prey.[16]

Unwittingly, Sir Harry Johnston had stepped on two of John Harris's corns—the Press and Sol. For a start, Harris believed in lobbying behind the scenes and not alienating the powers-that-be by untoward publicity. He was also daggers drawn with Plaatje. Plaatje had come to England in 1914 as secretary-general of the South African Native National Congress (later the ANC), to petition the imperial government against the new South African parliament's 1913 Natives' Land Act. Harris had sabotaged Plaatje's platform of getting more parliamentary votes for Africans in South Africa, by persuading the other delegates that what they needed was 'equitable segregation' through separate black institutions, leaving parliament and central government under white control. (This was the policy that the APS was currently advocating for Southern Rhodesia.) Plaatje was unconvinced, being perfectly well aware of how the legal doctrine of 'separate but equal' had been subverted in the United States, where the pretence of black equity camouflaged the actual intensification of white supremacy.

Back in August 1914, Sol Plaatje had stormed out of Harris's office and wrested back control of the Native National Congress delegation—though too late to have any effect, as the British government was thrown into war emergency. While other delegates returned to South Africa, Plaatje stayed on in England to further his literary career, writing his polemical book *Native Life in South Africa*, speaking on humanitarian platforms, and developing a keen interest in current studies of linguistics. Besides his acquaintance with Harry Johnston, Sol Plaatje collaborated closely with the phonetician

Daniel Jones—the real-life prototype for George Bernard Shaw's Professor Higgins—at University College, London. Their collaboration resulted in Plaatje's own Setswana becoming one of the languages that Daniel Jones used to develop the International Phonetic Alphabet, or IPA.[17]

It was thus vanity rather than good sense on the part of John Harris that made the APS pass up on the opportunity of making direct contact at Margate that summer of 1915 with Franz Taibosh through Sol Plaatje. Travers Buxton wrote to Harry Johnston: 'We are afraid that Plaatje is not altogether to be trusted and we should hesitate to ask him to look into the case.' Ironically, if Sol Plaatje had been trusted, he surely would have communicated with Franz Taibosh in more than one language. As well as revealing to the world that Franz was fluent in Afrikaans, the multilingual Sol Plaatje had grown up near Mamusa with Korana people and should thus have had some command of Franz's native tongue.

Instead, the APS went along to the Director of Public Prosecutions (DPP) within the Home Office in London, on 3 August, to ask that a police watch should be kept on the Dancing Bushman at Margate. Solicitor Morgan had told Buxton that only the DPP could institute a criminal action against Epstein for 'unlawful duress' on the dancer. On 2 September, the Home Office reported back to the APS that the DPP could find no cause for complaint, as Margate police reported no indications of cruelty or unlawful duress by Epstein (confirmed by the Home Office to be really a Mr Hepston from Dublin). Morgan added his ha'porth of advice four days later, reiterating that the society could not prove any duress without actually speaking to the Bushman direct—but the advice, once again, fell on deaf ears.

Enter 'Professor' George Cunningham. Towards the end of the first week of September 1915, Cunningham wrote to the APS and then came down to London for a long interview at a gentlemen's club, the National Liberal Club in Whitehall Place. His visiting card described him as 'Lecturer in Cinema Science at the University of Cambridge', while his telegraphic address was 'Cunningham Dentist Cambridge'. He told Harris that he should not be confused with another Dr Cunningham in Cambridge (apparently also a Rev.), and impressed on Harris that he was a member of the university Senate.

George Cunningham was an important founding figure in the New Dentistry of preserving rather than pulling teeth. After dropping out of medical school in his native Edinburgh and completing a first degree in Paris, he had crossed the Atlantic to become one of Harvard University's first Doctors of Dental Medicine in 1876. Thereafter he set up shop in Cambridge, and took an undergraduate degree at Downing College. Interested in all that was new, he has been described as 'a great traveller, bon viveur, after-dinner speaker, skilful writer, linguist, pioneer of Esperanto, and inventor of garden golf'. His Cambridge dental practice on King's Parade, filled with books and toys, specialized in attending to the needs of children. He sat on government commissions and developed a pan-European reputation, but began a 'sad decline' after the death of his mother: his practice had greatly shrunk by 1912, as 'he became over fond of the liquid for which Scotland is famous'.

Cunningham's current preoccupation was the use of cinematography for scientific and medical education. On 17 November 1913—soon after Franz Taibosh was in action at the New Examinations Hall in Cambridge— Cunningham organized a show of medical and scientific films for seven hundred doctors and nurses in London, at the West End Cinema in Coventry Street off Leicester Square. He selected most of the films from the Pathé Frères film library, and included in the programme the film that he had made with Pathé on the Cambridge Dental Institute for Children, arguing that dental care for children ought to be extended across the nation. 'Sir James Crichton-Browne, who presided, urged that it was high time the nation was awakened to the ravages of dental decay and the need of taking measures to arrest it. He was not one of those who believed that dental decay was an essential feature of our modern civilization, or that the superman of the future would have a swollen head and toothless gums.'[18]

George Cunningham's interest in the anthropology of a Wild Dancing Bushman is explained by his interest in scientific cinematography, rather than by his dentistry. Before cinema became synonymous with photoplays or feature films, there appeared to be a bright future for scientific and educational films. There was a proven market for films of African wildlife and native life, stimulated by Cherry Kearton's hour-long film *Theodore Roosevelt in Africa* released in 1911, which enabled Kearton to become a professional cine-lecturer touring America and the British Isles. The white hunter Paul Rainey followed with two films, made in the years 1912 and 1914, which 'probably did more to influence American ideas of African wildlife than any other pictures until the 1920s'. Films of African lions at a waterhole were being advertised in London during August 1913 under the rubric of 'Cinema College: a post-graduate course in natural history and how wild animals live'.[19]

Cunningham was evidently planning to use Franz Taibosh as the subject of a scientific film, in collaboration with Dr Duckworth of Jesus College, who was preparing his *Descrizione di un Boscimano del Sud Africa* for publication in Italy. Cunningham undoubtedly knew Duckworth, who had lectured at the annual meeting of the British Dental Association in Cambridge on 4 August 1913.

After the interview with Cunningham, Harris wrote to—but seems to have received no reply from—R. Douglass Vernon of Cambridge, who had raised the issue of the Wild Dancing Bushman's oppression a year earlier, asking him for confidential background on George Cunningham. '[Cunningham] was anxious to know the evidence which the Society had as he is interested in the Bushman and has, I understand, a contract with Epstein his captor in reference to the production of certain cinema films in which the Bushman figures ... He gives Epstein a bad character and is anxious to get the Bushman out of his hands.'

Cunningham had told Harris 'that there is difficulty in getting further "turns" for the Bushman and it seems therefore possible that the old man may before long be stranded in this country'. In a letter to Miss Goddard of Margate on 10 September, Harris suggested that the unwillingness of music halls to accept the act might be reinforced by placing public advertisements in the theatrical press. Three days later the APS wrote once again to W.P. Schreiner, the High Commissioner for the Union of South Africa, alerting him to the possibility of the Bushman being abandoned by his master.[20]

Harris had smelt a rat when he met Cunningham at the National Liberal Club. As Travers Buxton told Harry Johnston: 'Harris felt very doubtful about him and his motives ... we gather that he wants to get the Bushman out of [Epstein's] hands into his own possession.' Cunningham had evidently been unaware of Harris's Baptist missionary background as he regaled him man to man on the terraces of the club. Profanity, drinking, smoking and slurred speech would all have been marks against Cunningham, who no doubt had good if confused intentions. Not for the last time, Franz Taibosh had aroused the protective feelings of a potential patron, anxious to save Franz from himself and from the clutches of Paddy Hepston.

Cunningham finally bust his case with Harris by three communications on 17, 19–20 and 20 September. The first was a postcard blue-pencilled from 8 Maids' Causeway, Cambridge, expressing his disappointment that he had heard no word of progress from the APS:

I had delayed my own proposed action in the matter on learning that your Society was also concerned in this matter.

Delay may be a pecuniary loss to me.

V.E.Y. [Very Earnestly Yours]

Geo Cunningham

The implied threat of legal action to recover expenses probably did not escape Harris. No copy of Harris's immediate reply of the 17th was kept, possibly because it was rather terse. Cunningham's two replies to Harris, dated the 19th–20th and 20th, were scribbled in thick blue pencil on lined pages torn from a school exercise book. Full of insertions, hesitations and reiterations, each page is indented with erratic pressures of handwriting, suggesting the blue pencil has been periodically licked and stabbed downwards. The first letter verged on alcoholic incoherence. It began by berating Harris's reply as 'extremely disappointing', continued by referring to a certain Dr Lange of central London who could presumably vouch for Cunningham and his relations with Epstein, reiterated that 'Captain Paddy Epstein is a dangerous person', and added: 'I have no greater desire than to relieve "Klikko" from his present very unworthy & insulting position; both in his interests and ours.' A final sentence was appended at the bottom of the letter, enclosed in a rectangle of blue pencil lines: 'Your letter is cold, formal and official; it freezes.'

The second letter from Cunningham, dated 20 September, was headed with a blue pencil note 'to catch the 2 a.m. post' [*sic*, not 2 p.m.], with the word 'Failed' written in red next to it. The letter began 'Dear Harris' and referred back to the tale of the two Drs Cunningham of Cambridge that he had told Harris at the National Liberal Club, in words that can hardly have impressed the reverend reader: 'I did not know that you were a "Rev": ... hence I hope you will excuse my exclamation on reading yr letter—DAMN.'

Cunningham had evidently spent the day running round Cambridge looking for advice, and—notwithstanding his jumpy literary style (or was it misplaced humour?)—still thought he could come to terms with Harris:

I have seen the Chief of Police, my Trustees, editor of Cam. Daily News, & my solicitor before writing you. They cannot help me except by saying ... *Forge ahead! We cannot advise.*

Get possession of the Bushman & I undertake to talk with him in 6 weeks (& I believe read his handwriting which looks like shorthand). I may do in less time.

But do hurry up!

V.E.Y.
Geo Cunningham

Over the next month, George Cunningham continued to press the idea that the APS should get Klikko loose from Epstein. He even collared the APS solicitor and legal adviser, Carey Morgan, with a proposal that would have included Sir Harry Johnston as interpreter. (Cunningham had discovered that Klikko spoke 'the Taal', or Afrikaans.) However, Cunningham could not shift Harris's and Buxton's view that he was a bad (and possibly a mad?) man. 'We do not like the idea of his proposal of a small meeting in London at which Klikko should appear to meet Dr. Cunningham's friends, and, in Epstein's absence, get someone to communicate with Klikko in the Taal dialect. This seems to open the door to a good deal of expense and probably to very small results except to put something in Dr. Cunningham's pocket.'[21]

The delay was fatal, with predictable results. On 3 October 1915, Jane Goddard again visited the sideshow next to the pier at Margate. The next day she wrote to the APS. 'Yesterday I found that the "pleasure fair" where the Bushman has been exhibited as a side show for some months, has been closed. It will not re-open until June of next year. I suppose the Bushman has been taken away.' She suggested that if music halls were tired of his act, surely it would still be found at fairs all over the country. But the APS relied on informants, and no more word was heard on the case of the Wild Dancing Bushman.[22]

As for George Cunningham, after a few more years of alcoholic decline laced with erratic enthusiasm for the cause of dental education in the armed forces, he collapsed and died on a London street—and narrowly escaped a pauper's funeral were it not for the generosity of his old friends and pupils. Franz Taibosh was fortunate that his career was not tied to Cunningham's coat-tails.[26]

FROM DUBLIN
TO HAVANA

PADDY HEPSTON had failed to launch the Dancing Bushman as a turn in variety theatre in Britain, as an established act in Continental circuses, or as a subject for profitable academic display through educational films. The act had been reduced to the least prestigious and worst-paid form of popular entertainment, playing in fairground freak-shows. A greater and more profitable world of large-scale circus sideshows and seaside parks beckoned across the Atlantic. Franz would once again take on a prime role as Wild Man rather than as a dancer.

Franz was still wholly dependent on Paddy. He was acutely awake, listening and watching and learning, but was too intimidated by Paddy and unsure of the wider world to venture into communicating with other people. In his deep well of loneliness, he must have suffered private moments of terror and self-doubt in the silences that followed the excitement and exertion of soul-revealing performances. His middle passage to slavery had begun three years before in South Africa, and now continued in Europe and across the seas to North America.

Franz Taibosh and Paddy Hepston disappear beyond our ken once again between October 1915 and April 1916. We may assume that they spent the winter of 1915–16 in Ireland, possibly again venturing into parts of Great Britain within range of the Liverpool ferryboat. Otherwise, Hepston and his strange sidekick found refuge in the tight-knit Jewish communities of Dublin and maybe also Cork. It is noteworthy that the passport applications of M.P. Hepston and W.D. Bushman in April 1916 were vouched for by a Dublin police detective sergeant with the common British and Irish Jewish name of Fagan.[1]

The theatrical failure of the Wild Dancing Bushman act left no reason for Paddy Hepston's actor-brother Randolph Epsteyne to stay around. There is also the question of the whereabouts of Paddy Hepston's wife. Was the woman who cohabited with him in England in 1914–15 the same woman as the Mrs Epstein recorded at Kimberley in 1907? We certainly have no record of a woman living with Hepston after 1915. If they were together for eight years or more, did they now part in Ireland? Did her absence, or indeed her presence, have something to do with Paddy's drinking bouts and acts of unwonted violence towards his Bushman protégé?

Hepston's alienation of other people gives the impression of a troubled soul also alone in the world. It would not be surprising if the marriage had been fractious since the couple left South Africa, with a final split between wife and husband occurring in 1915–16 after Paddy failed to hit the promised big time.

◎

Irish society was increasingly divided in its response to the Great War. Conscription had deliberately not been enforced in Ireland, unlike in the rest of the United Kingdom, but great numbers of men flocked to join the forces in France. Recruits from north-east Ireland signed up as loyalists to keep Ulster part of the union with Great Britain. Recruits from the rest of the country did so largely as an escape from poverty. They were also induced by propaganda that described resisters as 'shirkers' and by the brouhaha of recruiting drives and fund-raisers replete with singing of 'When Irish eyes are smiling' and 'Belgium put the kibosh on the Kaiser'.[2]

An uneasy truce persisted between nationalists and unionists within Ireland, and was policed by the Royal Irish Constabulary and British army detachments. The unionist loyalties of the latter were reinforced by the fact that army officers, from the commander-in-chief Horatio Kitchener downwards, were 'as a class drawn to a very disproportionate extent from the Anglo-Irish gentry … whose unionism was hereditary'. Dublin Castle, the British security establishment in Ireland, looked weak. Irish National Volunteers were planning, with anticipated German help, to rise in rebellion and establish an Irish republic on Easter Sunday in 1916. But German imperialists, having previously sided with Protestant Ulstermen rebelling against England, were not really in tune with Catholic Irish republicanism. The majority leaders of the Irish Volunteers called off the national rising at the last moment, by a public notice placed in the Easter edition of the Dublin *Sunday Independent*. A minority decided to go ahead anyway.

An Irish republic was proclaimed on Easter Monday, 24 April 1916, at

Dublin's General Post Office, a magnificent building that was pounded to bits by British artillery. The rebels were reduced to surrender within a few days. By 1 May the Irish revolution was reported to be dying out, after ten million pounds' worth of damage to property in Dublin. Many more bystanders were killed than revolutionaries. Slum dwellers took the opportunity to raid shops in the city centre, much of which had been gutted by shellfire. British soldiers had to protect captured fighters from the abuse of infuriated Dublin housewives. But the arbitrary execution by firing squads of the captives so soon afterwards turned popular sentiment in favour of the republicans.[3]

Paddy Hepston and Franz Taibosh lived through the sound and fury of these events, probably in Dublin less than a mile south of the battle.

A British passport for Hepston M.P. was issued in London on 7 April 1916, and the British passport No. 89139 for 'Taaibosh Franz known as W.D. Bushman' was dated 13 April 1916.[4] Presumably the passports were delivered to Dublin some days later. That would have given Hepston and Taibosh only the barest of chances to leave just before the Easter rising of 24 April 1916.

The passport was simply an official sheet of paper identifying the holder and giving permission to travel overseas for a limited time, usually for one year, renewable thereafter. Given that it was wartime, with limited shipping available, Hepston probably had to satisfy the authorities that he was contracted to exhibit W.D. Bushman overseas. If that contract was for Cuba, it is unlikely to have been signed before July 1916, as the lively winter tourist season in Cuba did not begin until November. There was therefore a whole summer in which money could be made. Did Hepston and Taibosh go to Cuba after April, or did they first find work in another country?

Cargo ships to Cuba, with provision for a very few passengers, sailed out of Liverpool every three to five weeks. But as they took only one or two passengers, it is unlikely that Hepston and Taibosh went on them. It is also unlikely that Hepston and Taibosh could have boarded one of the large passenger liners that touched at Queenstown (Cobh) in Ireland on their way to New York. They would presumably not have met the criteria of social importance allowing British passengers on board in wartime. Nor are their names listed in the records of Liverpool's port as outward-bound passengers on any ship travelling overseas. But 'overseas' meant to a port beyond the Mediterranean, and thus did not preclude them from taking a ship to Spain.

In later years, Franz Taibosh gave other people the impression that he had once lived in Spain—witness his delight in guitar music and bursting into spontaneous gypsy dancing as an old man. Spain had a vigorous carnival and circus tradition, and was a neutral country offering Paddy shelter from being drafted into the British army. The Anglo-Irish Hanneford equestrian family took their Royal Canadian Circus from wartime England to Spain, where young 'Poodles' Hanneford was spotted by the American circus owner John Ringling in 1915–16, and the whole family was recruited for Barnum & Bailey for Easter 1917.[5] Hepston could have connected with the Hannefords through Irish funfair and circus contacts. The Wild Dancing Bushman could have been engaged in Spain by the Hanneford circus, with a subsequent arrangement for crossing the Atlantic in late 1916.

There is also a slight possibility that Hepston and Taibosh stopped off in the British colony of Jamaica. (This was the impression given to the writer Laurens van der Post in 1959, a possibility that Barbara Cook does not discount.) There is, however, no mention of a performance by a Wild Dancing Bushman in Jamaica during 1916 in (albeit incomplete) microfilms of the Kingston *Daily Gleaner*.

In Cuba the most likely circus to have recruited Hepston with Taibosh in 1916 was the new Santos y Artigas Gran Circo. In July 1916 Messrs Pablo Santos and Jesus Artigas of Havana had announced that their new circus—the biggest ever in Cuba—would open in Havana in November 1916, and would then tour the island for some months under imported American canvas. John Ringling promised to supply acts from Barnum & Bailey, and the Santos y Artigas would include a hippodrome, a wild animal menagerie and a sideshow. The Wild Dancing Bushman would have been an obvious new recruit for the sideshow. His act was not reported in newspaper reports of the Santos y Artigas Gran Circo in Cuba, but publicity usually focused on big-top (main circus) rather than small-top (sideshow) acts.[6]

Hepston and Taibosh were not alone as popular entertainers crossing the Atlantic for employment or vacation in the latter part of 1916. One of the passengers arriving in New York on the liner *Philadelphia* from Liverpool in July 1916 was Rosa M. Richter (Mrs George Starr), the former 'Zazel' of human cannonball fame. Another artist arriving in September 1916, on a French liner from Le Havre, was Mademoiselle 'Lady Little', a recruit for Sam Gumpertz's Dreamland Circus Sideshow at Coney Island near New

York. Acquired from her French parents for $4,000, she was twenty-three years old and twenty-five inches tall, and would often appear with Franz Taibosh in the future.[7]

The Caribbean island of Cuba was North America's winter playground for the rich and aspiring. It combined the security of a US-dominated territory with the naughtiness of a foreign land. In April 1915, Havana had seen the great title fight for the heavyweight boxing championship of the world, in which the exiled Jack Johnson was finally knocked out by a successful 'great white hope', Jess Willard.

Two or three Ward Line steamers arrived from New York weekly, while other Americans (Yankees all in Cuban eyes) arrived off the Peninsular & Occidental ferries from Port Tampa and Key West in Florida. Over the winter season the city was filled with the straw hats and 'Palm Beach suits' that were considered *de rigueur* for visiting Yankee men. Havana port tallied a record number of 14,267 disembarking passengers in November 1916, but the number dropped to 12,262 in December. The reason for a less good season than expected was said to be the fear of impending entry by the United States into the Great War.[8]

The tourist season officially ran until March, but the circus and vacation season of 1916–17 was cut short by insurrection elsewhere on the island. The conservative president of Cuba, Mario García Menocal, had been re-elected in 1916 after blatant electoral fraud. Liberal rebels led by José Miguel Gómez rose in revolt at Santa Clara and prepared to march on Havana in February 1917, but the rebels were cut off and eventually suppressed with US military help by March. The revolt sent many tourists packing from their hotels. In February 1917, the *New York Clipper*, 'the oldest theatrical publication in America', reported that the uprising in Cuba had panicked local circus proprietors: 'tent shows are the greatest sufferers. Before the disturbances, show business of all kinds was better than it has ever been.'[9]

In March 1917, *The Billboard* (subtitled *It Keeps the Show World Posted*) added: 'the Santos y Artigas circus suddenly closed its tour in Cuba on account of the uprising and shipped to Havana. Word now ... is that the management is planning to resume the route, in as much as Gomez has been captured and the revolution is believed to be over.'[10]

One of the American visitors in Havana over Christmas and New Year 1916–17 was 'the freak-show czar' Samuel W. Gumpertz, who was staying with his wife and two midgets (presumably another married couple) at the Plaza Hotel. At some moment Gumpertz spotted the Wild Dancing Bushman act. It was most likely at a stand of the Santos y Artigas circus outside Havana in the latter part of January. This fact should not be forgotten in Gumpertz's subsequent relations with Hepston and Taibosh: they were his discovery, and thus in a sense 'belonged' to him. Gumpertz was the expansive owner of the Dreamland Circus Sideshow on Coney Island, New York's premier seaside amusement park. He was always on the lookout for new acts, having gone on record in 1909 on how to keep the punters coming back again and again: 'Novelty, that's the answer. None of these park amusements is lasting … The only way to make an old show go is to hang out a new sign—and that won't work more than one time with the audience.'

In a March 1917 interview, Gumpertz concluded that 'the [Cuban] circus business is much overrated by the circus press agent. I have visited some of the circuses very often and found their business not what I call even fair. However I heard that they did big business for two or three weeks in Havana.' He could not recommend American circus people to work in Cuba outside Havana, as living conditions were only good enough in the capital. 'Cuba is a nice place for a rest, and I enjoyed myself very much,' he concluded, but 'as for thinking of taking a show to Cuba, that is out of the question.'[11]

Gumpertz was described as being 'as well known in the show world as almost anyone now engaged in catering to the masses'. Born in 1866, he had grown up in San Francisco, working in theatre there as a teenager before going on to the so-called Grand Opera House in Rochester, upstate New York. After managing a touring theatrical company, he gravitated into running amusement parks. In 1902 he was recruited to run the Lilliputia village for midget people at Dreamland on Coney Island, the world's biggest and most vulgar amusement park. It had a fifty-foot-high naked-breasted woman modelled in stucco above its main entrance; she was given wings to pass her off as an angel. Lilliputia was soon expanded into a full freak-show, and a Streets of Cairo exhibit (organized by the Lebanese tumbler George Hamid) was added, featuring acrobats, jugglers and belly-dancers. From 1905, when Gumpertz recruited Filipino (Ingorot) 'head-hunters', there were some 'genuine' ethnographic freaks. Gumpertz later softened the 'corn-country hog-seller' style of his 'boosters, shillabers, spielers, and ballyhoo talkers' by introducing them to the quieter and more persuasive marketing of his Hindu hypnotist, Omar Sami, said to have been really an Oxford graduate named Clarence.

The entire Dreamland lot at Coney Island burnt down in a great fire of 1911. Gumpertz responded within two days by setting up his Congress of Freaks in a tent on the burnt site, and contented himself in future at Coney Island with running 'the world's best freak show'. Gumpertz's Dreamland Circus Sideshow had its own large building on the old Dreamland site with an elaborate cast-iron front, flanked by a wax museum and a simulated Chinese opium den and other concessionary sideshows, each with its own barker and ballyhoo (come-hither). Gumpertz's artists included Bamboola the Wild Man from Borneo, standing in front of the show 'uttering grunts and meaningless ululations'—in fact a man from Alsace-Lorraine in blackface with frizzed hair and a big ring in his nose. By 1917 Gumpertz had diversified his investments with a stake in seaside amusements at Blackpool in England, and had plans for a Long Beach amusement park near Los Angeles.[12]

Gumpertz returned to the United States from Cuba in February 1917 in time for the annual convention of the Outdoor Showmen of the World at Chicago. The convention was rent by dissent against its president, Frank Spellman. Gumpertz set up a rival group, the National Outdoor Showmen's Association. *Billboard* interviewed Gumpertz in its issue of 24 February 1917. He boasted that his new freak-show at Coney Island for the 1917 summer season would far exceed anything yet produced by Barnum or the Ringlings. He would have not only Lady Little, the cute French midget, and Eddie Masher, the skeleton dude, but also Amok, the Philippine head-hunter, Professor Ajax, the sword-swallower, and 'the Australian Wild Man'. Franz Taibosh was the 'Australian Wild Man', given a moniker that was to re-occur.

Gumpertz made a second quick trip to Cuba in mid-March, no doubt to finalize arrangements with the likes of Paddy Hepston. The touring tented 'mud show' of the Santos y Artigas circus had packed up and returned to base at Havana.[13]

Coney Island
and Havana Again

UNDER THE HEADING 'Parks, piers, & beaches', *Billboard* of 24 March 1917, carried a full-page advertisement for the coming season of the Dreamland Circus Sideshow at Coney Island.

The Original Dreamland
Circus Sideshow
Coney Island, New York
20 Pits Living Curios
Real Shows for 1 Admission
Coney Island.
Homer Sibley, Lecturer
Capt. Epstein, Ass't Lecturer
N. Salih, Gen'l Manager
*Can always place a few
more good freaks*

The Original Eden Musee
formerly of 23rd St., New York
Now at its $50,000
permanent home in Dreamland
It truly
represents the world in wax.

S.W. Gumpertz, Inc Proprietor
N. Salih, General Manager

The lead feature in the sideshow line-up was a poor-quality photograph of Franz Taibosh, dancing for the camera with his hands in the air, looking more cuddly than ferocious. He was touted as about sixty years more than he really was, and seven inches less: 'The Australian Wild Dancing Bushman. Age 103 years: Height 44 ins; Weight 70 lb.'

Franz himself and Paddy Hepston arrived at New York on the *Philadelphia* out of Liverpool on 3 May—having made a quick trip to Britain to renew their passports, after leaving Cuba (according to Barbara Cook's notes) on 12 April. US immigration papers described Morris Hepston as a married forty-year-old British Hebrew last resident at Kimberley, South Africa, proceeding to employment with Gumpertz at Dreamland, Coney Island. Complexion:

dark; hair: black; eyes: brown. Marks of identification: 'Scar from bullet wound in right cheek'. By contrast Franz Taaibosh [*sic*] was described as a single sixty-one-year-old, born in 'Calahari Desert, Bechuanaland', his complexion 'copper colour' [thus spelt, not 'color'] and his identifying mark being 'Hair stretching like elastic'.

Franz Taibosh was to be the new star of the Congress of Curious People within the Dreamland Circus Sideshow building, through which spectators shuffled slowly on a twenty-minute tour led by 'lecturers'. Franz's most famous competitor as a Wild Man, old Zip the Pinhead, was away for the time being.

A declaration of war by the US against the Axis powers was just around the corner. Coney Island had its own vigilantes to protect it from alien sabotage, while its showmen nursed hopes that, like Blackpool in England, it would become a popular escapist destination for war worriers. Coney Island was covered in 'derricks, steam shovels, cables, trenches, hammers, picks, bull-tossers, hot air shooters, and several millionaires', all busy preparing pavilions for the coming season opening in mid-May. The great Spiral Wheel at Luna Park, looking like a giant upturned pudding basin on a tilt, was getting ready to spin its first trains on a 3,200-ft spiral ride into its dark interior on April Fool's Day. Gumpertz responded to talk that Coney Island would shut down at night in wartime as 'all bosh'.[1]

According to the *Clipper*, Franz Taibosh began dancing with the Twenty-in-One Amusements of Gumpertz's Dreamland Circus Sideshow on or about Wednesday, 14 May 1917. Dreamland pre-empted the weekend opening of the two other major amusement parks on Coney Island, Steeplechase Park and Luna Park.[2]

John Ringling, from the family that owned both the Barnum & Bailey and Ringling Brothers circuses, had developed a business relationship with Gumpertz in which they exchanged artists. He was an early visitor to Dreamland in May 1917, and came back in June with his sideshow manager, to arrange an immediate swap between Lady Little and a Japanese midget. Though Sam Gumpertz and John Ringling were rivals, they had a lot in common: both remained 'indifferent to encomiums and unperturbed by acrimonious assaults'.[3] It would be surprising if from the start Ringling did not have half an eye on Gumpertz's current star attraction, the Wild Dancing Bushman.

Billboard's 'Circus, menagerie, hippodrome & side-shows' page carried a long description of the Dreamland Circus Sideshow at the beginning of June 1917:

When one walks into the Dreamland Side-Show he [*sic*] is instantly struck with the idea that he is in a dream in reality and instinctively pinches himself to see if he is awake … Manager Smith walks around with a broad, good-natured smile these days, for, altho the season is very backward as Coney Island has had only a day or two of decent weather, the Dreamland Circus Side-Show has been visited by everyone on the Island, and all visitors have to admit it is the greatest ever … Sam Gumpertz has let his fancy run riot in framing up the show this season, and has all of the pits painted to represent old nursery rhymes … Homer Sibley is back again telling the customers all about the show and guiding them from pit to pit, and … everybody goes out boosting the show, for Sibley knows how to tell it to them. He is ably assisted … by Frank Bowen and they certainly make the strongest team of lecturers Coney Island has ever listened to.

The Wild Dancing Bushman, also referred to as 'Klikko, a real wild dancing Bushman from the Kalahari desert, South Africa', was picked out by *Billboard* as 'a riot'. 'His gag line is "Ooshwa," which means a friendly greeting, so Capt. Hepston, his manager says, and already "Ooshwa" has become a favorite expression by Coney Island visitors.'

Coney Island suffered severe rainstorms during the summer of 1917. One storm on 28 May led to the collapse of seating and the injury of eight people in Luna Park watching the Submarine Attack show, which played on fears of German U-boats attacking ocean liners. By the end of the summer, Dreamland is said to have played before as many as 30,000 people an hour, drawn into the hall with twenty pits or stages by the 'bally' (ballyhoo) at the front door. The 'entire S.W. Gumpertz Dreamland Circus Side Show' was contracted to appear over the 1917–18 Christmas season as the sideshow of the Santos y Artigas circus in Havana. Aerialist May Wirth and the Hanneford equestrians from Barnum & Bailey were also signed up by the New York agent of Santos y Artigas.[4]

The Santos y Artigas circus hired the Teatro Payret in Havana, and set up its tent tops opposite the theatre on a big lot. Billed as 'the Barnum and Bailey of Cuba', it performed under canvas at Havana for six weeks from 16 November 1917. 'Equestrians, acrobats and artists of the round top', such as the Hannefords and the Davenports, and 'freaks' such as the giant George Auger, arrived off Ward Line boats from New York and Miami. Franz Taibosh and Paddy Hepston set sail from Miami on 15 November.

From 6 January 1918, the Santos y Artigas circus divided into two touring sections under canvas, called Circo Azul and Circo Rojo. These two sections, blue and red, toured the island for up to twenty weeks till May, complete with their own sideshows and wild animal menageries, 'all-American bands and a crew of American canvas and property men'.

Franz and Paddy arrived back at Miami from Havana on board the *Carillo* on 8 January, registered as immigrant aliens in transit via New York, with the British consul in New York given as their address. Franz was described on immigration papers as a 4 ft 2 in dwarf British-African Black, with Mr S.W. Gumpertz of Brighton Beach, Long Island, as his guardian; and Paddy as British-English (though another passenger was marked as British-Hebrew). Because he was a dwarf, Franz was held back awhile for a further medical examination, which he passed.[5]

Cuba was to leave its marks on Franz Taibosh. In subsequent years, he was known for his trademark Cuban cigars, which he consumed in enormous quantity. His Cuban experience would also have reinforced any previous residence in Spain, including his lifelong partiality to the clapping and stamping rhythms and shouts of flamenco.

It was also during this Christmas season of 1917–18 that Franz Taibosh was 'spotted' in Havana by William Mann. Despite his professional role as a beetle and insect collector, with a recent Harvard doctorate in entomology, Mann had a great interest in zoos and circus sideshows. He was returning via Cuba from the British Bahamas, where he had gone on a visa valid from 25 May to 24 November 1917 for purposes of 'historical research and recreation'. (It appears to have been an intelligence-gathering mission, since he was reporting back to the US State Department; the mission may have had some relation to the fact that the United States had bought the nearby Danish Virgin Islands in January 1917.)

William Mann reckoned himself somewhat of an expert on the 'bushmen' who inhabited the mountainous interiors of Pacific islands. In line with his pro-Boer sympathies as a boy, he was no admirer of British colonial rule, but during 1916–17 he had spent nine months in British Fiji and seven months on the British Solomon Islands. On the island of Malaita, he remarked: 'I looked for "bush" men harder than for insects.' As a leading circus fan, Mann knew not only John Ringling personally but also Frank Cook, the Barnum & Bailey legal adjuster. He was also a good friend of William 'Blackie' Blackburn, former Barnum & Bailey menagerie boss and since 1890 the head keeper of the National Zoological Park at Washington, DC. (Mann himself was to become the zoo's director in 1925.)[6]

Frank Cook's daughter Barbara has confirmed that her father first learnt about Franz Taibosh from William Mann, who excitedly brought the Wild Dancing Bushman to Cook's attention. Mann contacted Frank Cook on his return to the continental United States. Cook was persuaded to rush down to Havana—probably just after Christmas spent with his daughter Frances in Albany, New York—to sign up this peerless new attraction for the Barnum & Bailey circus sideshow. Because of the war in Europe, there was a shortage of new circus acts and of 'freaks' in particular (most of whom, according to Gumpertz, came from Germany and points further east, though midgets also came from the Pyrenees and Belgium).

In Cuba, Cook persuaded Paddy Hepston that for the next summer season the Wild Dancing Bushman would do much better with Barnum & Bailey than with Gumpertz's Dreamland show. 'The Greatest Show on Earth' could hand out wages at a scarcely believable rate. Hepston agreed to a 1918 season contract with Barnum & Bailey at $200 (then £50) a week. (By comparison, an assistant manager in the Ringling–Barnum sideshow in the 1920s started at $30 a week, rising to $50 in the early 1930s.)[7]

Cook's triumph in booking the Wild Dancing Bushman for the 1918 season must have infuriated Gumpertz, who was expecting the Bushman to return to Dreamland. Cook as a clever lawman somehow got round Gumpertz's requirement that his 'freaks' sign option contracts covering the next season before they left to join Santos y Artigas in Cuba. Relations between Gumpertz and Cook over Franz Taibosh were now encumbered by an enmity that was to dog the subsequent career of the Wild Dancing Bushman.

Frank A. Cook had been born in Albany, capital of New York State, in December 1873. He became an investigator for the Eastern Life Insurance Company, checking on fraudulent claims and developing a sound knowledge of the law in the process. He also, no doubt from an early age, developed a love of the circus. In the later 1890s Frank Cook married, for the first time, and had two children. His daughter Frances was born in the year 1900, followed by a son called Edward.

Cook was recruited as an investigator by the US Department of Commerce and Labor, and then in 1909 swapped jobs and joined the Barnum & Bailey circus as its legal adjuster—a top management position with one of the two largest circuses in the United States. Personal tragedy may also have persuaded Frank Cook to take to the road for half of every year when he became a widower. From 1918, his eighteen-year-old daughter Frances took charge of the family home in Albany while he was on summer tour.

Every travelling circus needed a legal adjuster, or 'fixer', to assist the owners of the circus in negotiating the annual tour of stands in numerous towns and to settle the claims for damages that inevitably resulted. Cook was a very good fixer. He was not an attorney who had been called to any state bar, but a law agent with 'a vast legal knowledge ... extremely familiar with tax and license statutes of almost every State in the Union'. The legal adjuster was the most important of the 'advance men' of the circus, fixing bookings weeks ahead at 'stands' across the country, though not necessarily always in person but by telegraph and telephone. The key to circus profitability lay in arranging an itinerary that combined maximum audiences with minimum local expenses at each stand, and the lowest railroad costs between them.[8]

In his semi-novel *A Mantis Carol*, Laurens van der Post produced a fanciful alternative version of Frank Cook's first meeting with Franz Taibosh. Cook first saw 'Hans Taaibosch' in a shabby theatre at Kingston, Jamaica, dancing in the limelight for a 'bored, well nourished and well wined audience', who mocked 'his dancing and his shape'. This aroused Cook's New England puritan conscience. He went round to the Bushman's dressing-room and 'had him to himself long enough to confirm in a strange kind of English that he was most unhappy and in a plight from which he longed to be delivered'. At this point Captain Du Barry (the pseudonym for Hepston used in a 1922 circus biography pamphlet) barged in—a 'large, red-faced, beery, mustached' Englishman, professing to be a captain in the British army. Cook realized: 'Since Hans could not read or write, there was no formal written contract drawn up between him and his promoter. The captain's power over him came entirely from the fact that Hans had nobody else to whom he could turn for protection.'[9]

Laurens van der Post did not consult any member of the Cook family. There is no evidence that Franz Taibosh ever appeared on stage in Jamaica, though Barbara Cook thinks it possible. But the portrayal of Paddy Hepston as a large, beery and moustached bully seems to have come indirectly from Cook family tradition. In fact, though Hepston was a giant next to Franz Taibosh, he was only 5 ft 7 in high. He may have been red-faced; certainly he seems to have had a fondness for beer, as indeed did Franz. Paddy Hepston was of course an Irishman, not an Englishman, but Americans could have confused his South African accent with that of a Cockney Londoner.

Van der Post may be nearer the truth in suggesting that Franz Taibosh felt 'immediately at home' among circus people: 'unusually happy, humane and harmonious'. But Van der Post's idea that Taibosh found whitefaced clowns closest to his heart—'as if in their tumbling, constant humiliation and incorrigible capacity for laughing at their misfortunes, he saw his own unrecorded fate portrayed, and thus felt accompanied, needed, wanted and so became content'—can be seen as a rather outdated literary convention. In the great three-ring circuses, clowns did not appear as solitary individuals in the ring but came in packs working the crowds in the stands between acts.[10]

What can certainly be argued is that Franz Taibosh underwent some kind of long dark night of the soul, when he crossed the seas in bondage. Only later in America did he find himself again as an autonomous being. Franz survived because, as he leaped and whirled on stage, he took the laughter and shouting of audiences to be positive affirmation of his art. Children came to regard him as a benign dwarf with wizard-like powers.

11

JOINING BARNUM AND BAILEY'S CIRCUS

MESSRS MANN AND COOK were anxious to have their Wild Man certified as genuine. Before Franz left New York for Britain on 19 January 1918, they arranged for him to be examined as an anthropological specimen. Mr Neandros of the American Museum of Natural History in New York covered Franz from head to foot in white plaster, with straws inserted in his nostrils, so that a whole body cast could be made. (By the 1990s, the nude plaster figure was relegated to the storage attic of the museum, under a plastic sheet, with obscenities scrawled around its genitalia.)

A series of photographs was taken for the museum by J. Kirchner. A close-up of Franz's face and upper body, titled '37072 African Bushman', shows a man in about his forties with a strong neck and smooth slight body, male breasts slightly fallen, knots of muscle in the upper parts of slim arms. His face stares full on at the camera: fleshy but creased, with small moustache and no beard, topped by a full head of wig-like raggedy hair in small plaits. The epicanthic fold over his right eye seems to have been slightly damaged. The eyes are large and moist and wide apart, under a deeply furrowed brow, giving the subject an air of deep melancholy.

Eight other American Museum of Natural History photographs (negatives 37064–72) show Franz's full naked body, standing with his front and then with his back and his side to the camera. The photographs confirm that Franz had been circumcised. The most curious photograph shows Franz lying sideways on a couch like the Rokeby Venus, his stomach blown up to the size of pregnancy. It is evident that the museum had fed him a very full meal, testing the hypothesis that Bushmen possessed 'variable conditions of the abdomen—as a result of unfavorable diet, unrestricted gorging, and the frequent alternation between starving and plenty'. The dope sheet for the photographs, which may have been written some time later, reads:

Franz Taibosh photographed at the American Museum of Natural History in New York, December 1917. (Images 37072 & 37069, file 57.2, photos by J. Kirchmer, American Museum of Natural History, NY)

'Accidentally shot by an Englishman while hunting in Africa. Brought to the United States and exhibited in Barnum & Bailey's circus.'[1]

The visit to Britain was just for a couple of months, evidently to get new British passports for 'Morris Hepston' and 'Frantz Taaibosh' (rather than 'W.D. Bushman'), valid for one year up to 18 March 1919. Subsequent documentation states that both men left London on 27 March 1918. They arrived back in New York from Liverpool on the three-funnel American Line steamship *New York* on 5 April. Immigration records show that Barnum & Bailey had paid for their second-class cabin passages, and also record negative answers to new questions—whether a polygamist, whether an anarchist, etc. Both still have Kimberley, South Africa, as their place of residence. Forty-two-year-old Hepston is given Irish-Hebrew ethnicity, while sixty-two-year-old Taibosh is 'South African: African Black'. Hepston's complexion is now recorded as bronze, and Taibosh's simply as dark.

The Barnum & Bailey circus was due to open in New York on 25 March 1918, before Hepston and Taibosh were even on the high seas. A snippet of circus news appeared in the 'Under the marquee' gossip column by Circus Solly in the showbiz newspaper *Billboard* (now modestly subtitled *A Weekly Digest of Things Theatrical*) published on 6 April, by which time they would actually have arrived in New York: 'Paddy Hepston is reported to be on his way back from England with the Wild Australian [*sic*] Bushman for a special appearance with the side-show of the Barnum & Bailey circus.'[2]

The opening of the 1918 Barnum & Bailey circus season at Madison Square Garden, in the heart of Manhattan, was trumpeted as usual on the front page of *Billboard*. The Ringling Brothers circus, by contrast, came out more meekly at the Coliseum in Chicago, amid rumours that this was to be its last season before folding. The three-ring railroad circus had once been seen as one of the greatest American achievements, reaching its highest development through 'Yankee genius'. But a writer in the *New York Clipper* late in 1917 doubted whether railroad circuses could survive the war, as railroads, particularly in the South, were refusing to carry such civilian traffic. The Ringling Brothers, however, had the advantage of owning several railroads and could use this as leverage in negotiations with other owners. (The *Clipper*, meanwhile, increasingly came to regard carnivals and circuses as passé, eventually ceasing to cover any circus news at all in mid-1924.)[3]

By the time the Wild Dancing Bushman arrived to take his place in the Barnum & Bailey sideshow, the opening parade or 'spec' in the central auditorium would have been running like clockwork, paced with precision by the monocled figure of Fred Bradna 'in full dress-suit … black patent leather shoes and immaculate white gloves' and a silver whistle on a fine black cord around his neck. (For evening performances he wore a high silk hat.) Fred Bradna, who had been promoted to 'equestrian director' in 1916, was an Alsatian, preferring to present a more French *persona* despite his previous rank as an officer in the German army. His whistle controlled the performance, packing 'a greater whallop than the loudest cracking whip', cueing the acts in and out, marking important moments in the acts for the attention of the audience, and starting and stopping the music. With short blasts, he directed not only the performers but also the riggers and roustabouts, and gave key cues to the circus band.[4]

In his later memoirs, Fred Bradna remarked on the expectant hush in the audience that greeted his appearance at the beginning of every performance. Bradna's opening of the Barnum & Bailey 'spec' at Madison Square Garden was recalled by Tony Kline, who had joined Barnum & Bailey in 1916 as a 'tableau girl', a living statue on a horse-drawn cart, semi-naked but covered in glycerine and white zinc oxide.

> Bradna blew the whistle, a still, penetrating sound … the door-man pulled the cord opening the curtain … and the trumpeters on horse-back, at the head of the band, sounded off with a fanfare heralding the procession; the band struck up with the *Triumphal March*, specially written music for the production … following the trumpeters through the door, along the hippodrome track and the show was on.[5]

The great doors of the central auditorium opened at 2.15 pm for the matinée performance. This year's 'spec' (Display 1) was a 'romantic pantomimic pageant' entitled 'Aladdin and his wonderful lamp: a glimpse of Old China', employing just about the whole circus complement of fourteen hundred people, seven hundred horses, and whole herds of elephants and camels, all extravagantly dressed in gorgeous colours. The horse-drawn tableau carts featured friezes of characters from Chinese legend in bejewelled costumes. Yet the 'spec' was described as having been downgraded from the grander entries of previous years because of wartime stringencies.

After the opening 'spec', Franz Taibosh took his place in 'the procession of freaks' (Display 2), marching around the hippodrome track and waving to an audience up to eight thousand strong. Spectators were always amused by the fact some little people had to sprint periodically to keep up with the procession. The star in the lead was the French midget Lady Little, closely followed by Abomah, the black giantess, and Princess Wee Wee, 'the Ethiopian midget' (both African American women). The cowboy giant Jim Tarver and Zip the Original Pinhead were followed by 'a host of other human oddities'. Franz already knew Zip, Lady Little, Abomah and other people who had worked in the previous year's Dreamland Circus Sideshow—to which some would return after the Madison Square Garden engagement, rather than undertake the countrywide tour of the Big Show. We can imagine the mixed emotions of fright and delight in the head of Franz Taibosh as he marched round the track for the first time with the circus band blaring.

The 'freaks' were followed by three herds of elephants, and then by Signor Bagonghi, the Italian dwarf bareback rider on a Shetland pony 'who caused much laughter'—and whose name was hardly ever spelt correctly in circus publicity. The dozen acts or displays that followed around the hippodrome track included a complete Wild West show, with shooting cowboys and screaming 'Indians'. Display 14 consisted of the tableaux of seven revolving tables of beautiful grey horses and zinc-plastered humans frozen in action as 'equine statuary'. Display 18 was the Hanneford family, 'England's wonderful bareback riders', regarded of one of the hits of the show. Last on to the track came the clowns with their props, which this year consisted of an imitation British tank from the Western Front, Houdini's vanishing elephant (*sic*), and 'the eccentricities' of a Ford car with 'many political allusions', presumably to the eccentric views of Henry Ford himself. Among managers and staff behind the scenes, *Billboard* noted that Frank A. Cook was once again the circus's legal adjuster, with George Black as its resident detective ('secret service officer').

Experienced performers like Frank Bradna contrasted the good order of one-ring European circuses with the 'cacophonous jamboree of three rings all working at once to the noise of a brass band', and noted the brutal competitiveness of American circus management. The Ringlings would ruthlessly chop out from the tour under canvas any acts that did not succeed at Madison Square Garden. But the Wild Dancing Bushman act introduced this year was evidently a great success.

After its usual free show given for patients at Bellevue Hospital, the Barnum & Bailey circus left Manhattan for nearby Brooklyn, and then arrived at Philadelphia for 29 April – 4 May 1918.[6] From Brooklyn onwards the circus was performing under canvas, with all the complications of coming and going by railroad and setting up stands and striking tents on empty building lots near city centres.

Franz and Paddy slipped into the routine of the Barnum & Bailey circus. Even if Paddy took all his pay and kept him in virtual bondage, Franz would have benefited from the respect given to a performer. By contrast, Paddy Hepston is said to have been out of his depth among circus people—an obvious outsider or 'josser'. Robert C. Toll has remarked on how circus performers 'compensated for not belonging to the society around them by thinking of themselves as superior people … calling non-circus people "towners", "gawks", or "rubes."' The same self-deluding snobbery insisted that the circus had no mere barkers or spielers but 'lecturers' or talkers.

Fred Bradna noted that the circus was organized like a boys' boarding school on the move, with social ranks fixed from the beginning of the season and determining where each individual dressed for performances, ate, slept, travelled by train, and socialized during the many months on the road. After owners and senior managers came big-top performers (equestrians followed by aerialists and others down to the clowns), followed by small-top or sideshow performers. Skilled circus functionaries such as linesmen were on a par with sideshow folk, with large numbers of unskilled workers or 'roustabouts' beneath them.

Each circus rank and each person had an assigned place at a trestle table in the cookhouse tent. A flag flew outside for lunch between eleven o'clock and noon, and for 'dinner' from half past four to six. 'None are so privileged that they may eat when the flag is not flying, except the freaks, who show continuously and therefore must dine while the talkers are talking up new business. Freaks are allowed to eat in costume; clowns may sit down in their make-up. All others must dress properly.'[7]

Sideshow performers worked under the small top as often during the day as the talkers could drum up a crowd. Sideshow folk were ranked internally according to skill and intellectual capacity; many of them, owing to their mental as well as physical peculiarities, kept apart from other circus people. Clicko's individual rating would have been low among sideshow 'freaks' so long as Paddy Hepston claimed that he was incapable of proper speech and kept him apart from other performers.

Crowds flocked to the Barnum & Bailey small top in the hours before the main show began under the big top. The sideshow tent was made of striped canvas, seventy feet long, forty feet broad, and thirty feet high. The public side of the top, facing the circus midway, was lined by a banner-line of large and lurid canvas paintings portraying its main attractions. The tent was illuminated inside by electric arc-lamps. Admission into the sideshow was 25 cents. Clyde Ingalls or his assistant Frank Bowen—a former clown—was the outside lecturer who announced each sideshow performance 'in Chesterfieldian fashion' from the bally platform, next to the ticket booths, outside the tent. They and their assistant 'inside lecturers' then took the ticketed audience down the length of the platform stage inside the sideshow tent. Paddy Hepston spieled for the Wild Dancing Bushman.[8]

Writing in 1918, the circus historian W.J. Hilliar reckoned that the best circus sideshow was that of the Ringling Brothers circus, managed by Lew Graham, but the Barnum & Bailey sideshow, managed by Clyde Ingalls, came a close second.[9] Otto Ringling had only recently recruited Clyde Ingalls from a competing circus in Springfield, Missouri. Alva Johnston gave Ingalls a glowing tribute some years later:

> The side-show orator has to adapt his rhetoric to the size of the town, the state of the weather, the section of the country, and the streetcar and bus schedule. In New England, he addresses himself to the intellect; in the Middle West, to the heart; in the South, to the passions. The most gifted of the demagogues in this line is Clyde Ingalls, a Mark Antony for working on the feelings of a mob.
>
> Inferior side-show orators are flustered by dog fights, fist fights, squalling babies, drowning airplanes, pick-pockets, and pinchers, but Ingalls seizes on these interruptions and works them into the stream of his logic without any loss of momentum. The first great principle of oration, according to Ingalls, is to pick on the precise moment when mass skepticism, self-consciousness and thrift have been vanquished, and then stampede the crowd for the box-office before it can change its mood.

The Barnum & Bailey sideshow band was headed by Professor Wolfscale. The band gave a ten-minute concert to draw people milling on the midway to cluster round the front door of the sideshow tent. The band then provided incidental and background music for the promenading of performers inside the tent, stopping and starting on cue just as the much bigger band did for the main circus performers inside the big top. The sideshow band was all-black, while the main circus band was all-white. Though still in some respects a banjo band, the sideshow band included wind instruments and timpani, and had a musical repertoire considerably bigger than that of the old minstrel bands, including ragtime and boogie merging into stock jazz.

Beginning at Madison Square Garden, and then on the road, the Wild Dancing Bushman was now the centre-stage attraction inside the Barnum & Bailey sideshow. 'Captain' Hepston, no doubt in khaki with a whip in one hand and a solar topee on his head, introduced Franz, who leapt wildly up and down on the stage in his canvas-sided booth. Hepston boasted how he had captured and tamed the Wild Dancing Bushman. Franz rushed forward towards the crowd, snarling and screaming before launching into one of his frenetic dances. His genius lay in suddenly transforming his performance from raging savagery into cuteness: one can imagine him snapping his springy dread-locks at first menacingly and then humorously. (The secret of a Wild Man's wild hair is washing it in stout ale turned flat.)

Franz usually danced shoeless on the carpeted sideshow platform, but the 'Sunday School' rules of Barnum & Bailey obliged his lean muscular body to be covered by a large leopard-skin. The leopard-skin grew larger and looser in later years, as he grew older and danced less. But, even in old age, Franz's sudden 'ungodly yells' startled patrons out of their wits and rattled empty glasses.[10]

The upstart Wild Dancing Bushman replaced the venerable cone-headed Zip the Pinhead in the position of glory in the Barnum & Bailey sideshow. Zip was reportedly furious at the slight (though this story may have been trumped up by the publicity department). Jealous old Zip watched his youthful replacement as resident Wild Man like a hawk, to steal what parts he could from Franz Taibosh's act.

Zip noticed that the Wild Dancing Bushman was making a big impact on the bally stage in the midway outside the sideshow, using a ukulele as a 'prop' to attract crowds. People milled around Franz, and bought his ten-cent photo postcards like hot cakes as he strummed away, though it is doubtful that he could play anything but badly. This inspired Zip into competition. His manager, Captain O.K. White, bought him a fiddle in Zanesville, Ohio, and Zip spent the next six years of his life screeching it badly and attracting crowds of his own. Back at Coney Island, where he had once been exhibited in a cage like the pygmy Ota Benga, Zip now imitated the Wild Dancing Bushman: 'For a period he wore a white night shirt, which he whirled around with mock savagery, making threatening gestures', before dissolving into smiles and gentleness. Zip remained silent on stage, or answered questions by distorting his face and grunting hideously, but off stage he was known to be loquacious and to 'cuss a blue streak'.

Zip was the oldest and best-established 'freak' of them all. Fred Bradna called him 'probably the best freak in the history of The Greatest Show on Earth'. Or, in the words of Sam Gumpertz, himself the greatest of freak magnates, 'I should say that the best known freak in the country, and the most ancient, too, is Zip, who is also under contract to me ... he certainly is the one remaining connecting link between the show business of today and that of P.T. Barnum's time.'

Zip's real name was William Henry Johnson. He was an African American, who had started out as a monkey-man for Barnum, inheriting the title of the 'What Is It?' Whatever his publicity said, Johnson was not the original man about whom Charles Dickens enquired 'What is it?' in London in 1846. (That was Harvey Leech, otherwise known as the Gnome Fly, who died in 1847.) The name Zip was derived from the blackface minstrel song 'Zip coon' and the swaggerer it portrayed. Johnson had progressed through variants of Wild Man, billed as the Missing Link, as a Martian, and as an Aztec. He was to all appearances a simple-minded old fellow, with a 'pin-head' looking too small for his shoulders. But he was actually a canny businessman, managing his own chicken farm at Nutley, New Jersey, and other properties.[11]

Leaving Philadelphia at midnight on 4 May 1918, the circus went on to three days in Washington, DC. President and Mrs Woodrow Wilson came down to the circus lot on the Tuesday, and were clapped and cheered by the audience as they sat down in their decorated seats. An outsize US flag flew outside on the big top's rigging. According to Fred Bradna, Woodrow Wilson took to the circus like an excited child, while subsequent presidents Harding, Hoover and Coolidge were more restrained. Bradna added that there was a segregated section for black people when the circus played at Washington, DC, as elsewhere in the South, but Washington blacks remained the best and most appreciative circus audience found in any city.

The Barnum & Bailey sideshow made a record $3,350 in receipts on its first day at Washington in 1918. After the next two days in Baltimore, it was reported: 'Jim Tarver and George Agur [George A. Auger, 'the Cardiff colossus'] are mighty popular these days and the Wild Dancing Bushman is quite a sensation.'

Sam Gumpertz certainly thought so. He got back in touch with Paddy

Hepston to snap up the Wild Dancing Bushman once again for his Dreamland Circus Sideshow, on Coney Island, for the 1919 summer season. Signing himself 'Morris Hepston', Paddy Hepston sealed the contract with Gumpertz's Twenty in One Amusement Co. on 18 May 1918. Hepston was to receive $65 a week and half of all net receipts for items such as postcards sold, plus 'one room and board for two persons'.[12]

From Wilmington, Delaware, on 13 May, the Barnum & Bailey circus began a series of one-day stands (an afternoon matinée followed by an evening performance) in Pennsylvania and New Jersey, then on to New York state and Massachusetts. Boston provided a few days under an auditorium roof (27 May – 1 June) before the circus reverted to canvas. By 21 June the Barnum & Bailey circus was at Bridgeport, Connecticut, its regular winter quarters. On the 24th the circus arrived at Albany, capital of the Empire State (New York), where Frank Cook had his home, and there was much entertaining to be done. Frank Cook was also secretary and organizer of the circus men's masonic or friendly society, Lodge No. 35 of the Loyal Order of Moose (LOM), which moved with the circus and met for dinner and entertainment on Sunday evenings, when public performances were forbidden in most states. The LOM was noteworthy among such societies for the fact that it admitted Jews, and for its lighthearted naming of its officeholders as Dictator, Sergeant-at-Arms and Inner Guard.

After a two-night stand at Buffalo, near Niagara Falls, on 29 June, Barnum & Bailey moved on through Ohio and Illinois to Missouri and Kansas, where it spent more than two weeks in relatively small cities, before arriving in Colorado, reaching Denver on 15 August. Two nights later the circus entrained at Cheyenne and crossed Wyoming into Idaho, to play there on the 21st. Mindful of a recent tragic accident in which another circus train had run into the back of a stationary troop train, killing more than twenty soldiers, the Barnum & Bailey train made a public relations exercise of crossing with a troop train at a siding on the single-track line after Cheyenne. The 'boys' were given coffee, sandwiches, cakes, fruit and books, and gave back a hearty cheer as the circus train departed.

Passing through one-night stops in Montana, the circus arrived at Spokane in Washington state on 24 August, and then proceeded stop by stop to Portland in Oregon on 2 September and entered California after another very long haul. Anna Bourdillion, tattooed woman, caught typhoid and had to be left behind in a Portland hospital. John Ringling caught up with the circus in California and graced it with his presence, entertaining and being entertained by the local plutocracy.[13]

*San Francisco, September 1918: Clicko and a sceptical spectator inside
the tent; the 'outside lecturer' boosts the sideshow from the ticket booth.
(San Francisco Chronicle, 8 September 1918)*

The *Oakland Tribune* carried a Barnum & Bailey press release five days
before the circus arrived, for those people 'to whom the odor of tanbark and
sawdust is an incense'. The circus arrived at Oakland, across the bay from
San Francisco, on Friday, 6 September, parking itself between San Pablo
Avenue and 45th Street. The next three days, 7–9 September, including
performances on a Sunday, were spent in San Francisco. Five trains with
eighty-nine cars were shunted around the bay in the early hours of Saturday
morning, shedding their burden of hundreds of horse-drawn wagons which
took circus equipment and personnel to the empty lot rented for the circus
on Market at 12th Street.

At 10.20 on the morning of Saturday the 7th, San Francisco saw its last
Barnum & Bailey circus parade through the streets. (Some may have been
more impressed by another headline in that day's *Chronicle*, 'Beer making in
America to be stopped December 1st. Necessity for food and fuel prompts
action by United States'.) A three-mile train of brightly painted circus
wagons, circus animals and waving circus artists trundled up Mission Street,
turning on 3rd Street to return along Market Street to the circus lot. The
circus press-agents were particularly proud of elaborately carved wooden
wagons representing the four continents of Africa, America, Asia and Europe,
copied from the frieze on the four sides of the Albert Memorial in London

'by the American wood carver, Cox'. With no striking of tents that night, the roustabouts played cards and quarrelled, and one was killed by another with a mallet blow on the head in the early hours of the next morning.

An artist employed by the *San Francisco Chronicle* caught an image, albeit a crude sketch in thick pencil, of the Wild Dancing Bushman seated on stage in 'the hall of freaks' and holding out a card to a smartly dressed young black woman. 'He may be wild—but he certainly do look like the man that used to come for our ashes.' Another sketch is the head of the 'barker' or opener outside the sideshow, who is describing the 'most marvelous assemblage of extraordinary and remarkable monstrosities' inside.[14]

The Barnum & Bailey trains arrived in Los Angeles on Sunday, 15 September, but there were no performances until the next day on its lot at Praeger Park. The *Los Angeles Times* showed no great enthusiasm. It carried a press release about 'That famous American institution, the circus parade, [which] will burst with all its blare upon the downtown streets of Los Angeles next Monday morning', but referred to it dismissively as 'everything for the kiddies'.

Barnum & Bailey exploited the patriotic fervour of the war against Germany by pushing sales of Liberty Bonds and thrift stamps. Frank Cook did 'wonderful work' in registering 'several hundred men with the Show for the army'. The newspapers listed the names of American casualties in France, and were full of cartoons of the 'dough-boys' in the trenches. 'Americans bottled up Hun hordes in [St Mihiel] salient' was a typical headline; the story beneath called Germans 'the Boche'. The Russians under 'Nikolai Lenine' (*sic*) were referred to as 'Bolsheviki' or Maximalists, posing a new threat to Civilization. The Turks as enemies were identified simply as 'the Moslems'. Maybe this explains why two Los Angeles men, whom from their names we may identify as a Muslim and a Sikh, were passing as Hindus when they were arrested in a scandal over importing mail-order brides from Oklahoma.

Anti-German fever must have been difficult for ringmaster Fred Bradna as a former German army officer. It may also have been difficult for the terribly English-seeming young 'Poodles' Hanneford, the showstopper at almost every performance. He 'should' have volunteered for the British army, but as an ancestral Irishman he possibly agreed more with the sentiments of a current popular song, 'Now's the time to set old Ireland free'.

The next big leap was from San Bernardino on the western side of Los Angeles to Phoenix, Arizona, then arriving in Texas at El Paso on 26 September. After almost two weeks in Texas, the Barnum & Bailey 1918 national tour looped into Louisiana and then returned for a last week in

Texas. Clyde Ingalls reported that Texans and Louisianans were packing into the sideshow for four or five performances a day. The last stop was Houston on 20 October.[15] Barnum & Bailey was forced to call it a day in Houston because of the great influenza epidemic of 1918–19. The flu hit the circus in late summer and caused a frighteningly high death rate, especially among bandsmen infecting each other with their blasted breath. One of the seven Ringling brothers, Henry, was also a victim.

Imminent amalgamation of the more successful Barnum & Bailey circus with the less successful Ringling Brothers circus was firmly predicted. There was cynical talk in the entertainment press advocating the Social Darwinism of the 'survival of the fittest', at a time of economic recession following on from the bloodiest of all wars. The 'reckless and excessive prodigality of nature' dictated that 'thousands must be crushed, mangled, starved and killed [so] that a few may survive ... to this inexorable law of nature there is and can be no exception'.

For the first time, in 1918 Ringling Brothers retired together with Barnum & Bailey for winter stabling and training in Bridgeport, Connecticut. Reflecting on the fact that the Ringling hometown of Baraboo, in Wisconsin, had previously been their winter capital, Robert (son of Charles) Ringling observed: 'That puts the crepe on Wisconsin.' Plans were mooted for a winter victory tour by the two circuses to London and Paris but were dropped. Instead the circuses had to make do with joining a victory parade at Bridgeport's Sea Side Park, complete with clown numbers and a 'real Wild West performance ... that made people sit up and take notice'.[16]

During the 1918 season, it was Paddy Hepston's job to talk up Franz's act in the Barnum & Bailey sideshow. He told the latest version of the old story of how he had captured and trained the Bushman in the Kalahari. What Hepston said was recorded and printed in a pamphlet sold as part of Clicko's act from 1922 onwards. It contained the same old untruths as before: 'He was found ... in the Kalahari Desert. No other human being was seen in the locality at the time ... when discovered this Bushman was in pursuit of ostriches, and ... he was armed with the bow and arrow which he still carries.'

Captain Hepston (renamed 'Captain Du Barry' in the 1922 version) 'was shooting ostriches in the Kalahari Desert and wounded (as he thought) one, but it continued to run away and he mounted his horse and overtook it and then he discovered it was the Bushman disguised very cleverly as an ostrich, which he was trying to kill when Captain Du Barry appeared on the scene. The Bushman was wounded in the leg and was taken down to Kimberley by the Captain who got him well and looked after him.' The last part of the story contained an extraordinary admission of habitual cruelty. On his farm 'near Kimberley', the captain was said to have 'tamed' the Bushman 'by tying him to a post and whipping him every day for six months'.[17]

Every word, of course, was sheer invention, though Hepston's cheerful admission of his training methods was instructive. Franz Taibosh's characteristic response to the story in later years when the pamphlet, which he had been selling for years, was read out to him was 'bullshit!' Some years later there was an alternative version of Franz Taibosh's origins doing the rounds in the circus. As related by the equestrienne Dixie Willson, the story is remote from reality but has a grain of symbolic truth.

> I know the real life drama of Cliko, the chattering little 'wild man', who had been seized from among a dozen naked pygmies by an English hunting party in the jungles. The captain of the party, taking his prize by cage to London, had found himself with a lucrative dime-museum feature … the panic-stricken little creature [was] wild indeed, for never had he known any life but the freedom of tropic days and nights. Now he had only the defense of snarling teeth … his keeper of course found it good business to keep him as frightened, as mystified, as tantalyzed as possible. The captain made money and, after a few seasons in Europe, came to America offering his novelty to Mr. Ringling. So Cliko, caged and helpless, became one of the 'strange people' of the big show.

There is no good evidence that Franz Taibosh was ever caged. (It seems to be a confusion with Ota Benga, the 'Pygmy in the Zoo', who sometimes appeared inside a primate cage at Brooklyn Zoo in 1906.)[18]

Franz Taibosh was beginning to enjoy himself during the summer of 1918. He relished being such an attraction in the Big Show, and began to profess disdain for the world of carnivals and funfairs. Barbara Cook de Romain, who as a child knew him very well in later years, says that Franz could be quite a social snob, as well as a male chauvinist. Wintering once again with Paddy Hepston, after all the excitement and the adulation, must have been a great anti-climax for Franz. They settled in a boarding or rooming house at 38 Courtland Street in Bridgeport, where Hepston had taken a winter job with the American Housing Corporation.

During the latter part of 1918, the lethal influenza pandemic continued. We do not know about Franz's health, but one of the temporary victims of the flu was Paddy Hepston. He was probably hospitalized, as he had to ask someone else to go and check on the Wild Man back in his apartment. This began a chain of events that was to completely change Franz Taibosh's life. The visitor found Clicko to be 'as amiable and social as anyone could wish' but was appalled by the conditions in which he was living—though we may discard Dixie Willson's contention that Clicko was imprisoned in a cage, fed on garbage, and clothed 'in old and greasy rags'.[19]

It was now quite clear that the real 'savage and wicked monster' was Paddy Hepston, not Franz Taibosh. Franz's condition was brought to the notice of the Ringling management. Frank Cook, the legal adjuster, with the consent of the Ringling brothers and no doubt feeling moral responsibility as the original contractor of Hepston and the Bushman for Barnum & Bailey, was determined to take drastic action.

KIDNAP IN CONNECTICUT

THE BRIDGEPORT POST of Thursday, 12 December 1918 carried an extraordinary report headlined 'African Bushman remains abducted' on its front page. The other main news of that day was that President Woodrow Wilson was to arrive in France on Friday the 13th—'his lucky day'.

> No trace has been found by the police of Franz Taaibosh, Barnum and Bailey's African bushman, who is said to have been abducted from No. 38 Courtland-street where he lived with his manager Captain Morris Hepston. The bushman who is said to be over 100 years old was spirited away during the absence of the captain some time yesterday afternoon and although the police have searched the city for him he has not been located. Taaibosh is said to be a valuable freak attached to one of the side shows at the Barnum and Bailey circus and has been traveling with the show all summer.

The *Post* added: 'While Captain Hepston was at work for the United States Housing Corporation some one telephoned the house and when told that the captain was out said they would telephone later. When the captain returned about 4:30 the bushman was gone.'[1] Twelve years later, the same newspaper expanded the story further:

> The circus had returned from making its last stand in Texas, and Hepston brought the 'wild man' back to Bridgeport and put him in a furnished room. Roomers in the house noticed that the 'wild man' was poorly clad and they called the circus office, then on Norman street.
> Some of the men came down to the rooming house and found the little 'wild man' wearing women's stockings, a woman's undergarment, women's shoes, and a pair of Hepston's pants that had been 'amputated' in the legs to fit the 'wild man'.

The little savage pleaded to be taken away. He was munching on crusts of stale bread and showed the circus men a glass of water, they said. He made them understand that he was living on bread and water. He was taken to the circus quarters by the men and he has been with the circus ever since as a free agent.[2]

The items of women's clothing may be said to confirm the general emasculation of Frank Taibosh as a victim of Paddy Hepston. Whether they indicated any more intimate relationship between the two men can only be guessed at. A third version of the events on that day is contained in the words of Dixie Willson, who claimed to know 'the real life drama of Cliko'.

> When the season was over, the captain settled down in winter quarters, and there it was that some one realized his cruelty to the little African. The matter was brought to Mr. Ringling's attention and one day the captain came home to his boarding house to find the wild man's cage empty—the wild man had gone!
>
> Immediately detectives for the Englishman went to work and very soon placed the theft at the door of—the show's attorney, Mr. Frank Cook! A warrant was sworn out for Mr. Cook's arrest, but since no trace could be found of the wild man, no arrest could be made! Mr. Cook neither admitted nor denied the charge, [but] simply gave them *carte blanche* to prove anything they could.[3]

Cook family tradition expands on the events of Wednesday, 11 December 1918. Frank Cook arranged for an alluring female to divert Hepston in a bar, presumably the bar to which Hepston repaired after work each evening. While Hepston was engaged with the doxy in the bar, Cook and his chauffeur broke into Hepston's unheated apartment. They found Franz Taibosh sitting semi-naked under a horse blanket in a bare room, looking miserably cold and ill-fed, with the bones left over from previous meals scattered across the floorboards. Franz greeted them in a friendly manner. They wrapped him in Cook's fur coat, and carried him downstairs and outside to the car.

They drove straight to Albany, arriving in the early hours of the next day. Franz was deposited at the Cook family home, under the charge of Cook's daughter Frances. She nursed him back to robust health, while Frank Cook returned to face the music at Bridgeport.[4]

Dixie Willson is correct that 'The captain dogged the Ringling attorney's footsteps', seeing the kidnap as the outcome of a conspiracy on the part of top Ringling management. But she is incorrect in supposing that Franz was hidden from public view for the next two summer seasons. Ringling riches could buy quicker justice than that. The Wild Dancing Bushman was openly paraded at the Spring opening of the Barnum & Bailey circus on 29 March 1919, at Madison Square Garden, New York.

Whether or not 'his apprehensive black eyes [were] darting at the milling crowds', the little Wild Man in the leopard-skin was certainly 'well guarded … quite out of reach of the captain or the captain's men' when he appeared on the hippodrome track in the opening 'spec'. Hepston had turned to the British consul-general in New York for aid. The consulate is said to have reacted with surprising alacrity as soon as the Wild Dancing Bushman appeared at Madison Square Garden. Once again we have Dixie Willson's fanciful account.

> When Mr. Cook returned to his hotel after the matinée performance, he found officers and papers waiting, on a charge of 'forcibly detaining a British subject'.
>
> 'If my friend Mr. Taibosh is upstairs,' Mr. Cook said to the clerk, 'please ask him to come down.'
>
> And presently out of the elevator stepped out a smartly tailored 'wild man', polished shoes, derby and stick.
>
> 'You want me, Mr. Cook?' he asked, with a pleasant, odd little accent.
>
> And within the next five minutes the officers found that Mr. Franz Taibosh as a guest of the hotel had registered for himself, had paid his own bills there, carried a contract in his pocket signed 'on the dotted line', *for* himself, and *by* himself …
>
> 'Who *is* it I am forcibly detaining?' Mr. Cook inquired blandly of the law.

If the details of this charade are anything like true, there had been considerable preparation and rehearsal. Franz Taibosh could swagger with the best and was a born mimic, but he couldn't read, or write more than a squiggle, apparently could never keep track of money, and at this stage probably had rather rudimentary command of English. He may have understood English well enough but had so far had little chance of speaking in his 'funny little Bushman-English voice', as Hepston had kept him virtually incommunicado.[5]

The British consulate in New York investigated Hepston's guardianship over Taibosh, mindful of the fact that their passports, enabling them to be absent from Britain, had come up for annual renewal on 18 March 1919. Frank Cook undoubtedly used his social connections to catch and keep the ear of the British acting consul-general in New York. The latter wrote to his superiors at the Foreign Office in London on 22 April that 'there has been considerable correspondence at this Office' on the matter of Franz Taibosh. He added—what Cook must have told him—that Taibosh had *deserted*

Hepston to seek the *protection* of Cook. Frank Cook's superior class cachet obviously carried greater weight than the British nationality of Hepston.

A satisfactory answer must have been received from the British authorities, clearing the way for Frank Cook to obtain US Immigration permission (File 7897) for Franz Taibosh to remain resident for another eighteen months until 1 November 1920. (The file on the case at the Foreign Office in London has since been destroyed, and thus cannot be found in the national archives of England and Wales. But a copy of the consul-general's letter of 22 April 1919 survives in the South African national archives at Pretoria.)[6]

Hepston turned to Sam Gumpertz for help. Hepston had signed a contract with Gumpertz in May 1918 committing himself to supply the services of the Wild Dancing Bushman once more to the Dreamland Circus Sideshow, on Coney Island, as from 'on or about May 1, 1919'. Clause 14 of the contract had committed Hepston 'in the event of a violation of this contract, that an injunction restraining the Artist from performing for any other person may issue out of a court of competent jurisdiction'.

On 27 June 1919, 'Morris Hepston', with Gumpertz's backing, obtained a Bridgeport court order through his attorney against the Ringling Brothers and Barnum & Bailey circus, against the Ringling Brothers as a corporation, against John Ringling himself, and against Frank A. Cook. The order summoned the parties to court on 1 September, and ordered them to deposit $6,000 with the court, against the $5,000 being claimed by Hepston in damages.

Hepston as plaintiff identified Cook as the person who had entered his Bridgeport apartment the previous 11 December, and the circus as Cook's employer that now had the Bushman in its 'possession ... held and detained against his will'. Hepston claimed that the Bushman had been placed 'about a dozen years prior' in 'care, custody and control ... as his servant' by the British South African Government (*sic*). Damages were being claimed because of loss of income from his contract for the Bushman's services with Gumpertz. Perhaps Paddy Hepston believed that Franz, who had lived so closely with him for so long, genuinely pined to return. As for Gumpertz's backing Hepston, Gumpertz stood to lose control of a valuable property for a season or two. Subsequent events also suggest that he felt he had proprietary rights over Clicko as his discoverer and first employer in America. He might also have had plans of his own to wrest Clicko from Hepston, and was annoyed that Frank Cook had pipped him to the post.[7]

◎

Just before the start of the circus season, there was a big party thrown by John Bryce of 1310 Brock Street, in Albany, New York, for Frank Cook and his family and friends. *Billboard* reported, 'A great time was had by everybody.' This could have been, in a very real sense, Franz Taibosh's coming-out party—out of hiding for the summer season with the newly amalgamated Ringling-Barnum circus.

The amalgamation of their two largest circuses had been the Ringling brothers' solution to the current crisis in railroad circus economics: too many circuses chasing too few customers against the rising costs of transportation and labour. John Ringling was the very model of a super-capitalist: his investments in US oil and railroads were benefiting from the drainage of capital out of war-torn Europe, and now he was driving towards monopoly of the circus business. Ringling Brothers and Barnum & Bailey's Combined Circus would be the Big One which swept around the land, covering costs through the economies of scale and creating super-profits by sucking up local city audiences for just one really big 'circus day' a year. And every year the circus would have more and more acts and attractions to bring in those punters who were sated on previous attractions. Against the increasing competition of movies, records, radio and baseball in the 1920s and 1930s, the Big One would bloat itself annually until it finally burst.[8]

On 25 March 1919, *Billboard* proclaimed: 'The circus was born again here this afternoon', with the opening of the World's First Super Circus, at Madison Square Garden. The matinée began with John Agee, the equestrian director from the Ringling circus, blowing his whistle for the enormous doors at the end of the Garden to open. The grand entry procession, when all the animals and performers—including the 'freaks'—trooped around the hippodrome track, was followed by the parade of elephants, and so on down the list through acrobats picked out by spotlights, and equestrians starring daring young 'Poodles' Hanneford, to a final hippodrome race with fiery steeds and Roman chariots, in the manner borrowed from and immortalized by Fred Niblo's film *Ben-Hur*.

In the words of the circus historian Mark St Leon: 'The new circus brought together under one spread of canvas the largest array of circus artists ever seen in one place at one time. Among them were the three finest riding acts in the world: the May Wirth troupe, the Hannefords and the Davenports.'

Stars of the big-top show this year were equestrienne May Wirth and aerialist Lillian Leitzel. May Wirth exhibited genuine prowess and dexterity: 'a back somersault through a paper hoop and the same stunt with the hoop alight with fire', on the back of a galloping horse. Her tutor in this was Orrin Davenport, who also performed spectacular somersaults from one galloping horse to another. (Edwin 'Poodles' Hanneford held the world record for vaulting on and off a horse, twenty-six times in succession.) Lillian Leitzel was known for an act that was more a feat of resistance to pain than skill. Dressed in a spangled leotard, she spun by one arm on a rope to the tune of Rimsky-Korsakov's 'Flight of the bumble-bee', dislocating and relocating her shoulder on each spin or 'plange'. By the fortieth spin her hair would fly loose from its pins, spraying out long blonde curls.

· Lew Graham was the announcer of the main show under the big top as well as sideshow outside talker. Unlike one-ring circuses where the ringmaster doubled as announcer of acts and equestrian director, the huge hangar-like tent of a three-ring circus needed a dedicated announcer with a huge voice. Lew Graham obliged: 'His deep resonant voice, magnified only by his cupped hands, carried to the farthest reaches of that huge tent as he told of the wonders of this or that act which the audience was about to witness.'[9]

As equestrian director, John Agee struggled with the enormous task of keeping up the pace of performances. He was replaced as equestrian director in the third week by his deputy Fred Bradna from the old Barnum & Bailey show. Otherwise the initial Ringling-Barnum run at Madison Square Garden appears to have been a success from the start. Extra matinée shows were given in the morning, including a free show for sailors and soldiers back from the war, and another show for patients in Bellevue Hospital at the foot of East 26th Street. The clown Fred Egner, followed by his devoted geese, got the biggest laughs. After Manhattan the Ringling-Barnum went under canvas in cool weather at Brooklyn, showing off its new, bigger and better canvas tops. The circus was now more mechanized than ever, with sheets of folded tent canvas dispensed from great spools, and stakes driven in by power-hammers.[10]

The cold weather continued until May when the Big One moved on from six performances in Philadelphia to Washington, DC. The Ringling-Barnum train was reportedly three miles long. Frank Cook went on ahead and was entertained by the Elks, a masonic order popular among showmen, in chilly Philadelphia. Lew Graham's sideshow is said to have smashed all previous Ringling Brothers or Barnum & Bailey attendance records in Washington. As well as Graham, Ingalls and Vino as sideshow lecturers, there were two ticket-sellers, two doorkeepers, two men in charge of canvas, and two other personnel managers.

Franz Taibosh always reckoned that his best friends among 'freaks' were the giants and midgets. The 8 ft 4 in George Auger was known as the Welsh Giant because he actually came from Wales, but the title harked back to Barnum's spurious Cardiff Giant, a man-shaped piece of rock hewn from a quarry at Cardiff in upstate New York. Auger wrote comic music-hall sketches in his spare time, and was always the best of friends with midget people. Then there was the brother and sister act of German-born Kurt (Harry Doll) and Frieda Schneider (Grace Doll), who had come to America in 1916 with their mother Mrs Bert Earles as their manager. Younger sisters Frieda (Daisy Doll) and Elly Schneider (Tiny Doll) were soon to join the duo to constitute a whole 'Doll family', which adopted first the Earles surname and then the surname of Doll in the 1930s.[11]

A newspaper clipping probably dating from May 1919 tells of a correspondent called Russ Simonton who joined the Barnum & Bailey sideshow team over lunch one day in the cookhouse tent. Simonton noted that George Auger, the star of the sideshow, sat down opposite his friends, the midget Dolls. Grace Doll berated the giant good-naturedly, and prattled on about a love-letter mailed her by a farm boy called George Plum. Simonton discovered that 'Freaks are regular folks, with regular troubles and regular laughs'. George Auger said: 'We may be out of the ordinary, but we have brains and feelings.' One of the photographs that accompanied the text was: 'Clico (lower right), Australian bushman, shaves himself with a safety razor.' (The same photograph was later used by another newspaper with a caption explaining that he was eighty years old and had left fourteen wives in Africa.)

Simonton was told again and again that the real freaks under the freak top were the spectators on the ground, not the performers on stage. But this did not stop Simonton from including the nonsense that 'Clico, last survivor of the Australian bushmen' was holding a conversation over the lunch table with the chimpanzee Congo, 'the lowest example of human life'. It is noteworthy that Franz Taibosh was now being given the semi-personal name 'Clico' in circus publicity, even if it was still unclear if he was a Bushman of African or Australian provenance: at least 'Wild Dancing' had been eliminated from his title.[12]

The Ringling-Barnum sideshow band had eighteen musicians, under the firm and professional direction of Professor P.G. Lowery. His wife sang with the band as soprano. Lowery was already an institution when he took on the combined circus sideshow band, after two decades of circus experience and a stint with the US Army. The 1921 season was to be his last before retirement. He was fondly recalled many years afterwards by Fred Bradna, director of the main circus band, who had once been a neophyte compared to Lowery's infinitely greater experience: 'Boy he could blow that horn. A first-rate musician. And the first black man to graduate from the New England Conservatory of Music. When he and his gang blasted off for the bally, well, that was sure enough windjammin'.'

The *Billboard* correspondent Circus Solly, in his 'Under the marquee' column, put the sound of the sideshow ('kid show') minstrel band at the very core of that glorious feeling which characterized circus life, as it played on the lot over the hours before the big top was opened: 'hearing the galloping rat-tat-tat of the "kid" showband (while you look for the "flag" at the cookhouse).'[13]

From Washington the circus progressed to Wilmington, Delaware, where a commotion was caused in the inaugural street parade when a wild animal tried to run off. After that night's show, local notables entertained the circus doctor Doc Shields, Frank Cook, Clyde Ingalls and other circus managers. Such receptions were commonplace for top circus people like Cook, since in most places circus day came but once a year. Usually the receptions were for men only, and only the best liquor was served. Performers were usually not invited, but it was to become evident that Frank Cook was taking Franz Taibosh along to such parties as his entertaining sidekick.

Frank Cook was known as 'Papa Cook' among circus folk, and as 'Cookie' among his intimates. After his death, *Billboard* simply called him 'the king of the fixers'. In a get-rich-quick age, even 'Sunday School shows' (rather than 'grift shows') like the Ringling Brothers' circuses were obliged to indulge in a little bribery and corruption at the level of local politics. Cook is said to have lived by the classic showbiz maxim of 'the show must go on'. He had to negotiate the lowest possible licence fees ('readers') and lot rentals, and had to bribe local officials with free passes to shows. 'In all my years of trouping,' remarked one old circus trouper, 'I don't believe I ever heard of a local official buying and paying for a ticket, and that included his family.' Local policemen even ate free meals in the circus cookhouse tent.

Cook maintained an enormous range of influential contacts and friends in the eastern and middle states of the US and in the Canadian provinces. Freemasonry was an essential part of such networking. As well as being secretary of the Barnum & Bailey chapter of the show-business masonry, the Loyal Order of Moose, he was a member of the Masonic Lodge of St Cecile in New York. Top managers like Cook travelled around with a bunch of free passes in their pockets. In return these managers shared in the lavish entertainments with which municipal dignitaries celebrated their annual circus day.[14]

The weather turned stifling hot in early June 1919 when the circus reached Syracuse in upstate New York, where thousands of people lined the streets to witness the parade of the world's biggest-ever circus. One of the brightly coloured circus wagons, drawn by a team of horses, got temporarily stuck under a low bridge. At Utica, the next city east of Syracuse, the geese clown Fred Egner died of unexplained causes, aged forty-five. By the time the circus made Boston, 'Bean City', on 16 June, after a two-hundred-mile railroad 'jump', the weather was cold and drizzling. But Boston was a 'straw house', meaning that there were more people than fixed seats, so bales of straw were provided as extra seating.

The Ringling-Barnum circus continued to break its attendance records in Connecticut, through Waterbury and New Haven until it reached Bridgeport, its home base, on 27 June 1919. Here, in the hometown of so many circus staff and performers, there were special celebrations. Maybe the circus managers also wanted to cock a snook against the court order obtained against them by Hepston and Gumpertz that same day. The circus baker excelled in the quality of his cream puffs, and Franz Taibosh was invited to preside at a management party for Charles Hutchinson, the circus treasurer.[15]

A story about the party appeared in the *Bridgeport Post*, under the headline 'West End in uproar when Clicco runs wild. Rubber haired toastmaster escapes with Bill Steinke's benny'. Bill Steinke was the *Post*'s cartoonist and columnist who put in a guest appearance as a circus clown; his 'benny' was his top hat. These were also known to be the last days of hard drinking, as Prohibition would soon come into effect throughout most of the United States.

His name is Clicco. He bears no relationship to any of the new temperance drinks. But today he is the source of vows by many West Enders to hereafter climb on the wagon for good, whether school keeps in or not after July 1.

It all started when some friends of Manager Charlie Hutchinson of Ringling Bros. and Barnum and Bailey Combined Shows decided to give him a 'Welcome Home' Party at his home in Elmwood Place after the midnight hour this morning. As a novelty, Clicco, the rubber haired negro, was requisitioned from the show to act as toastmaster, chairman and general fun maker. Clicco was in good spirits and his merry antics brought out many a hearty laugh.

During the course of the merriment Franz, no doubt more than a little tanked up, put on the silk top hat belonging to Bill Steinke, and ran off into the night wearing it.

Fred Bradna, ring master for the Ringling circus, was the first to miss the Para haired kaffir. 'He's gone! Clicco has vamoosed!' cried Fred. 'Hurry, he's gone!' cried Mrs. Fred, who was also among the throng.

'Who's gone?' chorused those in the other room.

'Clicco.'

Bill Steinke forgot to look for his hat. Charlie Hutchinson forgot his too in Elmwood Place, Bridgeport. Mayer turned a somersault. Suckley, assistant to John Ringling, jumped to the phone. Jake just ran to the door.

The party adjourned to the drizzling rain and stygian darkness ... The quest took the group through the principal streets of the West End. At Park Avenue, a policeman was found apparently holding up a last-week-in-June celebrator by the arm. 'Did you see him?' chorused the party, excitedly.

'See who?' shot back the cop.

'Clicco, the rubber-haired man.'

'Gosh, I was just trying to figure out whether this was a man. I kinda thought it was the guy with the smoked glasses. I don't need him anymore,' spoke the policeman, promptly turning Clicco over to his keepers. Bill Steinke's silk lid was a little battered, but Clicco looked as debonair as ever. He wore no coat and his white shirt shone out brightly in the night. His suspenders were hanging down.

'Click-click-click, clicko-clickee-clicka,' which means 'It's great to be lost,' said the rubber haired man as he sat down to a feast in the Hutchinson home shortly after two bells.[16]

Independence Day, 4 July 1919, was celebrated at Harrisburg, Pennsylvania, as the circus continued to jag across the north-east. The Ringling-Barnum culinary chef, Ollie Webb, provided dishes of Maryland chicken and English plum pudding, washed down with lemonade, for the staff and performers' dinner-dance. Music under the elaborate decorations in the dining tent was provided by Penn Harris's Ladies Jazz Orchestra, and circus medic Doc Shields led everyone in the long twisty line of a conga dance.

Bastille Day, 14 July, saw the circus caught in a great wind and electrical storm at Akron, Ohio, just as the roustabouts were about to lower the big top that night. The top was left up in the rain and got so waterlogged that it sagged and broke two centre poles, damaging the tent and interior lighting. Franz Taibosh would have been perfectly familiar from his childhood with the violence of electrical storms on the great plains of South Africa but was no doubt snug in his rail coach bunk.

On the way from Parkersburg, West Virginia, on 20 July, a former detective with the circus, now chief of police and fire-chief of the small town of Nitro near Charleston, intercepted the train. He drove off his with 'old companion' Frank Cook, Doc Shields and others for a chicken dinner. They whiled away the evening in autos and motorboats, eating corn on the cob and blackberry and lemon pies, until they rejoined the circus at Charleston for its performance on the 21st. Perhaps another adventure for Franz Taibosh as their butler.

On 24 July the Ringling-Barnum circus proved its 'Sunday School show' credentials by performing at Columbus, capital of the 'Bukeye State' (Ohio), during the Methodist Centenary Exhibit. Frank Taibosh may have had a chance to visit two women and three men featuring as a 'Kaffir Quintet' in local churches, presumably Xhosa-speaking Methodists from South Africa.[17]

The climax of Ringling-Barnum's first summer was its stand at Chicago, the Ringling brothers' business base, from 9 to 17 August 1919. It was the first circus allowed to parade inside the Loop, the central business district, for twenty years. Not for the first time the circus was considered a distraction from current civil discontent. Chicago streetcars and elevated railroads had been on strike, and racial conflict between competing black, Polish and Lithuanian meat-packers in the stockyards was being blamed on Bolshevik agitators. In the first few days of August, troops of the Illinois National Guard blocked central Chicago between the university and the stockyards, and workers reluctantly returned to work.

News from the rest of the world reflected similar tensions. General Ironside was pressing a futile British expeditionary force on the Archangel front against Soviet Russia; Sinn Fein was stealing British army rifles in Northern Ireland; Liverpool was racked by riots and London police were on strike; and Jews were being massacred at Odessa, then part of Poland. Henry Ford was successfully suing the *Chicago Tribune* for the preposterous libel of calling him an anarchist antagonistic towards capitalism.

Against this background, the *Tribune* welcomed nine days of the circus with a touch of irony as a story which 'may bore the children, but it will interest the grown ups'. The Big Show was given a prime pitch on the lakefront, in Grant Park, between Van Buren and Harrison streets, near the shopping district where patrons would be most numerous. The 'riotously emblazoned cars' of the circus trains, which had departed from South Bend in Indiana the previous evening, began to draw into the Chicago railroad yards in the early hours of Saturday, 9 August. '"Here she comes!" yelled one of a crowd of grimy youngsters who gathered in the vicinity of Eighteenth and South Clark streets this morning long before daylight began creeping into the railroad yards. "Hey, Mick-e-e-ee! Cir-cus!"'

When the horse-drawn wooden circus wagons began to rumble up Clark Street, 'an endless, cavorting, shrieking, laughing juvenile procession streamed behind red and gold wagons, trailed tarpaulin-draped cages, or trotted at a respectful distance behind softly padding elephants as they moved from the freight yards across the Van Buren street bridge into Grant park.'

More than 300 wagons were employed in moving the circus with all its paraphernalia to Grant park. Besides the main tent, there are twenty-eight smaller ones ... There are five troupes of trained seals, a man [Monsieur de Long] who skates on his head from the apex of the tent to the ground, aerialists, acrobats, equestrians and plenty of trained dog and pony acts, and clowns for the little ones.

The main show under the 600-ft big top opened to the public at 2 pm on that Saturday, an hour after the sideshow and menagerie tents were opened. On the following Monday twelve hundred riders and costumed marchers, with seven hundred horses and forty-one elephants, paraded in a three-mile procession and pageant of all nations down Jackson Boulevard, La Salle and State streets in the Loop: the 'sun glistening on golden spangles' amidst the 'blare of red-coated musicians'. Ringling-Barnum donated its declared profits in Chicago to a soldiers' and sailors' memorial fund, and US army veterans paraded through the Loop on the following Saturday demonstrating their opposition to the recent riots. Lew Graham expressed his satisfaction that the Chicago newspapers had had a field day, and the sideshow had again broken all its attendance records.[18]

By early September 1919 it was announced that the Ringling-Barnum circus would keep on going that year into November, milking the return to boom conditions in circus entertainment. The only dent in confidence was a railroad crash en route to Oklahoma of a thirty-car section of the circus train, which hit open switch-points, smashing four cars and killing twelve horses. More than seventy other horses were injured and some had to be put down.

Texas in early October proved to be full of rain: there were a number of washouts when tents could not even be erected. It was fine when the circus arrived at San Antonio, but the scheduled performances were then cancelled because of heavy rain. Paris, Texas, produced the following jottings from a circus man: 'So this is Paris! Nowhere to go and the town tied up ... all that the folks do in Paris is to promenade the main drag until they get sleepy and then go to the cars.'

Bets were now being taken on when and where Ringling-Barnum would end its first season. Advance crews of billposters plastered Alabama, Virginia and the Carolinas, Georgia and Tennessee. But too many stands were lost to 'rain and mud' in Alabama, and the overflow crowds in Virginia and the Carolinas were a welcome fillip for circus finances: the 'side-show has also been getting a good share of the business'. In Georgia the weather turned cold and audiences began to drop, so the season was ended on 1 November in the coastal port of Savannah. The circus's number one car then led the circus train back to winter quarters at Bridgeport, Connecticut. Once again there was no truth in a rumour that the whole circus would be shipped to England, for a Christmas run at London's Olympia exhibition hall.

Ringling-Barnum had covered roughly ten thousand miles on the railroads in 1919 as far west as Denver, Colorado. But rail travel had been temporarily nationalized under federal government control, to facilitate wartime transport of troops and materiel. The railroads would revert to the control of their separate owners in 1920, and rail rates would inevitably rise.[19]

1919 was Franz Taibosh's first year of freedom from Paddy Hepston. The British authorities had recognized Frank Cook as his guardian. Cook ensured Taibosh had all creature comforts, including those of the flesh; they partied and ate and drank and used the services of brothels together. As Taibosh's manager, Cook dealt with all money matters. In essence the arrangement was that, in return for Taibosh's summer pay minus pocket money, Cook would provide Taibosh with a winter home.

The two men might party and eat together but did not live together in the summer season. Cook had his own stateroom in a management car that was rarely hitched to a circus train but travelled separately; Taibosh had his bunk in a dormitory Pullman car with other sideshow performers. Each season he would have been allocated an upper or lower bunk according to his rank, closer to or further from the wheels of the wooden car. The rail cars of both big-top and small-top artists were in the last circus train that left the siding by one o'clock each night after a stand—preceded by a first train with cooks, canvas-men and stake-drivers ready to set up on a new lot, and second and (from 1919) third trains with the show's livestock and grooms, wardrobe staff, and the patent collapsible seating for the big top. The last train carried circus performers; management were the last to board.

Wholesome food was an obsession with most circus people, who expended so much energy in physical activity every day. Franz was no exception. There was food to be had on the overnight trains, with waiter service and better cuisine in the restaurant dining-car, and plainer fare (in some states with beer) in the 'pie car' or coffee wagon—a 'privilege' (private concession) held by Joe Millar. This car, hitched on to the back of the train, served as a social centre where performers could snack, smoke, gamble and unwind into the early hours of the morning. When Franz ate and drank in these places, or bought goods from other concessionaires within the circus, such as the candy butchers who sold confectionery, he used a circus form of 'tick' or credit note; he did not trust himself with cash.

Franz is said to have become the 'pet' of managers and top artists, moving freely among them. They gave him the large Cuban cigars he characteristically smoked. Until the onset of Prohibition, he might also be taken out for a drink to a local hotel at a weekend. His favourite drink was beer; he got much too sozzled on hard liquor. Not surprisingly, his command of the English language greatly improved in his first year of liberty, and he became known as a chatterbox, in the distinctive lilting tones of South African Coloured English derived from Afrikaans.[20]

Franz spent the winter of 1919–20 with the Cooks, father Frank and daughter Frances and son Edward, in their Albany home. The alternative would have been to stay with other circus folk in or near the Bridgeport winter quarters.

It is not known if Franz and the Cooks attended the circus high-society wedding of the year at the Little Church Around the Corner—the Episcopalian Church of the Transfiguration, also headquarters of the Actors' Church Alliance, in New York City—when Frank White from Wirth's circus in Australia married May Wirth. (She stayed on with Ringling-Barnum despite being offered $1,000 a week elsewhere.)

Franz and the Cooks could possibly also have attended the rather stranger marriage of Lillian Leitzel's ex-husband Clyde Ingalls, Ringling-Barnum ringside announcer and sideshow manager, to a Czechoslovak dancer, a former 'Ziegfeld girl', at a Baptist church in New York in early 1920. It was strange because Ingalls and Leitzel had recently travelled overseas as a couple, together with circus band-leader Merle Evans. Evans and Leitzel had been stricken by sea-sickness, releasing Ingalls to chase other women around the ship, causing Evans much later to remark: 'He was always on the prowl for new dames. Never understood why Leitzel got hooked into him. She so out-classed him. But I'll say this for Ingalls. When it came to announcing an outside bally, there was no equal then or now.'[21]

13

'I AM AN
AMERICAN GENTLEMAN'

ENCOURAGED AND SPONSORED by Sam Gumpertz, Paddy Hepston had not given up on his attempt to regain possession of Franz Taibosh. The case was not heard as prescribed in the superior court of Fairfield county, at Bridgeport, Connecticut, on 1 September 1919, because the plaintiff wished to modify his complaint. Hepston's attorney submitted the amendments to the court on 12 September 1919. A new paragraph had been added, stating that Hepston had not been allowed access to the Bushman since 11 December 1918. More significantly, two existing paragraphs had been amended: one to add that the 'said Bushman was and always has been of inferior mentality', and the other to change the word 'possession' of the Bushman to 'employment'. The latter amendments must have been designed to undermine reports of Taibosh's obvious contentment with his new position, and to counter any charges of enslavement against Hepston.

On 19 January 1920, Hepston as plaintiff pledged a bond of $50 against legal costs, but the defendants did not formally respond to the court until April 1920. Meanwhile, Hepston applied to the British consul-general in New York for another year's renewal of his British passport, from 18 March 1920. He was summoned to the consul-general's office, where on 13 April he successfully pleaded to remain overseas to pursue his case at Bridgeport.

On 23 April, the Barnum & Bailey circus (continuing as a legal entity) launched its counter-attack. It put a motion before the court at Bridgeport, challenging Hepston to substantiate his claim that the South African government had given him the Bushman as his servant and had permitted them to leave the country together. The circus asserted that Hepston was in violation of the US criminal code on two counts: for importing into the US a slave or person 'to be held to service or labor' (section 248), and for kidnapping or enticing any person 'to be sold into involuntary servitude, or held as a slave' (section 268). Hepston was required to provide certified copies of his and Taibosh's passports and of the contract with Gumpertz.

The plaintiff's attorney responded six days later with copies of passports and of the Gumpertz contract. On the two more substantive points, the response was that Hepston had signed a document at Kimberley in South Africa on 25 July 1912, giving him 'care and custody' of the Bushman, on the promise that he would be returned to South Africa. But, unfortunately for the plaintiff, Hepston had 'received no copy of said agreement'.

On 3 July 1920, the Fairfield county superior court accepted Hepston's attorney's plea that the defendants be summonsed to appear before the court, and set a trial date for 1 September 1920. Summonses were delivered on 23 July on the Barnum & Bailey circus, on Frank Cook, and on John Ringling.[1]

Thereafter there was a curious legal silence—and the case lapsed for a full decade until 1930. Presumably Hepston and Gumpertz were dissuaded from pursuing their case by private contacts between the attorneys on both sides. The counter-accusations of kidnapping and enslavement were too strong to be easily refuted. It would have entailed expensive work by attorneys instructed in South Africa. What could they have proved? Merely that Hepston had registered Taibosh with the civil authorities at Kimberley as his employee under local Masters and Servants legislation (not as his 'batman' with any military authorities as he claimed), and that Hepston had agreed to some vague guarantee of repatriation for Taibosh. As for Hepston's contract with Gumpertz of 18 May 1918, it specified Hepston himself not Taibosh as 'the Artist', contracted to supply 'the services of the Wild Dancing Bushman'. It still begged the question of Hepston's legal relationship with Taibosh.

As for Paddy Hepston after 1920, 'within a year or two he had vanished from the scene'. A further year's extension of his British passport would have expired in March 1921, and there is no record of his applying for a new one. The only record we have is of a Morris Epstein arriving at New York off the White Star liner *Majestic* from Southampton on 21 November 1923. He was a married man like Hepston and aged 47 (though Hepston would not reach that exact age for another two and a half months), but was a United States passport-holder previously resident in Baltimore, Maryland. We cannot entirely eliminate the possibility that this was indeed the same man as Paddy Hepston.

In 1920 Frank Cook was recognized by the British consul-general as Franz Taibosh's *de facto* guardian. US Immigration obliged by extending Franz Taibosh's permission to stay from 1 November 1920 to 1 December 1924. Cook gave Taibosh the option of returning to South Africa. But Taibosh preferred to stay on and live the life of Riley in the circus, rather than return to life as a farm worker (or, more likely, an impoverished urbanite) in South Africa. This settled, from that moment onwards Franz Taibosh and Frank Cook 'spent all the summer months travelling the wide circus beat of America'.[2]

The most notorious incident in American circus history occurred during the hot summer of 1920, in Minnesota, while Ringling-Barnum was still touring New England. With post-war unemployment persisting, racial tensions were by no means confined to the South. The John Robinson circus train arrived at Duluth on Lake Superior on Wednesday, 16 June 1920, at 3.35 pm. As the tents were being set up, a seventeen-year-old white girl claimed that she had been gang-raped by roustabouts—and she picked out no less than seventeen black men at an identity parade. Three of the arrested men were dragged from jail that night by a white mob and lynched on telegraph poles; the other fourteen were only saved from lynching by Minnesota state troopers with machine guns. The circus's response was outrageous: it sacked its remaining black employees, and boasted that it was now an all-white show.

Ironically, on the very morning of the Duluth outrage, President Coolidge made a speech claiming that the US constitution guaranteed a class-free society. Four days later, Chicago policemen shot dead two members of a Garveyite 'Abyssinian' group merely because they were burning a US flag. The *Chicago Tribune* perversely put the blame for the incident not on Marcus Garvey but on W.E.B. DuBois, 'the Karl Marx of the colored race'.

Billboard's 'colored entertainment' columnist, J.A. Jackson, pleaded for circus and carnival managers to protect respectable 'Negro professionals' from white ruffians, and to distinguish these performers from the derelicts and rotten apples found among unskilled roustabouts and nondescript canvas-men pretending to be artists.[3] Being a black performer was generally a problem outside the circus, not inside it. Circus artists took pride in being true cosmopolitans with 'a freemasonry amongst them which is peculiarly their own ... and as a rule keep strictly to themselves'. On the circus sideshow in particular, *Billboard* observed: 'The midget that stands smoking that big, black cigar is married to a blonde girl twice as tall as he is. And yet this heterogeneous conglomeration of human opposites seem to get along sociably and amicably. In fact, in all probability, there is less dissension among side-show people than in any other branch of show business.'[4]

Franz Taibosh was generally protected from racial hostility by only venturing outside the circus in the company of other performers. In the Deep South, his problems were as much cultural as racial, as people who shared his colour did not share his culture. He delighted in telling the story of going to church one Sunday evening in Mississippi. Forced to sit apart from his circus companions, he found himself seated in the black section of the congregation. But wherever he sat, everyone moved away, fearful of the 'wild man' from Africa. Franz thought it extremely funny that, even as he sat in his enforced isolation, the preacher was appealing for the congregation's money to convert their heathen brethren in Africa.[5]

During the 1920 season the Ringling-Barnum circus proceeded from the north-east to the Mid-West, down to Texas, and ended up on a tour of Louisiana, Alabama, Tennessee, Georgia, Florida and South Carolina, closing at Richmond, Virginia, on 27 October.[6]

After the season's end, Franz Taibosh was taken to Columbia University's School of Language in New York, so that his language could be studied. He was introduced to a twenty-three-year-old white South African linguist called Gerard Paul Lestrade, on his way to Harvard University to study Hebrew, Chinese and Arabic. Lestrade amazed his hosts by complete and rapid communication with the Bushman in a strange tongue, and then had to explain that they were conversing in Afrikaans, not in any of the Khoesan languages.

Lestrade concluded that Franz Taibosh was not a Bushman from the Kalahari but a 'Hottentot' or Coloured person from the Cape, because of his fluency in Afrikaans. Unfortunately no copy is known to survive of Lestrade's master's dissertation written at Harvard under Professor Tozer, on the Bushmen and Hottentots of South Africa. He may have used Franz Taibosh as an oral source. Lestrade went on to become the first professor of African languages (as opposed to philology) at the University of Cape Town.[7]

Franz Taibosh presumably played his part among the 'strange people' in the last-ever Ringling-Barnum circus parade through the streets of Manhattan, on 27 April 1921. The two-mile procession of performers, with their animals and horse-drawn wagons, attracted half a million spectators. The parade was led by Fred Bradna as grand marshal: 'feeling like a Pied Piper luring to destruction the children of Hamelin ... down Fifth Avenue and into the old Madison Square Garden, where it was swallowed up, never to be seen again.'[8] Until 1925 the Ringling-Barnum circus continued to open annually at the old Madison Square Garden building on 22nd Street—built in 1889 and 'a spectacular block-long building of yellow brick and terra cotta, topped by a controversial nude statue of the goddess Diana'.

Ringling-Barnum generally confined its annual circuits to the eastern half of the United States, including the Mid-West. But 1922 was one of those years in which it proceeded through Canada to California. At Los Angeles, newly expanded into a great city, the 'celebrities of picturedom turned out in full force to see the greatest show on earth ... Each night found many of them seated in section F, eating peanuts, popcorn and drinking soda pop.' The cowboy star Tom Mix outshone all others in bright white flannels and an enormous hat. Douglas Fairbanks, Mary Pickford and Charlie Chaplin— the royalty of Hollywood—were all in attendance. Harold Lloyd was most intrigued by the antics of trained dogs. But Fred Bradna remarked on Los Angeles being the most difficult circus stand, because the Hollywood movie crowd knew all the tricks of audience manipulation, including how to dampen applause. Stars also expected free passes to the circus and to ride elephants in the 'spec', and sulked when they were turned down.

Charlie Chaplin was appalled to see the way that the massive circus completely dwarfed and devalued the clowns. The great French clown Marceline was reduced to just one of the clowns running around the enormous arena, 'a great artist lost in the vulgar extravagance of a three-ring circus'. Memory of Marceline helped inspire Chaplin's later film *Limelight*. The ageing English clown Fred Stelling explained what hard work it was trying to keep people laughing in the aisles of the big top while other acts were proceeding in the rings and stages below: 'Some days the Pallenberg Bears [roller-skating and bicycle riding] seem to get all the attention and I am ignored and I go off without a hand of applause. That makes me feel a bit blue naturally, and I say to myself as I go to the dressing tent, "Well, what's the use anyway? ... I'm only a clown trying to take some of the gloom out of life."'[9]

Crossing and re-crossing the continent by train, Franz and other circus folk had to endure the vagaries of the North American climate. At Omaha, Nebraska, on Friday, 28 September 1923, gunmen had to shoot holes in the canvas to drain it, as the big top sagged under the enormous weight of rainwater.[10] In 1924—otherwise considered one of the Ringlings' best years for range and quality of performance—it rained for eight days almost continuously in Brooklyn and then in Philadelphia and Washington, DC, where show people sloshed about in galoshes. At New Castle in Pennsylvania, the sideshow tent was almost blown down by a storm when hundreds of spectators were enjoying the antics of Clicko and other 'freaks'. In panic people ran out into the muddy fields beyond. That same day in neighbouring Ohio up to seventy people, mostly children, were killed when buildings collapsed in a cyclone at Lorain near Cleveland. (There was then so much looting that the military had to be called in to restore order.)

Some days later, ushers and property-men had to quell mass panic when heavy wind and a thunderstorm suddenly hit the big top during a matinée at Sioux City in Iowa. 'Jerked and tossed by the wind, tent poles leaped from their mooring and hopped into the air, weaving back and forth with the big spread of canvas.' Merle Evans's military-style band played steadily on against the howl of the wind and the beat of the rain. The performance recommenced when the gymnastic star acrobat Lillian Leitzel, famous for 'her nerve and grit and endurance', was carried into the big top, standing on the shoulders of two men who had trudged from her dressing-tent through ankle-deep mud.[11]

Franz and other Ringling-Barnum 'freaks', supplemented by performers on loan from Gumpertz at Coney Island, were featured in the 'spec' parade at each Madison Square Garden opening. Thus, in March 1921, giant George Auger, wearing a red suit with flower buttonhole, lifted one of the midgets in the air for the first big laugh of the evening, as the 'strange people' marched round the track. The next laugh was for the burlesque midget-rider Count Bagonghi dressed as Madame Spangletti, dashing along the track on his tiny Shetland pony. Outside main arena performance hours, the sideshow operated continuously in the subterranean chamber beneath the arena, where the 'freaks' were also photographed as a group during the annual four-and-a-half-week season in the Garden.

The sideshow featured wild animals as well as people. The big new attraction in 1921 was 'John Daniel', an evil-looking gorilla 'that naturally snorts red flame and vinegar'.[9] Other sideshow artists that year—besides 'Cliquot, an African bushman; Captain George Auger, Cardiff Colossus' and Signor Bagonghi—included 'Mr. and Mrs. Doll, tiniest terpsichoreans; Captain Fred Walters, original blue man; Miss Gibbons and Master Cradock, tattooed folks; Three Brothers "Hoehne," world's fattest trio; Mlle. Gabrielli, original half lady; Mlle. Clifford, sword swallower; Mame Gilmore, queen of serpents; Krao, "Missing Link"; [and] … "Zip", Barnum's original "What Is It?"'

All Freaks But Us, Say Side-Show Freak Folk

Miss Otisa (lower left) here poses with Patsy, her python pet. Clico (lower right), Australian bushman, shaves himself with a safety razor. The Doll family—Mr. Harry and Mrs. Grace—is a mere double handful for George Auger, "Cardiff colossus."

BY RUSS SIMONTON,
N. E. A. Staff Correspondent.
WITH THE GREATEST SHOW ON EARTH, May 00.—"He'll be one of us for a few days," announced Clyde Ingalls, assistant side-show manager of the circus to his freaks gathered at the cook house table for lunch.

the giant who has a special berth on the train and yet has to sleep with his legs "rolled up."
"You do a thing and I'll fix you!" threatened Mrs. Doll with a "dangerous" treble in her wee small voice. "You know what I did to you last time."
The giant subsided.
Otisa explained.

New England, May 1922: Daisy and Harry Doll on the arms of George Auger; Franz (with safety razor) is referred to as 'the last survivor of the Australian bushmen in America'. (Chindahl papers, Circus World Museum, Baraboo)

Clicko's good friend, the Welsh giant George Auger, chaired the Side Show Social Club that met on Sundays and after weekday performances. The club had its own 'dues, rules, and a big party at the end of the season'. Sideshow people, said Carrie Holt, the circus fat lady, were 'just like a big family ... I had a grand time. I was in everything even if I was fat.'

Franz alias 'Cliquot', with higher billing in publicity, further aroused the jealousy of old Zip the Pinhead by swaggering around the nightspots of New York in the company of Frank Cook, attired in formal evening dress and smoking large cigars. In response Zip puffed out his chest and began to march around the Madison Square Garden arena each evening in a tuxedo, chewing a large cigar in imitation of circus boss John Ringling.[12]

Serious rivals to Zip joined Ringling-Barnum in August 1922. Two new Pinheads, albino twins named George and William Muse, about forty years old, joined the sideshow in August 1922. They were promoted as 'two Ecuador white savages' and given the names Iko and Eko, and are remembered strumming their guitars and 'laughing and singing until the train started to roll' on humid summer nights. However, as far as Franz Taibosh was concerned, they were soft-minded simpletons. Franz chose to mix with people of better intellect, notably midgets and giants, with whom he could easily converse and crack jokes.[13]

Franz's opinion echoed those of circus managers about sideshow performers: 'They were often moody and most of them were illiterate ... [and they] succumbed quickly to professional jealousy ... Most of them kept out of the public eye, lest they exhibit their wares free.' Ringlings' threefold criteria for hiring 'freaks' were laid out by sideshow manager Lew Graham: 'the abnormality must be remarkable, if possible unique; it must be exploited by an accompanying talent or dexterity; and it must be inoffensive to public taste.' Ringling-Barnum rarely gave employment to self-made freaks with deliberate disfigurements.[14]

The Ringling-Barnum sideshow was said to be 'the largest, most novel and most interesting' ever by 1924. A new middle section had to be added to the length of the sideshow tent to accommodate the crowds. The sideshow now employed eight staff as ticket-sellers and lecturers. The all-black sideshow banjo and jazz band numbered eighteen, this year under the baton of Thomas May.

The gentle giant George Auger died in December 1922, but Franz made a new friend during 1925 in 'Alice from Dallas', a placid, good-natured woman weighing between 550 and 720 pounds—whose great thrill in life was being flown around in airplanes. Above all, Franz retained close friendship with the German-speaking Doll family of midgets—Harry, Daisy, Grace and Tiny. He addressed the sisters in informal Afrikaans fashion, as he did other young women, as 'my Dolly'. Blonde Daisy Earles was the tallest and most glamorous, described as 'a perfectly formed little darling who looked exactly like a miniature Mae West'. According to Barbara Cook, Franz had a crush on Daisy that went entirely unrequited. There was no question of messing with Miss Daisy: she had a large husband who acted as the family's chauffeur and protector. Such friendships also help to explain how Franz became fluent in German.[15]

Circus performers scattered during the winter—some to charity Masonic or Shrine circuses in the States (such as the 'Moslem Temple Circus' of Detroit), some across the ocean to the two Havana circuses or to Bertram Mills's circus in London, some out west to work in Hollywood movies, and others to winter homes in New York or Bridgeport or Florida.[16]

Frank Cook and Franz Taibosh, by contrast, hobnobbed with the rich and famous before and after repairing to stay with Cook's daughter Frances at Albany, up the Hudson River, over Christmas and New Year. Frances kept house at Albany while Franz and Frank enjoyed themselves downstate in New York City and elsewhere.

Over the winter of 1921–22 Franz and Frank spent time with John and Mable Ringling at Miami in Florida. This was in itself a great privilege, since John and Mable usually never entertained circus people socially. Photographs taken of this Florida holiday show Franz on a Miami golf course, wearing a loud check coat and vest (waistcoat), plus-fours stuffed into woollen stockings, and brogue shoes. Franz was 'still young enough for the bone to be visible beneath the skin', directing an untroubled gaze towards the photographer.[17]

During the summer season that followed, Franz would have seen relatively little of Frank Cook, who usually travelled ahead of the circus stands. It therefore came as something of a shock when widower Frank announced his forthcoming marriage to Lulu, from the famous family of Davenport equestrians. Franz appears to have worried himself sick about the implications of losing Frank Cook's companionship, which would cast him adrift once again. This might explain the item from a *Billboard* correspondent writing within a few days of the circus closing at Greensboro, North Carolina, on 1 November 1922: 'Our old friend, the Bushman, suffered an attack of severe indigestion during the closing hours, but at the present is swiftly recovering.'

Frank Cook married Lulu Davenport on 22 November 1922, at Elgin in Illinois. Franz was packed off to stay the winter with Frances in the Cook family home at Albany. When the Ringling-Barnum circus toured near Albany the next July, Frank Cook was reported 'doing his usual home-town entertaining': 'if there is any person, man, woman or child, who don't [*sic*] know and love Frank Cook in Albany we have failed to discover him.' Frank Cook's insistence on maintaining close ties with Franz Taibosh may help to explain why Lulu's ardour for her husband cooled. The marriage seems to have been over by the summer of 1924, though formal divorce was to take ten more years.[18]

Franz Taibosh's 'temporary' permission to stay in the United States as an alien immigrant was once again, and finally in lieu of deportation, extended by US Immigration from 1 December 1924 to 11 November 1927. No doubt this was due to Frank Cook's efforts, as by this time Frank (without Lulu) and Franz had resumed their winter idyll together and with Frank's daughter Frances at Albany—once again playing the life of the idle rich and using up Franz's summer pay. Franz called Frank 'Papa', but nothing particularly subservient or childlike should be read into this. 'Papa Cook' was his usual nickname in circus circles.

Franz played the butler and licensed jester at Frank's parties, serving drinks and making jokes, though he had to be restrained from taking more than his fill of now illegal liquor. The characteristic that endeared him to Frank Cook's friends was his extraordinary capacity for observation and mimicry of foibles. Self-important lawyers, artists, businessmen, scientists and priests needed to meet Franz but once before he was able to perfectly imitate and puncture 'their pretensions and preoccupations and other crustations of custom and conformity'.[19]

Photographs, seen thirty years later by Laurens van der Post, sum up the high life of Franz Taibosh over the winter of 1924–5. One photograph showed how Franz had absorbed Frank Cook's passions and prejudices. Franz was seen on the morning after the presidential victory of the Republican 'dry Yankee', Calvin Coolidge, in November 1924. He sits sunk into a chair in an expensive dressing gown, pointing at the headline in a newspaper that he cannot read, but with an 'expression of utter resolution and unmistakable happiness'.

The second photograph was taken at a ski resort in Vermont. Franz stands in thick snow, dressed in a warm sweater, woollen bobble-hat and gloves, ski sticks in his hands and long skis on his feet. It was all a charade, as he could not ski at all. But he loved snow: 'The first flake of snow would send him off dancing into the snow with delight ...' Coming from a continent known for its jungles and deserts, few would have believed Franz when he said that snow reminded him of his childhood.

Another photograph taken later in 1925 has Franz suave and fashionably dressed, under a wide-brimmed hat, standing in New York's Pennsylvania railroad station. He carries a briefcase and wears the flapping trousers known as Oxford bags above two-tone black-and-white 'co-respondent' shoes.[20]

Franz's penchant for puffing long cigars was famous. 'He would take a long, deep pull at his cigar, and draw the smoke somewhere deep into himself ... There he could sit, calmly talking away ... until some minutes later one would notice the thinnest and bluest little swirls of smoke appearing at his nostrils.' It is said that Franz inhaled cigars so deeply into his lungs that the smoke emerged minutes later through every orifice in his head, including his ears. (Had his eardrums been perforated at some stage by illness or violence?)

Laurens van der Post suggests that the smoking of tobacco or cannabis was something akin to a religious sacrament for Bushmen, 'partaking of the divine breath' and being reinvigorated by fire. Franz Taibosh could thereby 'rediscover some of the feelings of the first man at his first fire ... being so delivered from the fear of the darkness and the cold which had hitherto enclosed his uncertain life'.[21]

Franz's sexual needs were usually met quietly within the close-knit circle of circus folk during the summer tour. During the off-season, and less frequently in the summer, Franz Taibosh accompanied Frank Cook to plush whorehouses, where Franz (always a comic turn in company) was treated as a pet by the working girls.

In the words of one of the Ringling nephews, life with the circus was 'hardly conducive' for 'a celibate existence'—though there were strict rules about casual contact between the sexes posted by the Ringling management, and an absolute prohibition on unmarried cohabitation. (By contrast, the tradition in 'grift shows' was an initial 'choosing day' when each performer chose a bunkmate for the whole season.) Among touring Ringling managers there was nothing unusual about visiting brothels. John Ringling taught his nephews how to pick up women in a bawdy house, and how to smuggle them into grand hotels.[22]

Franz Taibosh's lack of a wife gave circus press-agents a new publicity angle in August 1925. An Albany, New York, newspaper, the *Knickerbocker Press*, carried the headline: 'Savants off on African hunt for mate for Albany bushman'. The story began with a racially insulting press-agency report on the sailing for Africa of three scientists from Colorado 'to penetrate the Kilahari desert of Bocheanaland [*sic*], inhabited by the African bushmen ... probably the lowest race on earth ... the smallest living race known and whose resemblance to highly developed apes is remarkable'. The newspaper then suggested the scientists might find a wife for 'the only African bushman

Frąnz Tarbosh, the Only African Bushman in America,
Garbed as Savage of the Desert, and in Store Clothes

This little fellow, butler for Frank A. Cook, 65 North Pine avenue, is shown dressed as "an American gentleman," (left), and in native costume. Franz is with Mr. Cook in Minnesota, "on the road" with the Barnum and Bailey's and Ringling Brothers' circus.

Publicity for the 1925 Denver Museum expedition to the Kalahari suggested
that it was going to find a mate for Franz, a winter resident of Albany, NY.
*(*Knickerbocker Press, *August 1925)*

in America, [who] spends five months each year in Albany at 65 North Pine Avenue, the home of Frank A. Cook'.

Knickerbocker Press interviewed Frank's daughter Frances, who kept house for Frank and Franz in Albany—mistakenly referring to her as Mrs Cook. She told the newspaper that Franz was 'fully Americanized, an accomplished dancer, and his favorite sport was shoveling snow'. The *Press* published two photos of Franz, one as a smiling dancer waving his arms in a large cat-skin dress, and the other in smart evening suit and bowtie.

Franz ... is satisfied and proud of his position, Mrs. Cook said last night. He is fond of children, and entertains those in the neighborhood with tales, strange orations in the tongue of Bocheanaland, and by exhibitions of native dancing.

He is an efficient butler, Mrs. Cook said, and to her knowledge he has never dropped a tray ... Franz is extremely devoted to Mr. Cook and his family, with whom he has been for many years.

How did he while away the winter recess in Albany, aside from shoveling snow? He spends much of his time perfecting himself in the latest American dancing steps. He owns an Airedale dog, 'Bobs', and spends much time in training him.

Did he not wish to go back to Africa?

Near the Kilahari [*sic*] desert ... Franz has three brothers. He says, however, he has no desire to visit them. When he is asked by a curious visitor as to his nationality or origin, Franz replies: 'I am an American gentleman.'[23]

14

Sam Gumpertz Takes Over

THE NEW MADISON SQUARE GARDEN building on Eighth Avenue, where the Big One opened during Holy Week in 1926, was described as the Grand Canyon cast in concrete. 'Its concrete levels and iron framed seats, brass rails and steel girders, make the word "fireproof" mean something … Tireless ushers direct the bewildered patrons … thru the subways and concrete caverns.' Circus performers came to hate it as much as the old Garden for its damp underground halls and chambers, and always looked forward to fresh air under canvas after five weeks.

The Big One had now grown from a four-ring to a five-ring circus. For equestrian director Fred Bradna, 'Never was the circus greater, or more fun. Salaries boomed in tempo with the extravagance of the era.' The sensation of the season was beautiful Australian (secretly part-Aboriginal) Winnie Colleano, 'who introduced a turn in which she swung from the bar of a high trapeze and caught herself by the heels, then turned a somersault into the safety net'. The clown teams delighted audiences with thrilling mini-dramas: 'the burning house' with clown firefighters (later seen in the film *Dumbo*) and 'the comic wedding'.[1]

Although there was no end in sight to big-top and small-top extravagance, the year 1926 was marked by three deaths that presaged the end of an era for freak-shows and for the Ringlings: the deaths of Krao Farini, Zip the Pinhead and Charles Ringling. Krao died on 16 April. A hirsute-faced South-east Asian woman, kindly and intelligent, she was much loved among circus folk. Billed as the Missing Link, she had been adopted as a young girl by the impresario Gilarmi Farini. Her personal devotion to Farini was not unlike that of Taibosh to Cook.

Zip the Pinhead died on 30 April. 'Grizzled and gray, feeble of step and plainly exhausted', he had been stripped of his brick-red coat and hurried to

Bellevue Hospital after parading in the 'spec' at Madison Square Garden. His last recorded words, to his sister, were: 'Well, we fooled 'em a long time.' Franz Taibosh was one of the honorary pallbearers at Zip's funeral in Bound Brook, New Jersey.[2]

Charles Ringling died on 3 December 1926. Ringling-Barnum was now under the sole and erratic charge of John Ringling, with 'Mrs Charlie' (Edith Ringling) a strident voice in the wings. But 'Mister John' was too busy extricating himself from the collapse of the Florida real estate boom to pay much attention to the running of circuses, which he anyway regarded as 'a never-ending stream of cash'. He preferred mixing with friends in high places and consuming fine food and drink, sleeping late and confining office work to a few hours in the afternoon. His phlegmatic management style was 'frosty toward even his closest associates'. He neglected to turn up for meetings, and when he did he came unprepared and found fault by picking on small details. Now he 'created confusion and ill will among some of his oldest and most valuable employees' by announcing that contracts for the next year would in future be signed right at the end of the previous year's tour in October, rather than in August as before.[3]

John Ringling also had the idea that circus artists and circus animals in training over the winter would attract tourists to his new city at Sarasota, south of Tampa on the west coast of Florida. He was constructing a waterside palace for himself, and was building up a collection of 'old masters' and a museum to house them—the germ, he and his wife hoped, for an art school and a future university. European aristocrats, finding themselves cash-strapped after the Great War, were happy to sell off their outsize Renaissance religious paintings to Ringling.

John Ringling's biggest catch, induced to settle in the 'Sarasota colony' during the winters, was his newest best friend, Sam Gumpertz, though it was their wives, rather than the men, who were really close. Gumpertz became Sarasota's greatest publicist, and shared with John Ringling similar tastes in expensive vulgarity. A journalist who met John Ringling at this time in Sarasota was less than impressed when Ringling spat on an expensive hotel carpet. 'Mister John' blinked nervously when he spoke, constantly chewed on a cigar stump, and was fat and puffing as he shuffled along, but was always dressed sartorially.[4] Though he probably exaggerated the Ringling riches, Fred Bradna noted in his autobiography: 'By 1928 Mr. John was one of the ten richest men in the United States. His day-to-day control of the circus, never tight, became even more relaxed. All of us on the show, enjoying the highest wages Ringling had ever paid, and the best working conditions, thought as he did that the good life would last forever.'[5]

Publicity postcard of 'Clico Wild Dancing Bushman', 1928.
(Author's possession)

◎

Franz Taibosh's permission to stay in the United States as an immigrant alien, extended from his arrival in April 1918 after previous months of US residence in 1917, finally expired on 11 November 1927. With ten crime-free years of temporary residence to Franz Taibosh's credit, Frank Cook started arrangements for certification of permanent residence.

The 'South African Bushman' reverted to top billing of the Deluxe Side Show at Madison Square Garden on 7 April 1928. Franz was now considered 'a fixture on the show', though his easy familiarity with top managers caused some resentment. He crossed and re-crossed the caste or class lines that divided circus communities. Nobody but John Ringling's closest associates had ever dared call him anything but Mister John, but Franz was allowed to call him simply John. Franz was also accused of bossing around show employees 'as though he was the manager, which he thought he was'. (The suggestion that Franz was mentally deluded is unfair, and seems to be a confusion with laconic old Zip, who *pretended* that he thought that he actually owned the circus.)[6]

In 1928 a new publicity photocard of 'Clico, Wild Dancing South African Bushman' was distributed by the circus. Looking fiftyish in years, he stood to attention in outsize leopard-skins, his feet clad in heavy boots. The copy of this picture in the Ringling Museum of Art is marked on the back: 'this wild African bushman was actually captured from the headhunters by Capt. Hepston'. Other photographs taken around this time show Franz cheerfully posing with the Doll family, and proudly displaying two or three police badges pinned like medals on his sleeveless leopard-skin tunic. It was part of Frank Cook's job to soften up local police forces in advance with free tickets for police families, and no doubt these badges were trophies of that special relationship.[7] Whatever stereotypes of degraded savagery Clicko represented in public, in private Franz Taibosh lived a highly privileged life.

Franz spent more time alone or playing with his pet dog Bobs in the Cook household at Albany over the winter of 1928–9. Frank Cook was off elsewhere courting a woman younger than his daughter Frances—Evelyn Joyce, the daughter of old Jack Joyce the circus equestrian. Evelyn was herself an accomplished dressage rider.

There was a second romance in the Albany household which could hardly be kept from Franz, as the suitor frequently came a-calling. Frances Cook, now twenty-nine years old, was being courted by Patrick K. Sullivan, a clean-living Irish-American electrical engineer. Both Frances Cook and Frank

Ringling–Barnum annual group photograph of freaks in the basement at Madison Square Garden, New York, 1929. Franz Taibosh stands in the middle of the bottom row, between the fat woman and fat man.

Cook were to insist that their future partners, Pat and Evelyn respectively, accept Franz Taibosh as part of the family. But Franz must have had doubts at this time as to his future. Could he now be finally cast off as a discarded pet or plaything?[8]

Ringling-Barnum was caught on the hop by its main rival, the American Circus Corporation (ACC), which secured a pre-emptive booking of Madison Square Garden over Easter 1929. The Big Show had to bear the humiliation of opening its annual season in the barely completed Coliseum building across the Harlem and East rivers in the Bronx. This involved John Ringling in much grief and wrangling, exacerbated by the death of his wife Mable in a New Jersey sanatorium, from terrible burns in June 1929 after a boating accident for which her friends Evie and Sam Gumpertz blamed Ringling. Eventually, in September 1929, Ringling was obliged to go very heavily into debt to buy out the complete American Circus Corporation. He was now king of the heap, owning five more North American circuses (Sells-Floto, Hagenbeck-Wallace, John Robinson, Al G. Barnes and Sparks). But his moment of triumph was followed within six weeks by disaster when the stock market crashed in October 1929, thereby destroying his multi-million investment in railroad stocks.

Then, on 30 December, John Ringling made a worse blunder, by marrying the snooty millionairess Emily Haag Buck, a woman who despised show business and alienated even generous-hearted Evie Gumpertz, who had been restraining her husband's growing secret antipathy towards 'Mister John'.[9]

As soon as the Ringling-ACC deal was announced, on 12 September 1929 Franz Taibosh and some other circus artists were transferred by train from the Ringling-Barnum stand at Los Angeles to join the ranks of the ACC's greatest asset, the Sells-Floto circus.[10] Two nights later, Franz was settling in with new 'strange people' at San Antonio in Texas. The roll-call of the Sells-Floto sideshow described Clicko as both 'bushman' and 'fire-eater'. Fire-eating is relatively easy to learn, as long as the fire-eater has the gumption to close his or her lips around a flaming torch head ... and does not mind an occasionally burnt mouth, or petroleum from the torch upsetting the stomach. But it appears that Franz did not like it much.

The Sells-Floto circus crossed into Louisiana, and then circled around Mississippi, Alabama and Tennessee, to close in Kentucky on 14 October.[11] A photograph taken of Franz with Sells-Floto shows a rather miserable-looking man standing alone in outsize leopard-skins, with a circus wagon and horses in the background. His shadow, projected by wintry sun on to the circus tent, looks like that of an African traveller dressed in buckskins on a cold Karoo morning.

Franz was unhappy. Previously content to live out his life within an American circus cocoon, he may have been having thoughts of returning home to South Africa. The relationship between Frank Cook and Evelyn Joyce had become serious, leading to a form of marriage contract in late 1929—of necessity a common law arrangement, given the continuing resistance of Frank Cook's second wife, Lulu Davenport, to granting him a formal divorce. (Evelyn and Frank's only child, their daughter Barbara, was born two years later, in 1931.) Because of the marriage, Franz was told that he could no longer live with the Cooks over the winter of 1929–30, and that an arrangement would be made instead for his employment over the winter season.

Without recourse to Frank Cook or old friends remaining with the Big One, Franz must have felt very lonely in his new show. The only authority figure that he knew in the Sells-Floto circus was 'Poodles' Hanneford. A great athlete with an air of jovial authority and a popular after-dinner speaker with a refined English accent, Hanneford was now also a film star (*The Circus Kid*, 1928). He was in constant social demand from local dignitaries. These demands on his time no doubt made him less accessible to Franz. Hanneford organized a gala banquet on the last Sunday night of the tour, in Peducah, Kentucky, with cowboy star Tom Mix acting as master of ceremonies. We do not know if Franz was present on this occasion, or other details of his life at this time. All that we do know is that Franz Taibosh suffered a cerebral stroke 'towards the end' of 1929. The South was not warm this winter but cold and wet, and Franz was more than middle-aged. The stroke may have followed a chill after sweaty exertion.

News of Franz's plight reached the Cooks. Frank rushed to Texas and collected Franz, taking him back for Frances to look after him in North Pine Avenue, Albany. Fortunately, the stroke was only partial. Franz was nursed back to health over the winter by Frances, who was by all accounts a remarkably kind and competent woman. Franz almost completely recovered the use of all muscles, except on the left side of his face. His left eye appeared a little 'lazy' after sleep, especially at breakfast, for the rest of his life.[12]

◉

Frank Cook's 1930 Christmas card. (Barbara Cook de Romain)

Frank and Evelyn were staying at a hotel in Sarasota in the last week of October 1929 when the stock markets crashed. Frank was in Sarasota because John Ringling had called his chief men together to formulate next year's plans for both Ringling and former AAC circuses. Pat Valdo (formerly of the Valdo Brothers, clown violinists) was appointed Ringlings' new director of personnel, and was delegated to seek out new circus acts for the big tops. Frank Cook took upon himself the task of travelling around the US and Europe to recruit new and supposedly better 'freaks' and novelty acts for the little tops.

The Ringling management was taking heed of 'freak czar' Sam Gumpertz's maxim that showmen should constantly change their shows and add new features 'to make the box office click'. But by becoming the chief Ringlings scout for new 'freaks', Frank Cook set himself up for a new rivalry with Gumpertz, who was boasting that Coney Island boomed while circus business staggered.

The showbiz newspaper *Billboard* ('Old Billy') reported in December 1929 that Frank Cook had been negotiating deals in Virginia, Washington DC, and points in the Mid-West; and was rumoured to 'sail shortly' for Europe 'on an important business in connection with the Big Show'. At the end of that month, no doubt accompanied by Evelyn, Cook took ship initially for London, where he checked out the 'novelties' of Bertram Mills's winter circus. There was not much to see: the circus clowns were still led by the ancient 'joey' Whimsical Walker; other artists under the big top were already booked for the next summer in America. Of 'freaks' there were none, as they had been regarded in England over the previous three decades as subjects for pity and pathology rather than as objects of popular entertainment. Cook's only significant signing was to arrange for the return of giant Jim Tarver to America.

Frank Cook then went on to Paris and Berlin, where colonial exhibitions and *völkerschauen* were the traditional sources of ethnological novelties and 'freaks' from France's empire overseas and Germany's hinterland in Central and Eastern Europe. Cook spent several days in Paris with his new wife, 'looking over the circus acts in the local houses'. He signed up two distinct 'wonders' from French Equatorial Africa (Ubangi-Chari, the later Central African Republic): plate-lipped women, and pygmies from the Ituri forests, both of whom came with French managers.[13]

Frank Cook's success broke the decade-long truce with Sam Gumpertz over the guardianship of Franz Taibosh. Gumpertz's ambition was maybe bolstered by the evidence of neglect that had led to Taibosh's stroke, and by the belief that John Ringling might now back him instead of Cook. Gumpertz flattered John Ringling's ego by initiating and organizing an annual Sarasota pageant in March 1930, as the publicity curtain-raiser for Ringling-Barnum trains making their way from Sarasota to the opening show in New York.

That same month, Sam Gumpertz revived Paddy Hepston's case of 1919–20 in the Fairfield county superior court at Bridgeport. The Ringling Brothers received copies of the original complaint and its amendments, and their attorney sent his formal reply to the court on 27 March 1930: 'All of the allegations ... are denied.' Gumpertz had successfully restarted the case on behalf of Hepston, but where was the plaintiff himself?

Franz Taibosh was back in the Ringling-Barnum show for 1930, but again did not appear at the opening show held at the Coliseum in the Bronx, on 31 March. His temporary absence could have been on doctor's or lawyer's orders: residual weakness since his partial stroke, or Cook's struggle with Gumpertz over guardianship of Franz. He was subsequently advertised as being on one of the twenty-five platforms of the 'Deluxe Side Show', but as a lesser attraction than Frank Cook's novelties.

The Ubangi women—dubbed 'maids with outboard lips' or 'jazzlip maidens' from the 'darker parts of Darkest Africa' by the publicity department—joined the sideshow after its opening in the Bronx. 'Much to the consternation of those who had brought children, and to the delight of the more sophisticated, in paraded … a single file of thirteen women, all nude to the waist. Whether anyone noticed the odd-shaped lips that night is doubtful.' Evidently they had been told to bare their breasts, but from the next night onwards they wore shawls, and were subsequently covered from knee to neck in buttoned dustcoats, looking like so many office-cleaners, were it not for their distended lips.

The Ubangi were fed on, and therefore smelled of, a diet of raw fish and bananas. The Ubangi patriarch in charge of the women is said to have pocketed all their pay. They were matrons rather than maidens, pining for their children left behind in Africa, sullen, quarrelsome among themselves and uncommunicative with others. They considered baring their mature breasts to be shameful. Hence when they were angry they sometimes stripped off their tops to shame the offender. According to Barbara Cook, Franz Taibosh came to dislike them intensely. Apart from their lips, they were hardly exotic and certainly not erotic. He considered them not show people at all, but smelly outsiders, and took every opportunity to avoid them. Time hung heavily on the hands of the plate-lipped Ubangi women. They feared they would never get back to their children in Africa, and two of them attempted suicide in front of automobiles.[14]

Four Ringling-Barnum trains with both Frank Cook and Franz Taibosh on board arrived at Omaha, Nebraska, early on Sunday, 24 August 1930, to set up two Monday performances on a lot at 30th and Wirt streets. A small graphic advertisement in that day's local newspapers featured an exaggerated sketch of a Ubangi woman's plate-lipped head, with the caption '1000 new foreign marvels. The greatest educational feature of all time. Tribe of genuine monster-mouthed UBANGI SAVAGES. World's most weird living humans. From Africa's darkest depths. New to the civilized world.' Events that Sunday evening were afterwards recalled by Albert Tucker:

'Clicko' sneaked out of the hotel and along with some circus 'candy butchers' [concession vendors] he made a tour of some night spots. Next morning Papa Cook discovered him missing from his hotel room and, before a search was started, word came from the police that they were holding a wild man at the station. Cook rushed down and sure enough there was 'Clicko' with his suit in shreds, his face swollen and nursing a big black eye. The gold watch he had prized was gone and the police had thrown the book at him: fighting, disorderly conduct, drunkenness, and resisting arrest, to mention a few charges; besides, the desk sergeant said that he had kept the police station in a turmoil all night.

Tucker continued with invented dialogue that did not catch Franz's form of English but gave the gist of the tale.

> Papa Cook took one look and said, 'What's the matter, boy, where have you been?' 'Clicko', rubbing his eyes and moving close, threw his arm fondly around Cook's shoulder and sobbed in a low voice. 'Papa, Clicko's been a bad boy; he went to see nice mama and had too much hot water' (his term for liquor).
> 'Where's your watch?'
> 'I gave it to my nice mama and she give me plenty hot water and a big kiss.' Now he was chuckling.
> Papa Cook, his eyes narrowing to a hard glint, his mouth set tight, turned to the police: 'I guess a couple of years in jail is what he needs.'
> 'No, no papa! Clicko no want jail, no more drink hot water. I always be good boy,' he sobbed as Cook winked to the police. By this time the cops were smiling. Papa Cook whipped out a book of passes for the show, asked each officer how many he needed for his family. Then he and 'Clicko' shook hands all around, walked out to the street, and were whisked away in a taxi to the show grounds.

The 1930 season ended with three successive stands in Alabama, at Tuscaloosa, Birmingham and finally at Montgomery on 10 October.[15] 'In the South, he was really a problem', Albert Tucker recalled of Franz Taibosh:

> I recall one time in Tuscaloosa, 'Clicko' came out to the Side Show bally platform, yelling as he danced up the steps. The band jazzed the 'Twelfth Street rag'. It was circus day in Dixie, cotton pickin' time; the folks had money in their pockets and were in spending mood.
> That night the crowds were pouring onto the circus lot. The big show doors hadn't opened yet, so the side show was doing the entertaining; the barker was about to make an opening and turn the crowds into the side show.

The colour of the girls involved in the following story was not specified. If they were white, the sight of a black man chasing them in 1930s Alabama would indeed have been 'really a problem' for him and the circus.

> 'Clicko' pulled on his kinky hair and let it snap back, at the same time smirking and ogling the girls, standing in front of his platform. They howled with laughter and he made a move as if he were coming down off the bally stand. This must have frightened the girls and they ran screaming, probably thinking he really was a wild man. The band kept right on playing, but a gleam came in 'Clicko's' eyes.

He threw himself off the platform and down the dirt road, giving out with his familiar yells; he chased the girls, and was soon lost in the darkness.

We found him about an hour later, in front of a country store, surrounded by a group of wide-eyed natives, asking them for 'hot water'.

Clicko, according to Tucker, 'really loved the girls'—presumably regardless of colour, though his preference was for a mature black woman. As Tucker put it, 'when he was asked what kind of a girl he wanted for a wife, he would always shout, "A big fat mama."'[16]

Franz loved performing, and probably also feared that he was crowding the newly married Cooks out during winter. Hence he was signed up for two months in a New York City dime museum, and was meant to leave for eight weeks in Europe on Thursday, 4 December 1930, until the latter engagement was cancelled for Franz to appear in court at Bridgeport, Connecticut. No doubt he would otherwise have spent Christmas and New Year with the Bertram Mills circus in London or on tour on the European Continent.

Franz arrived in Bridgeport from New York City on the morning of Monday, 1 December, and waited in the rooms of the Ringlings' attorney, Alexander L. Delaney. He was now ready to step into the witness box before Judge Frederick M. Peasly. The *Bridgeport Post* misleadingly referred to Franz as the Wild Man of Borneo—'one of Barnum's most famous freaks of a quarter of a century ago'—now billed as an African Bushman by a New York museum, where he 'had ceased taking his turnips and cabbage raw'. A longer story the next day added:

> He entertained a group in the attorney's office by singing and dancing and smoking cigars. He is reported to be 104 years of age and the Smithsonian Institute of Washington upholds his claim. The skin of his face is drawn over the bones like parchment, his teeth are worn down almost to the gums, and he wears what might pass for a beard in an African forest ... he performed a tap dance in the law office that would have made a mother proud of her 10-year-old son. Then he inhaled great puffs of cigar smoke and laughed at the sensation he produced. He 'sang' in English and he uttered a series of clicking sounds that he said were words in his native tongue ...
>
> He has been exhibited as the 'Wild Man of Borneo', the 'African Bushman', the 'World Renowned Pygmy', and the 'African Pigman'.

Gumpertz had begun legal proceedings on behalf of 'Morris Hepston' without locating his whereabouts. The court proceedings began that afternoon with Delaney moving that the case be struck from the docket because Hepston was dead. Hepston's attorney, Henry C. Burroughs, denied his client was dead but could give no proof to the contrary. Delaney asked the court to declare Hepston legally dead. He convinced the court that Morris Hepston had returned to the British Isles during the 1920s, and had been deceased for three years. Hence, on the afternoon of 2 December 1930, the plaintiff's attorney withdrew the 'said cause of action'.[17]

In fact, there is no record of Hepston's death to be found in the official registries for either Ireland or England in the 1920s and 1930s. (The Morris Epstein who died of heart disease in the London Hospital at Whitechapel on 14 December 1925, aged fifty—two years younger than Paddy Hepston—was a master tailor who left a widow called Ethel in Grosvenor Road, Richmond, Surrey.)

The *Bridgeport Post* of Tuesday, 2 December 1930 carried a front-page photograph of Franz Taibosh under the heading 'Wild Man and two friends': 'The little "Wild Man from Borneo," christened Franz Taaibosh by his German friends [*sic*], is shown above flanked by Attorney L. Delaney and William Conway of the Ringling Brothers, Barnum and Bailey Circus. Said to be 104 years old, the now civilized "wild man" came to the city to testify in a lawsuit over him between the circus and his former manager.' Wednesday's *Bridgeport Post* reported that 'disappointment was registered by many in the County court house building when it became known that [Franz] would not take the stand'.[18]

The circus world was shocked when feisty Lillian Leitzel died in Denmark in early March 1931, after a fall when a metal ring broke during a performance. The news would still have been fresh when Ringling-Barnum opened its 1931 season at Madison Square Garden on 4 April.

It was the first time in three years that John Ringling had managed to book the Garden for the grand opening. But his triumph was muted by the fact that the date was in doubt because of the priority booking given to a possible ice-hockey play-off match. There was no time for a dress rehearsal; the high rigging for acrobats in the big top got tangled during the opening 'spec' displays, distracting the audience from the parade of freaks. Once again *Billboard* declined to give its front page to the opening of the Ringling-Barnum circus season, despite the fact that it had a lion and tiger act for the first time since 1926. Ringling-Barnum went under canvas during the third week of May in Brooklyn, on a lot between Flatbush and Nostrand avenues. Thereafter the circuit concentrated on choice cities where big audiences could be expected, and was extended once again to California, thus gambling for receipts from larger audiences against increased costs of travel.[19]

At the end of the 1931 season, Franz Taibosh was happy to spend the winter once again with Frances Cook at Albany. Frances was still dating Pat Sullivan, who came into town from Glens Falls, on the Hudson River above Albany, where he worked for the power company. Little is known about Frank Cook's son, Edward Cook, who also lived in Albany, where he remained for the rest of his life.[20]

Evie Gumpertz died in July 1931, and her death removed any semblance of affection between Sam Gumpertz and John Ringling. Wily old Sam fuelled the discontent of the Ringling brothers' widows (as inheritors of their husbands' holdings) with John Ringling's autocratic management and circus losses made in 1930. John Ringling found control of his empire slipping into the hands of the widows whom he despised. The crunch came in 1932 when he defaulted on the one million dollars still owed to the former proprietors of the American Circus Corporation.

Gumpertz saw his chance and made his move. The immediate debt was covered by Gumpertz's business associates, on condition that John Ringling pledge all his personal assets to them until he paid off his debts. Sam Gumpertz and the Ringling widows turned Ringling Brothers into a limited stock company, with Gumpertz as senior vice-president and general manager. 'Mister John' remained nominal president for a mere $6,000 a year salary, but had no authority within the circuses.

'In truth,' remarks circus historian W.C. Weeks, 'Ringling and Gumpertz were now enemies, except in public. Ringling regarded his long-trusted friend as a conspirator.' John Ringling began a lonely slide towards bankruptcy, hounded by Emily Buck's divorce lawyers and by the new Internal Revenue Service for millions in back taxes.[21]

Photographs of Sam Gumpertz at this time show a trim and benign-looking middle-aged man with glasses and a smile on his face. He certainly excited genuine affection among some of his employees. 'Sam Gumpertz was a wonderful human being and I am glad that I was privileged to know him,' reads one testimonial. But he was also a ruthless manipulator, determined to bring everyone and everything under his control.[22] Gumpertz made a point of befriending midget show-people. He had already tried twice to obtain guardianship over Franz Taibosh—and would try to do so again. Was it control mania or some genuine compassion for Franz that drove him? He seems to have always got on well with Franz Taibosh as an individual, but Franz had the knack of exciting genuine affection in everyone who knew him well.

As for Franz, his immigration status in the United States was at last assured on 7 June 1932, when a Certificate of Registry (i.e. a permanent work permit) was issued in his name by the US Department of Labor and the Immigration Service.[23]

In the latter part of 1931, Frank Cook and Evelyn Joyce withdrew to live in Canada, where Evelyn gave birth to their daughter, Barbara. Evelyn Joyce then rejoined the Ringling-Barnum circus for the 1932 season, as a rider and bareback dancer in the Tommy Atkins equestrian act. Like other circus folk, the Cooks would have left their baby meanwhile with relatives or on a 'baby farm'.

The 8 April opening of the 1932 Ringling-Barnum season at Madison Square Garden was back on the front page of *Billboard*, which remarked on the disc-lipped Ubangi who jogged round the hippodrome track in blue sweaters. The original Ubangi women imported from France in 1930, after Frank Cook's negotiations, had been 'turned over' with five new women and three accompanying men. Unlike their predecessors, they could speak an international language, French, and thus got on better with other circus folk.

The sideshow performers were photographed by flashlight once again in the Madison Square Garden basement, standing around their main platform. Jolly Ollie the fat woman was seated in the middle, flanked on either side by one Doll (Earles) sister, two Ubangi women smartly dressed in sweaters and waist-cloths, and Eko or Iko. Sky High (Jack Earl) stretched his arms over diminutive Major Mite and Habib the Egyptian fire-eater on one side, and over Harry Earles and Clicko on the other. Clicko, wearing socks under his sandals and a leopard-skin tunic down to his knees, stood with legs apart to reduce his height.[24]

After the failure of Franz as a fire-eater, Frank Cook had supplied the Sells-Floto circus with a 'fire-eating pygmy' for the 1932 season. He inherited the name Bamboola from the 'original' Wild Man from Borneo, who had first appeared at Coney Island in 1911. The 1932 Bamboola was really Bobo, husband of Kiki. The showman Harry Lewiston later recalled how shamelessly he 'talked up' this Ituri pygmy couple to the crowds with entirely spurious facts: 'These tiny people live among monkeys, apes, chimpanzees, and other creatures of the simian world. To make themselves more at home in this kind of jungle environment, the less intelligent, the less thinking power they have, the better off they feel themselves to be! Let me put it this way: you don't have to be stupid to be an Iturian pygmy, but it helps!'

Lewiston would then jab his bandaged finger towards Kiki, who on cue flashed her triangular filed teeth and let out a weird laugh.[25] Kiki, like Franz, was thus complicit in the showbiz libels propagated about African peoples. Franz loved to parade up and down, shuffling and shouting in his Wild Man act, next to the outside lecturer or 'talker' inducing patrons to enter the sideshow tent. Circus folk noted 'his positive adjustment to circus life and his overall happiness ... In his own way he was part of the amusement world—a showman of sorts.' In truth Franz Taibosh did not consider himself a 'freak' at all, as he was not mentally or physically defective.[26]

High Life with Frank and Evelyn

EVELYN COOK got to know Franz Taibosh better during the summer of 1932 when they were touring in the same circus, and began to accept the idea of the old man as part of the marital ménage. Hence Franz spent the first part of the winter in New York City hotels with Frank and Evelyn, living a life of glamour and luxury. The big event at year-end was the opening of the six-thousand-seat Radio City Music Hall at the Rockefeller Center, featuring vaudeville and circus artists and long lines of high-kicking Roxyette (later renamed Rockette) show-girls. One can imagine the sensation created as a distinguished-looking older gentleman with grey hair, a pretty young woman with furs draped over a low-cut dress, and an old but athletic little African in a glittering white tuxedo swept down the aisle to their seats, greeting friends and smiling and nodding to acquaintances.[1]

For the second half of the 1932–3 winter, Franz stayed with Cook's newly married daughter Frances and her husband Pat Sullivan, at snowy Glens Falls on the upper Hudson. The Sullivans, a devout and welcoming Catholic couple, provided the real home for Franz Taibosh for the rest of his life. They also took on much of the responsibility for bringing up Frank and Evelyn's daughter, Barbara. In later years, Barbara Cook said that her half-sister had been a better mother to her than Evelyn.

Sam Gumpertz as general manager did his best to restore Ringling-Barnum to prosperity, keeping a sharp eye on everyday operations. John Ringling was 'conspicuously absent' at the opening in Madison Square Garden on 8 April 1933, which *Billboard* relegated to page five. Gumpertz played to a matinée audience of ten thousand, with the Durbar of Delhi as his 'spec', described lavishly as 'full of vigor, illumination, sparkling women, a cavalcade of mounted animals and drawn floats' preceding a 'golden painted pachyderm, [with] a gilt-covered girl at top'. Otherwise the first eight displays were identical with those of 1932. The show dragged on for three hours and twenty minutes, and could definitely have been speeded up. Clicko was last on the list of the sideshow, which now boasted the Ituri pygmies in place of the Ubangi women.

Ringling-Barnum's business over 1933—including its fiftieth jubilee celebrations at Baraboo in Wisconsin and a venture into eastern Canada—was described as merely 'okeh' (okay) in the trade press. In truth it was disastrous, as the circus lost so many stands to rain, as well as being rusticated from its customary pitch at Soldier's Field, Chicago, during the 1933–4 'Century of Progress' World's Fair. The year also saw a boom in adult rather than family entertainment with the end of liquor prohibition; beer drinking was re-legalized in New York in May 1933.[2]

Clicko was temporarily released to exhibit himself at the Chicago World's Fair. The fair had Oriental, Mexican, Navajo, Irish, Moroccan and (Florida) Negro model villages, a midget town, a Ripley's 'Believe It or Not' Odditorium, and beauty shows ballyhooing for the Miss America pageant. A magnificent Italian pavilion celebrated eleven years of Fascist rule under Benito Mussolini. After a month, the fair drew in up to a hundred thousand visitors daily. A Plantation Show of 'brown-skin girls' added spice to the Streets of Paris exhibition, where fan-dancer Sally Rand appeared as a naked Lady Godiva 'complete with a white horse and strategically placed long-haired wig'. Dick Hood's Folies-Bergère had nude female silhouettes grinding their way through a new dance every ten minutes. Mayor Kelly of Chicago toured the girl shows, objected to a few, and opined: 'It's alright to give the visitors a thrill, but I don't intend to have them walloped.'

The Darkest Africa 'educational' show opened in the heart of the midway on 4 July, 'with an immense gaudy carnival side-show front that makes it a great flash', boasting 'firewalkers, pygmies, and various savage tribes'. Beer and sandwiches were available at Darkest Africa's coconut bar, which boasted the best bartenders of the fair.[3] Harry Lewiston, the director of the Darkest Africa show, recalled that the canvas banners outside the show depicted 'life in Africa in its most primitive form—of course, highly exaggerated'. The main attraction of the show for men was the chance to see so many women naked from the waist up.

The show opened with a small number of Gold Coast (Ghanaian) men from the docks, whose drumming was so persistent and whose dancing was so poor—'little more than hopping around'—that they were soon let go. The show was re-staffed with seventy African Americans of all shapes and sizes and colours, led by a proud 'Zulu' king: his warriors and maidens resplendent in feather headdresses and tooth necklaces, with bits of ivory in their noses, jabbering at each other in loud gibberish. The king's witchdoctor sidekick was a gay black man chanting mumbo-jumbo spells and muttering curses. Lewiston lectured the crowds in the persona of Major Lewiston, 'the famous authority on Africa', dressed in long boots and riding breeches, and a pith helmet, in the style of Frank Buck. 'As for the stories that went with all this, and the other rigmarole, such as the burning hoop jumping, [those] came almost entirely out of my head. It's true that I bought some books on Africa before the show opened, but a perusal of them soon indicated that they would be of little help … And who could question what I had to say? Wasn't I the great "Major Lewiston"?'

Lewiston's employees had to endure fire-walking or, rather, fire-running along a long bed of hot coals. There was a high turnover of men with badly burnt feet, but new labour was easy to come by in Chicago at a time of economic depression. Employees were kept in camp during their engagement, so they wouldn't blab their true origins in local bars. When the weather turned cool, they sat half-naked and shivering in front of open fires, and 'It was a relief when we finally closed up shop, and left the education of the American people to the schools.'[4]

Franz Taibosh exhibited himself in 'one of the huge display halls' at the World's Fair, where he was seen by a visiting South African, Ernest Malherbe, on Sunday, 8 October or Monday, 9 October 1933. He found the 'diminutive' Bushman sitting alone on a pedestal and looking rather bored. 'I approached him and asked him in Afrikaans, "My boy, what are you doing here?"' Franz enthusiastically embraced Malherbe, calling him 'baas', i.e. boss or master, the respectful form of address for a white man: 'Baas, ag baas, jy praat my taal! [you speak my language].' Malherbe then repeated, 'What on earth are you doing here?'

> He said, 'Ag, Baas, I just sit.'
> 'Is that all you do?' I asked him.
> 'No, Baas. I think.'
> 'And what do you think about?'
> 'Oh Baas, just of food and women ("kos en meide").'

Malherbe used this story a few years later to justify the provision of educational services to bored South African soldiers in North Africa, who otherwise had nothing better to think of than grub and girls.[5]

Franz Taibosh must have seen the bronze sculpture of a 'family group of South African Kalahari bushmen' at the Hall of Man in the nearby Field Museum. A man stood with bow at the ready, a woman seated next to him with a baby on her back, three ostrich-eggshell water containers beside them. Malvina Hoffman's sculptures of 'primitive races of the earth … from living models' were unveiled in the Chauncey Keep memorial hall of the Field Museum on Tuesday, 6 June 1933. A student of Auguste Rodin, Hoffman had previously sculpted the figures that adorn the façade of Bush House in London, opened by New York property developer Irving T. Bush in 1925. The models for the Bushman woman and child were photographs of pretty young women at a pond taken by the Vernay–Lang Kalahari expedition in 1929.

Hoffman had rejected using Franz Taibosh for a model in the family group. The Field Museum made a series of photographs of Franz in 1931, but she preferred a younger and slimmer figure for the man in her group, in stereotypical stance with bow and arrow. Hoffman's sculptures were said to embody 'the wedding of art and anthropology', as they strove 'to represent the most beautiful representatives of a race in the manner of an artist, rather than the ugliest in the manner of an anthropologist'.[6]

Once again Franz spent some weeks before Christmas with Frank and Evelyn Cook, and their small daughter Barbara, then rising three years old, before going on to stay out the winter with the Sullivans at Glens Falls. The Cooks had rented a luxurious penthouse apartment at the top of the Forest Hotel, near Madison Square Garden, for the winter half of the year, leaving it to the writer Damon Runyon in the summer, where 'he wrote his Broadway columns and stories and which provided background for *Guys and Dolls*'. Evelyn later remembered 'huge closets, a large double bed that didn't shake, [and] a bathroom with endless hot water and other luxuries we lacked in our [rail-car] stateroom traveling with the Big Show'. She added: 'The lobby of the Forest Hotel was filled with colorful fauna [*sic*], so walking through the lobby with a three-year-old child and an African Bushman in tow presented no spectacle.'[7]

Continuing depression depleted audience pockets, and Ringling-Barnum had a pathetic opening at Madison Square Garden on Friday, 30 March 1934, alienating Christians with a matinée during the Good Friday watch

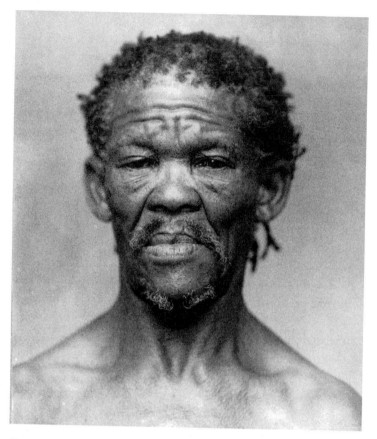

Franz Taibosh photographed by the Field Museum at Chicago in 1931.
(Anthro Coll., album 404 neg. 67644, Field Museum of Natural History, Chicago)

service, alienating Jews with an evening performance after the beginning of Passover, and attracting tiny audiences of 'the unregenerate'. But at least *Billboard* now restored news of the event to its front page, though it was critical of the 'minimum of new stuff' in the main show and longed for new ideas in the sideshow.

There was more than a hint of desperation in the fact that the Ringling-Barnum publicity department resorted to the oldest chestnut in circus press-release lore. On 12 April the *New York Evening Post* carried the story 'Circus odd folk threaten mutiny. They won't be called freaks, that's the long and short of it'. Meanwhile, *New Yorker* magazine carried a multi-part series by Alva Johnston entitled 'Side-show people'.[8]

Evelyn Joyce Cook many years later recalled the social whirl during the

Bronze bust of Franz Taibosh by Malvina Hoffman, c.1932.
(Field Museum of Natural History, Chicago)

inaugural weeks of the circus in 1934, when circus people were invited to after-show parties as trophy guests by patronizing New York plutocrats. Frank handed her four hundred dollars one morning at breakfast to buy herself 'a knock-out of an evening dress today ... How about black chiffon? You look great in black with your red hair. And get a dress with no back and one of those floating skirts.' They were invited that night to the Gay Nineties Club by the heiress Louise Launsdale, reputedly worth forty million.

'Oh no! Is she the blonde who sits in the front row of John Ringling's box, with her feet on the rail, smoking cigars?'
    'That's the one. Pretty blonde, too.'

After that night's circus performance, Evelyn and her husband piled into a taxi with Franz in tow, plus the clown Felix Adler, some dwarf clowns, and Felix's pet pig which managed to rip Evelyn's dress. 'Now Franz, remember!' she admonished him, 'you are to drink *only* beer, no hard liquor. Understand?' Franz replied, 'Ach forschstand Maw' (Ek verstaan, ma), glaring at her with sparkling black eyes.

'You know it's useless,' Frank interjected. 'He'll drink anything offered to him.' As Evelyn observed in her draft memoirs: 'When sober, the Bushman had beautiful manners, but hard liquor caused his civilized exterior to crack and fall away like an old shell and an unpredictable individual emerged.'

At the entrance to the club, they were greeted by Louise Launsdale, dressed in a pink-and-white suit with a plunging neckline and a turban on her head. 'She walked unsteadily towards the Bushman, wrapped her jeweled arms about him, kissed him and pressed his head close ... She hugged Franz affectionately and he, nothing loath, stood leaning quietly against her soft cushioned bosom.' Suddenly releasing Franz, such that he nearly lost his balance, she rushed over to Felix, who stood there in full 'joey' makeup, and kissed him and his pig on the snout.

Inside the club the circus people, wont to tuck into hearty meals after performances, were given plenty to drink but virtually no food. Franz entertained the guests with his satiric imitations of important people, and with samples of 'his clicking, explosive tongue', but then disappeared from view until the early hours of the morning, when he burst into the almost empty downstairs bar of the club, weaving unsteadily and howling so uncannily, after taking a deep breath, that the bottles on the bar rattled. (Evelyn characterized his howl as an extended yoo-hoo.) Besides the barman, there was only a louche young man chatting up Evelyn in her daring barebacked dress. Ever the guardian of his guardian's interests, Franz deduced the worst and raged at Evelyn.

'What de hell de matter, Maw. Ye got nudding on! Dat no is nize. Ach no lack dat!' Then he shouted 'Ye go home, Mama Cook!' That 'Mama Cook' let me know that he had remembered his manners and I enjoyed the first laugh of the evening.

'Franz, come here. I want to introduce you.' I turned to where my companion had been seated. He had disappeared. I never saw him again. I looked at the barman and read his thoughts. 'And *he* is not my husband!'[9]

Frank Cook and his previous wife, Lulu, were finally divorced by decree on 8 February 1934. He then formally married Evelyn Joyce in Chelsea Presbyterian Church in New York on 27 May 1934, in time to gratify her dying father, Jack Joyce, the famous horse-trainer. The wedding was not revealed to the press until after old Jack died, a month later. *Billboard* reported: 'The couple spent a few days in New York this week and will rejoin the show shortly. Mrs. Cook intends to retire from circus business and establish a home in midtown New York. She will accompany her husband on his quest in Africa for freak attractions, a tentatively planned trip which was supposed to have been made last fall.'[10]

On 13 June 1934, the entire personnel of Ringling-Barnum, more than a thousand people, were photographed in bright sunlight in front of their tops at New Haven, Connecticut. Up to twenty clowns sat on the grass in front of the seated management: Gumpertz in bowtie in the middle, Bradna in top hat to his left. Franz Taibosh sat in the fourth row, between a clown (maybe 'Spader' Johnson) and 'Princess Oskoman, Indian guide and seer'. Behind them there were at least ten rows of people. Serried ranks of uniformed personnel and cooks stood behind them. Right at the back was a mass of roustabouts, many of them black men, some of them seated on the wooden circus wagons.

Ringling-Barnum was reported 'clicking' in the Mid-West in 1934, stressing its suitability for children. But, once again, there was no run at Chicago, where the World's Fair had entered its second year.[11] On 19 August, the Ringling-Barnum circus made one of its longest 'jumps' ever on the railroad, from Wichita in Kansas to Denver in Colorado, a total of 565 miles. Los Angeles was the highlight of this trip, with a circus lot on Wilshire and Fairfax avenues 'within 10 minutes of everything'. The show was a sell-out with 'straw houses' (people sitting on straw bales) from its first matinée till its fifth evening performance. 'The movie folk attending comprised the who-is-who in the flicker colony ... Norma Shearer, Wallace Beery, Douglas Fairbanks, Ginger Rogers, Gary Cooper', and others including Charlie Chan—but not Charlie Chaplin. The circus was admired by Hollywood for its 'clockwork efficiency' and it was reported that the sideshow had had a big five days, 'running every night until after midnight'.[12]

Franz Taibosh made a new friend in the sideshow's new assistant manager, Harry Lewiston. They shared the privilege of a lower sleeping-berth in the open compartment of the sideshow rail-car. (Clyde Ingalls as manager had his own compartment or 'stateroom' at one end of the car.) Described on the cover of his posthumous autobiography as an 'incredible scoundrel', Lewiston had previously worked in 'grift shows' where he learnt to shortchange customers with folded bills and palmed coins, while distracting them with a flood of talk. On joining Ringling-Barnum, he was struck by the huge size of the sideshow with a bally platform and ticket-stands in front of sixteen lurid 20 ft-high canvas banners of the show's main attractions, and a 320-ft-long sideshow tent. 'The huge side show tent held, I suppose, two or three thousand people. Two inside lecturers kept the show going from morning till night, so the audience, which always stood since there were no seats, was changing constantly as people came and went.'

The most impressive 'inside lecturer' was Peter Staunton with a huge black moustache, said to be a Yale graduate, who spiced his talk with quotes from Shakespeare, from the fashionable contemporary poet T.S. Eliot, and from the old showman P.T. Barnum. Like Clyde Ingalls, who walked around the lot sipping from a white coffee cup filled with Old Quaker whiskey, Staunton was a talented alcoholic who would have found it difficult to hold down a conventional job. Lewiston assisted Ingalls in talking up the coming attractions on the outside bally platform, flanked by five wooden ticket-stands (manned by Ingalls, Lewiston, King, Staunton and McCauley) selling 25-cent entrance tickets. 'Every few minutes, I was up on the platform barking for all I was worth, then reaping the results by hopping down into my booth and selling a string of tickets ...'

Lewiston was out to impress his boss, but Clyde Ingalls proved a hard taskmaster. On the 4 July holiday at Fitchburg, Massachusetts, Ingalls tore a strip off Lewiston in public for introducing Clicko as a 'pyg-a-my'. 'You son of a bitch, are you the one I appointed as my chief assistant? Where in hell did you ever go to school?' When Lewiston pronounced Italian as 'Aye-talian', Ingalls loudly corrected him on the bally stand. Ingalls was particularly jealous when Lewiston's cash take exceeded his own. Both were past masters at the carnival ticket-seller's trick of putting a customer's change to one side on the very high ticket-box, hoping the customer would not see it and neglect to collect it. (The rule was to hand it over quickly if there was any protest.) Ingalls allowed Lewiston to shortchange customers in return for half his extra take, though shortchanging customers had become more difficult since 1929 when new smaller coins made people check their change more carefully.

Professor Arthur A. Wright's Side Show Band, seventeen talented African American musicians under his baton, mostly playing banjos, started outside the ballyhoo with a ten-minute minstrel piece. The band then followed the crowd inside the tent, playing music on cue for artists in the performance booths. Franz himself often paraded on the outside bally stage, helping to sell tickets in front of the banner line, as a 'teaser' for his mini-show before repairing to his own booth inside.

Lewiston had his doubts that Franz Taibosh was really aged 104. He thought Franz 'looked nothing like an American Negro' but appears to have swallowed the line that Franz was the 'only genuine African Pygmy brought to this country'. He exaggerated Franz's shortness and fatness, and was not impressed by his Afrikaans-accented English:

> He could speak only rudimentary broken English, and his development was such that he could not be allowed out alone or he might have wandered off. He was 'owned' by Frank Cook ... [He] was three-and-a-half feet tall, was almost as round as he was tall, and loved to smoke big, black cigars. Always cheerful and seemingly happy, he was the pet of many of the circus executives, who were always bringing him his favorite smokes, or a bottle of beer, his favorite refreshment.[13]

In November 1934 Gumpertz announced that the gross take of his three big Ringling shows (Ringling-Barnum across the country, Hagenbeck-Wallace in the Mid-West and South, and Al G. Barnes in the West) was thirty per cent up on 1933. Georgia's *Augusta Chronicle* floated the idea of 'The circus as an index to progress': 'President Roosevelt and his recovery must be getting somewhere. The circus is feeling it and it is our private opinion that virtually every line of business in the country is feeling it, only some of them are so used to complaining of an ache in the midsection that they can't quite get around to admitting they are better off.'[14] The return of Ringling-Barnum to profitability would have helped the Cooks to relax and live the high life again that winter. Franz Taibosh once again divided his time between them in New York, and Frances and Pat at Glens Falls.

The circus year of 1935 began with Gumpertz's announcement that Frank Cook would be the manager of Ringling Brothers' Hagenbeck-Wallace circus, expanded from what had been basically an animal show. Gumpertz 'was emphatic ... that Cook's appointment to the Ringling No. 2 show management was in recognition of his long service ... and as a reward for his loyalty'. This was a coded message to people aware of the struggle going on between Gumpertz and John Ringling, as Cook was known to be a buddy of the latter. A further press release added: 'Show officials said here today that in Cook Mr. Gumpertz had a man who knows the circus business and who had gained the respect and confidence of officials, performers and workmen alike and who knows them all.'

The Cook family, with small daughter Barbara in tow, repaired to the town of Peru (pronounced Pee-ru), Indiana, the winter base of Hagenbeck-Wallace. The family guests in Indiana no doubt included Franz Taibosh for a time. Evelyn Cook joined her brother Jack Joyce, Jr., in the equestrian team, working ménage and high-school horses. By March 1935 the horses were ready to be shown off to the newsreel cameras of Fox Movietone and Universal News Service.[15] Hagenbeck-Wallace's big feature was the lion-tamer Maria Rasputin, reputed daughter of the Mad Monk himself, discovered by Frank Cook working for a small circus in France. Frank Cook met her off the German liner *Bremen* in New York, and took her on to Indiana.

Franz Taibosh reported for duty as usual for the Ringling-Barnum opening at Madison Square Garden in April 1935. Governor Harold G. Hoffman of New York presided. Mrs Charles Ringling sat in one box. Frank Cook sat in another with his wife Evelyn Joyce Cook 'and her two children'—obviously including Barbara, but who was the other child? The Doll family led the Parade of the Freaks, and 'Clicko, African Bushman' could be spotted among 'the armless girl, the contorting boy, the robed Hindu fakir [with a good Muslim name, Mohamed Khan], the team of fat ladies, Susie the elephant skin girl, the snake charmer, the tattooed lady ... and the bearded madame'.

After the show, guests and performers, no doubt including Franz together with the Cooks, partied with a circus fans' club under a big top in New York's Gotham Hotel. Within a few days the Hagenbeck-Wallace was to take its first forty-car train out of Indiana for its inaugural in Chicago. Franz would probably not see the Cooks again for some months.[16]

Frank Cook had to be recalled by Gumpertz from the Hagenbeck show, even before the month of April 1935 was out, to act once more as legal adjuster for Ringling-Barnum. Cook's successor as legal adjuster at Ringling-Barnum had evidently been an instant failure in arranging and negotiating the circus's itinerary and engagements. Gumpertz was prepared to sacrifice the No. 2 show's interests to ensure a successful season for the No. 1 show. Anyway, the sudden move must have gratified Franz Taibosh. Though Franz worked, changed and slept in separate quarters from the big bosses of the circus, he was now once again able to spend some time with the Cooks during the circus season's progress across the States.

This could well have been the time when, as Evelyn Cook recalled many years later, Franz came to Frank and asked him for four dollars—'$2 for beer, and $2 for the local whorehouse, where apparently the girls thought he was "cute".' Austin King, a new inside sideshow lecturer in 1935, found Clicko a bit of a headache: 'He would ramble off the lot and head for the nearest pub whenever he wasn't watched. Then a big-top jig would be dispatched to retrieve him. King said that after one of these bouts Clicko was lifted back on his platform and as Austin extended his arm to introduce [the] inebriated pygmy, Clicko fell off the back of the platform.'[17]

Franz would also have had other things to think about. Death stalked Ringling-Barnum from Pennsylvania to Wisconsin that year: many circus people took ill with typhoid, and had to be left behind in local hospitals when the circus moved on, and some died. There was an atmosphere of secret fear within the circus, until the Wisconsin state medical officer diagnosed polluted drinking water that had been taken on by the circus trains in Pennsylvania. The polluted tanks were emptied, sterilized and refilled.[18]

The revamped Hagenbeck-Wallace show, deprived of Frank Cook's management, went into the red during its 1935 season. Gumpertz was desperate to ensure that at least his No. 1 show should be in the black. (The No. 3 show, Al G. Barnes, was doing okay on the West Coast.) Using Cook's skills as legal adjuster to set up new dates, Gumpertz extended Ringling-Barnum's normal season to take in more venues. The last stand after Jacksonville was at Miami on 11–12 November 1935, hot on the heels of a hurricane. It had taken a railroad trek of 15,000 miles to bring the Ringling-Barnum circus to profitability, whereas the Hagenbeck-Wallace show had completed more like the normal 10,000 miles. Hagenbeck-Wallace had suffered from its concentration on industrial cities worst hit by depression, while Ringling-Barnum had managed to spread its load. It was a personal triumph for Frank Cook, but the accumulated stress led to the collapse of his health at the end of the season.

At the beginning of November 1935, Frank Cook was reported ill with influenza, at the Victoria Hospital in Miami. Influenza led to pneumonia. Rather than head north to New York City for the winter, he went first to convalesce at Sarasota with the rest of the circus winter folk. It may be assumed that Evelyn, Barbara and Franz accompanied him.[19] After the sojourn at Sarasota, Franz went with the Cooks to their New York penthouse at the top of the Forest Hotel. Evelyn decided to retire from the circus to live in New York all year round, with Frank and their daughter Barbara, while Frank would use the New York office of the circus corporation to do his long-distance legal work by telephone.

Evelyn's old friend Dorothy Herbert came to stay in the same hotel. She was another circus equestrian who was spending the winter learning how to act at the Paramount Pictures dramatic school in New York. She spent most of her time with Evelyn when not attending school. 'They had all of their meals sent up from the dining room and I usually ate the evening meal with them, after which Frank would retire. Evelyn and I would then either practice my script for the following day or play cards until bedtime.' Franz was no doubt gratified to have two glamorous young women around, as well as a child of whom he was extremely fond. But Dorothy Herbert's memoirs tell us that Franz was frustrated and 'quite hard to handle when cooped up with nothing to do'. She found the little old man with a wrinkled face, who looked a hundred years old, to be 'a pest to have around'.

> Evelyn would get me to take him for walks down the avenue, which would not have been so bad (even with people staring), but he had an awful habit of suddenly running up behind ladies and pinching them, then jumping up and down laughing. Most of the ladies did not find it funny. Neither did I, so I learned to keep a close watch on him. Another annoying habit was his cigars. He smoked almost constantly and the brands he liked most were black and smelly.

Franz went to stay after Christmas with Frances and Pat Sullivan, who had moved down river from Glens Falls to Claverack near Hudson town on the Hudson River, south of Albany.[20]

Over Christmas the circus community was alive with rumours that Hagenbeck-Wallace would soon close down, and Gumpertz did indeed announce in the first week of 1936 that it would fold. This was also the time that Gumpertz entered into agreements on behalf of the Ringling shows with labour unions, with serious long-term implications, beginning with the Billposters Union in January 1936. Gumpertz did his best to come to terms with the new labour militancy, but a certain sourness persisted into the 1936 summer season. There was scandal over tampering with performers' mail and telegrams, to intercept alternative offers of employment. The biggest potential problem was the depression-driven casual labourers who swelled the ranks of circus roustabouts, with miserable living and working conditions, and who joined and left the circus in constant turnover from town to town.[21]

After being filmed at Sarasota by Fox Movietone, Hearst Metrotone, Paramount News and Universal News newsreels, circus performers and

Franz and a baby elephant. Franz was probably photographed reluctantly as he feared elephants and horses. (Chindahl papers, Circus World Museum, Baraboo)

animals entrained for New York in March 1936. The Madison Square Garden opening was picketed by some discontented theatrical workers, and lacked the zip of former years. John Ringling appeared in person, and 'stormed about the premises, angrily criticizing everything about the show ... Gumpertz virtually kicked him out of the Garden.' (Ringling returned to Sarasota, with his tail between his legs, and 'sat in his Rolls-Royce for hours on end, staring blankly into space'.) *Billboard* waited three weeks before it found room for an unusually restrained front-page splash. Franz was described on an inside page as 'the perennial Clicko, African Bushman'. In Barnumesque terms, always in search of novelty, 'perennial' was the ultimate show-business insult.[22]

1936 was to be Franz Taibosh's last full season with Ringling Brothers and Barnum & Bailey: the season ran from 8 April in New York until 11 November at Tampa. There were 394 performances in 218 days, by 1,608 circus people of 49 different nationalities travelling 16,370 miles by railroad. This summary of just one year indicates how extensively Franz Taibosh travelled the United States and Canada for year after year over nineteen years with Ringling-owned circuses. By 1936 his act was old hat and it was probably a bit of a bore—little more than a shuffle for a dance, and uttering perfunctory yells that had lost their bloodcurdling edge.

Frank Cook was tired, too. He probably never completely recovered from the previous winter's illness, and leaned increasingly on his assistant in the legal department, Eddie Vaughan, during the course of the 1936 season. A photograph of Frank Cook with his four- or five-year-old daughter Barbara, taken some time in 1936, shows a faded man advanced in years, looking more grandfather than father.[23]

At the end of the 1936 circus season Franz Taibosh went again to the Cooks' penthouse at the top of New York's Forest Hotel. Frank Cook, however, took ill with a heart ailment, and Evelyn Cook spent most of her time taking care of him, leaving little Barbara and Franz at a loose end elsewhere in the apartment. Frank Cook's condition worsened. In early December 1936 Franz was sent upstate to stay at Claverack with Frances and Pat Sullivan, with whom he celebrated Christmas. At some stage he was joined there by little Barbara. The bed-ridden Frank Cook was transferred from the Forest Hotel to the Polytechnic Hospital in New York.

The news of John Ringling's death from bronchial pneumonia, on 2 December 1936, can scarcely have helped Frank Cook's morale. John Ringling had dreamt to the end of wresting back control of the family firm from Gumpertz and his Brooklyn backers. Said to have been once worth a hundred million dollars, John Ringling lay delirious and dying in a small apartment at 270 Park Avenue, New York, a 'pathetic, tragic figure' who, it was said, 'would have had difficulty raising $100 in cash'.[24]

Frank Cook reached the age of sixty-three on 16 December 1936. He died in hospital on 11 January 1937. The funeral service and cremation were arranged by the St Cecile Masonic Lodge, at the Park West Memorial Chapel in New York City. Two hundred and fifty circus people, from Ida Ringling downwards, came to the funeral together with family and friends.

Twelve men acted as honorary pallbearers bringing the coffin into the chapel, which was adorned with floral tributes. A male voice choir sang. After valedictories, the coffin was committed to the flames. Beverley Kelley, as if addressing Frank, said: 'There has been an expression going round these many years that you were a good friend and a dangerous enemy.' Messages of condolence flooded into the Ringling–Barnum circus. Frank's previous wife, Lulu Davenport, could not attend the funeral. She was recovering at home in Chicago after being seriously ill with influenza in the Grant Hospital.

There was an air of gloom among Ringling–Barnum people at the winter quarters in Sarasota, Florida. First, old John Ringling had died, the last of the founding brothers, and now, a month later, Papa Cook. What was going to happen to the circus? Sam Gumpertz issued a statement to the press, that Frank Cook 'had more friends than any other circus contact man on the American continent'.

Five-year-old Barbara could barely remember her father in later years. It must have been very different for Franz. He had lost the guardian who could protect him from the predatory sharks of show business, his closest companion for the last eighteen years, and his soul mate in an alien land. Franz and Frank had been strange doppelgängers, so different in their backgrounds and life-skills but united by empathy and shared humour.

No doubt Franz could now see his own end in sight. But he had inherited from Frank a sense of duty and responsibility to look after the child Barbara and the widow Evelyn. As for Sam Gumpertz, with Frank Cook as well as John Ringling out of the way, he could now see his way to seizing complete control of the circus and its sideshow. For the third time, he initiated moves to take over the body if not the soul of Franz Taibosh.[25]

16

'I Inherited a Bushman'

On his deathbed, Frank Cook asked his Evelyn to look after Franz Taibosh, and to give him the option of returning home to Africa. Evelyn Joyce Cook recalled this four decades later when she wrote a manuscript entitled 'I inherited a Bushman', as part of a creative writing course at a New York college, fragments of which have survived with Barbara Cook de Romain.

Franz could have retired back to the Cape Province in South Africa, where he probably had relatives at Middelburg—including one, possibly his brother Hans, who also worked for a circus, Boswell's, in the 1920s and 1930s. More likely Franz would have stayed in Cape Town, living a comfortable life in a city that was to some extent immune from the racial segregation of the rest of South Africa. He would have been among people who looked like him and spoke his language; but, illiterate and innumerate as he was, ostensibly rich and probably drinking too much, he would surely have been fair game for tricksters. Instead, Franz chose to stay in America to pursue the only career he knew. He enjoyed the security of the circus and its sideshow, and he took very seriously the idea that he was now 'the man' in the depleted Cook household.[1]

Sam Gumpertz resumed his bid to take over the guardianship of Franz Taibosh. He used his clout as manager of Ringling Brothers to bring Evelyn Cook to heel, denying Franz (and maybe Evelyn herself) employment that year until she conceded victory to him. Evelyn's brother Jack Joyce, 'noted horse and pony trainer', also got into legal trouble at this time. He tried to wriggle out of a contract signed the previous year with Cole Brothers circus, possibly to stay with his sister in the Ringling-Barnum circus. The Cole circus brought the law down on his neck to enforce the contract.[2]

Frank Cook's daughter Frances Cook Sullivan led the counter-attack against Gumpertz with the help of a local lawyer at Hudson, New York, named Lewis E. McNamee. On 8 April 1937, Frances petitioned the notary public of Columbia county at Hudson, one Freda Roehm, for the appointment of a committee to establish the guardianship of Franz Taibosh. Franz was now residing with Frances and her husband at Hudson, and he was said to be 'of the age of approximately one hundred and ten years and now is incompetent to manage himself and his affairs'. Frances's petition outlined what was known of Franz's background, with rambling perorations on the nature of Bushmen in South Africa. No doubt on the advice of the attorney, while acknowledging Franz's 'delightful sense of humor ... honesty, generosity, sensitiveness and loyal devotion to those he loves', the petitioner was at pains to stress the following:

> When the alleged incompetent first came to Mr. Cook he was unable to speak a word of English and could only prattle in his native tongue. He now, however, understands many English words and can carry on a conversation with your petitioner and her husband. It is impossible, however, for the alleged incompetent to carry on any sort of intelligent conversation with a stranger. The said incompetent also is unable to differentiate between the various denominations of money, particularly paper money.

Somewhat disingenuously, considering Franz's command of a Germanic language like Afrikaans, the petition claimed: 'To the knowledge of your petitioner, no one in any English speaking country understands the Bushman language as used by the said alleged incompetent. That, as a result, he is unable to make himself properly understood or to properly understand other people with whom he comes in contact.'

Besides, Franz 'desires to drink of intoxicants to excess and this, together with the other facts above set forth, makes him incompetent to manage himself and his affairs'. The petition went on to state in conclusion that Franz's only personal property was the contract with Ringling-Barnum that entitled him to $30 a week for up to eight months in a year, and that he was 'upon information and belief, a single person and has never married and has no next of kin and heirs at law'.

The case was heard before the acting county judge, Jonathan D. Wilson, in the courthouse at Hudson on 12 April, with Franz Taibosh present. Lewis McNamee put the case to the judge, who ordered that it go before a jury seven days thence at eleven o'clock in the forenoon. Franz Taibosh (stated to be of Joslen Boulevard, Hudson) was sent formal notice of the trial, served by the notary public and attested by a commissioner for oaths.

Franz actually appeared before the court, and must have given sufficiently good or, rather, bad evidence to convince the court. McNamee said his piece and no one in court raised any opposition to the proceedings. The jury then produced its answers to four questions put to it by Judge Wilson. First, that Franz Taibosh was indeed 'incompetent to manage his affairs'. Second, that he possessed no 'real property'. Third and fourth, that his annual income amounted to $960.00, and that that constituted the sum total of his 'personal property'.

The next stage was for the court to consider a court order 'confirming the findings of the jury … and for the appointment of Frances Sullivan Cook' as the person to whom 'the person and estate of the said Franz Taibosh' was to be committed 'upon the filing by her of the security required by law and direct by the Court, and for such other and further relief as the Court may deem proper'. The hearing of the case was slated for 1 May before the substantive judge of Columbia county, Ransom H. Gillett. Judge Gillett then ordered that Frances should be the 'committee', i.e. trustee or custodian, of Franz Taibosh's person and estate, upon payment of a surety of $1,000 to the court.

Frances signed her agreement to the arrangement, but her stepmother Evelyn Joyce Cook expressed immediate disagreement. As far as she was concerned, her late husband had entrusted her and not his elder daughter with the care of Franz Taibosh. On 27 May Evelyn Joyce Cook (giving her address as No. 1 West 67th Street, New York City) deposited an affidavit with the Hudson court, stating her long-term acquaintance with Franz Taibosh over 'about the past 10 years'. She objected that Franz Taibosh had never been a legal resident of Columbia county and thus was not subject to its court. Instead he had resided for nineteen or twenty years 'with Frank Cook in the City, County and State of New York' or 'under the guidance, control and management' of Frank Cook while touring with the Ringling Brothers and Barnum & Bailey Combined Shows.

Frances evidently consented to relinquish her legal guardianship over Franz. It was her attorney, Lewis McNamee, who formally approached Judge Gillett in the Hudson court on 27 May with Evelyn Cook's counter-petition. Gillett ordered all previous proceedings to be 'set aside, nullified and declared void'. Frances was repaid the substantial bond money she had given in surety, and the legal status of Franz Taibosh reverted to the *de facto* succession of Evelyn Joyce Cook to the late Frank Cook as guardian.

Frances Cook Sullivan must have felt somewhat bruised by the experience of being deposed by Evelyn Joyce Cook. But she at least had the satisfaction of having deterred Sam Gumpertz from muscling his way in to take over Franz's guardianship. Meanwhile, Evelyn faced the added problem of the second Mrs Frank Cook, Lulu Davenport, putting in a claim on Frank Cook's will.[3]

So long as Sam Gumpertz remained in charge at Ringling-Barnum, there was no hope of Clicko being re-engaged in its sideshow. From January until May 1937, Franz sheltered with the Sullivans at Claverack. He then moved to New York City to live with Evelyn and Barbara Cook at the Hôtel des Artistes on the Upper West Side, on 67th Street, not far from Central Park and the American Natural History Museum, where his whole-body plaster cast of 1919 was sometimes displayed.

The Hôtel des Artistes had been built in 1913 to house Bohemian artists 'who had moved beyond their romantic garret stages' into inhabiting 'luxury co-ops' or 'sumptuous duplexes'. Its reputation was sealed in 1934 by the unveiling of murals of gorgeous athletic nudes, posing as wood nymphs, on the walls of its downstairs bistro, the Café des Artistes. It became quite the place to be for fashionable rich young New Yorkers, and also 'prohibitively expensive'. Chilled water was piped to every apartment. Residents, equipped only with tiny kitchens, sent down raw ingredients to the bistro kitchen to be cooked and returned by 'dumbwaiter' elevator.

Though Franz only stayed at the Hôtel des Artistes for up to six weeks initially, he was to return there periodically and became a well-known figure among the occupants—that is, until Evelyn Cook had spent the fortune inherited from Frank Cook and could no longer be a tenant and the freest-spending of merry young widows—a lifestyle that Franz Taibosh undoubtedly enjoyed sharing while it lasted.

Franz Taibosh was transformed from ward of Frank Cook to grandfather figure for Barbara Cook. He also kept a watchful eye on Evelyn, on behalf of the deceased Frank, while she kept an eye on his drinking and smoking. She would not countenance the idea of the old man bringing a woman to his bed, or his going out to find women elsewhere.[4]

While he was precluded from rejoining the Ringling-Barnum circus, there were other dissidents from the Gumpertz régime whom Franz could join. Harry Lewiston, former assistant manager of the Ringling-Barnum sideshow, had broken away to set up his own 'traveling museum', and was desperate to recruit good acts. Harry and his wife Rose rented an apartment in Chicago (3224 Greenshaw Street) as their home and office, and got to work signing up 'freaks' to tour Canada with Patty (Patrick) Conklin's carnival that summer of 1937. Conklin's All Canadian Shows were to kick off at Hamilton, Ontario, 'the Pittsburgh of Canada', in June, going westwards as far as Alberta before returning east to Ontario, culminating in a stand at the Canadian National Exposition in Toronto.

Harry and Rose Lewiston induced a number of performers from the Big Show to join them: Mel Burkhart, the human knot; the sword-swallowing John and Vivian Dunning who had now taken to swallowing lighted neon tubes; and Stella Card Rogan, the tattooed girl. (A subsequent neon-swallower employed by the Lewistons became so enthusiastic in responding to audience applause in Detroit, that he took a bow, and had to be rushed to hospital to remove the slivers of broken glass in his gullet.)

The Lewistons contacted Evelyn Cook, or as Harry put it later, 'I had also had a talk with the "owners" of Clico the African pygmy and they wanted him to go with our show, mainly because I was willing to pay more for him (his own pay remained the same—a glass of beer once in a while and all the cigars he could smoke.)'[5]

Franz felt himself to be a burden on Evelyn Cook and on Frances and Pat Sullivan, and very much wanted to work, as had been his wont to do each summer, his pay covering his winter expenses with the Cooks, as well as indulging his sheer pleasure in performance.

Letters preserved by Evelyn and Barbara Cook show that Harry Lewiston sent a draft contract to Evelyn Cook (at 1 West 67th Street, NYC), 'as per instructions of your wire', dated 10 June, asking that the 'freak known as African Bushman' join the Lewistons at Winnipeg by the 19th. No doubt after further telegrams, Evelyn replied on 23 June to Lewiston at Moose-Jaw, Saskatchewan, enclosing two signed copies of the contract as revised by her attorney, Edward J. Garity, of 258 Broadway, with the Bushman's name given as 'Franz Taibosh'. She would take him as far as Montreal, to ensure that he got across the border with his 1932 US Certificate of Registry but no passport, and then put him on a train west. 'It is only after serious consideration that I have decided to let the Bushman go with you, and I feel certain that you will take good care of him, and see that he is well protected, and under no circumstances will permit him to leave the show unless he is accompanied by me.' The agreed pay was $30, to be sent each week to Evelyn.[6]

On 5 July 1937, Rose Lewiston ('Madame Zindar') reported that 'Clico' had arrived safely at Carman, Manitoba, starting work on 30 June. 'We have Dick Disco, whom you no doubt know, he did the Punch and Judy on the show, staying with Clico nights, and when the show moves, I personally take him to the trains. He eats all he wants, and gets his cigars, but nothing to drink, since Mr. Lewiston and I know him perfectly.'

Conklin's All Canadian Shows with Lewiston's World's Fair Freaks moved on to the annual Yorkton show on the prairies of Saskatchewan, near the Manitoba border, between 12 and 14 July. The *Regina Leader-Post* of Tuesday, 13 July reported on 'Crowds throng fair opening at Yorkton' on the previous day. 'Despite drouth [drought] and promises of little or no rain, Yorkton and district turned backs on despair and came out Monday to give Yorkton's fair its biggest opening for many a long day.' Attendance records were broken, restaurants overcrowded, all parking spaces filled with cars, and the drought broke on the third and most crowded last day of the fair, with heavy rainstorms coming from the south.[7]

All in all, it was the sort of show that Franz would have enjoyed: 'throngs of youngsters ... roundly applauded the gymnastic Radke sisters and the whirlwind Rajah Arabs, thoroughly enjoyed the Scotch music and dancing of the Saskatoon girls' pipe band, and shrieked long and loud at the clowning of the Carr brothers and the indiscriminate kicking of the comedy mule.'

Lewiston's World's Fair Freaks moved on for three more days of the Saskatchewan annual fair, at Melfort north-east of Saskatoon, and then to Lethbridge in Alberta where the fair was greeted by torrential rains.[8] On 18 July, Rose Lewiston enclosed two weekly cheques in a letter to Evelyn Cook, adding the words: 'Clico is well, and very happy, and says he likes it better than the Barnum and Bailey Show, and to say hello when I write to you.'

Business was not particularly good in the Canadian west. Conklin's All Canadian Shows with Lewiston's World's Fair Freaks returned eastwards, playing at two Manitoba venues, followed by a 1,900-mile 'jump' back to Ontario, where they played at the Canadian National Exposition in Toronto.

Toronto was 'unusually busy' but posed a problem for the Lewistons. They had to delete Stella Card Rogan's hoochy-cooch and striptease as a 'blow off'—the extra show for extra money tacked on to the main show. In the prim tradition of the Ringling Brothers, Stella Card Rogan had never before revealed the whole of her tattooed body to an audience. So Lewiston had made her striptease the climax of his museum's 'blow off'. While women and children were diverted to a Punch and Judy show, their menfolk were induced to part with 25 cents for the 'artistic tableaux' featuring the shadow of a woman undressing, with three more dancers in succession on offer—the first showing a little breast for 25 cents more, the second showing more flesh for 50 cents, and the third completely nude for a dollar. That was how really good money could be made in show business.

Rose Lewiston wrote to Evelyn Cook on 13 September that Conklin's would close on 7 October, but the Lewistons wanted their World's Fair Freaks to continue playing all winter in the US in 'store shows, shrine dates, etc.', when 'Cliko' would be paid the winter rate of $20 a week. She added:

> Cliko is apparently very happy, although the last three weeks have been hard and have been the hardest we had this season … everything is done to make him comfortable. Sunday I took him to the hotel, and he had a nice bath and dinner in the dining room. He likes Mr. Lewiston very much … With best wishes from Clico, Mr Lewiston and myself …

The Lewistons 'told all personnel to plan for winter work … to play auditoriums, empty stores', when World's Fair Freaks was to become an independent touring show. They chose an empty store as near the Toronto city centre as possible and ran it as a temporary dime museum, meanwhile scouting around for more venues over the border in the US. (Most performers slept in the store overnight to save on accommodation expenses.) After six weeks at Toronto, World's Fair Freaks began its winter tour and crossed the international border. By December 1937 they were playing at Pontiac, Michigan.

> When Harry Lewiston's World Fair Freaks played here the location was downtown and the attendance was good, with the following attractions: Carlson Sisters, fat women; Leo Kongee, man who tortures himself; Stella Rogan, tattoo artist and torture box [*sic*]; Marvin Burkhart, anatomical wonder; Leona Harris, fire-eater; Click [*sic*], Bushman; Mrs. Jerry Burkhart, snake enchantress; Professor Disco, magician; Madame Zindar, mentalist; and in the annex Leo-Leona. The troupe entertained the Fisher Body Works strikers and the local 159 of the Auto Union.[9]

The exhibition of Leo-Leona the hermaphrodite was illegal in most states, as was Rose Lewiston's fortune-telling. The industrial strikers were a sign of the times. Lewiston's was not a 'Sunday School show' like Ringling-Barnum.

It was more in the tradition of the old grift shows, but Harry Lewiston differed in not wanting his customers to feel cheated. He had learned from Clyde Ingalls the principle of 'always giving the customer more for his money than he expected', unlike other shows which disappointed customers by giving less than they had paid for. Customer satisfaction was the best way to generate enthusiastic word-of-mouth advertising. But Lewiston did indulge in typically mendacious advertising on cards distributed to barber shops and bars. The cards portrayed a Ubangi woman with the word 'Freaks' coming out of her mouth, and heavily featured the words 'Everything, everything ALIVE' (to assure people that they would not see a row of pickle bottles as in some other freak shows). Other text spuriously invoked the name of the sports journalist which was by now synonymous with freakery, Robert L. Ripley.

Probably influenced by Rose, a religious woman, Harry Lewiston liked to think of himself as a good employer, paying better than Ringling-Barnum and providing good food prepared by a full-time cook travelling with the show. Lewiston also instructed his people to be polite rather than rude to the 'rubes', not to treat all the customers as suckers, as did so many carnival folk. Freaks must not talk on stage and thus spoil audience illusion, and announcers had to talk to approved scripts learned by heart. Rose also inspired him to make good money by selling cheaply printed Bibles in aid of Freda Pushnick, a legless and armless woman who was exhibited as an unexpected attraction at the end of the show. Harry Lewiston then did his own performance with his pet pythons, after which he sold 'genuine' snake oil.

In Joliet, Illinois, where they exhibited for two weeks in December 1937, the World's Fair Freaks were arraigned before a court for the exhibition of 'obnoxious persons', under a local law of 1866, but the prosecutor accepted a $200 bribe instead. Also at Joliet the infant boy adopted by Rose and Harry was circumcised in accordance with Jewish law. At Toledo, Ohio, where there were blizzards, Harry Lewiston paid a bribe of $800 to escape imprisonment for exhibiting a hermaphrodite. At Hamilton, Ohio, Rose and a colleague were fined $50 for illegal fortune-telling.

Harry Lewiston found it difficult to move around in advance of the show to rent new locations. Neighbouring stores would object to a noisy dime museum, and local police and other officials had to be squared. But by January 1938 the Lewistons were doing well enough to hire their own 'advance man', an alcoholic with a melodious voice called Paul Sprague.[10]

Freed from the totalitarian oversight of Ringling-Barnum, Franz enjoyed himself on the road with the Lewistons. A showman named Smythe who worked for Lewiston in these years later recalled: 'Clicko, a saddle-colored, four-foot high Australian [*sic*] bushman, who was with the show for several seasons [was] a flawless example of what a performer should not be in his private life'.

> Clicko was both an inebriate and a wolf. Attired in a leopard cloth, he looked like something that should have been decorating a lawn, until he started to jump up and down and yell. Smythe was never able to tell when Clicko was drunk, until the little Bushman, in flawless English, started to make indecent proposals to the ladies in the audience. Then it was too late.[11]

The 1937 Ringling-Barnum season had opened in April without Clicko, for a twenty-three-day run at Madison Square Garden. (The opening was delayed at the last moment by an ice-hockey play-off that took precedence.) Gumpertz's old opening 'spec' was repackaged with a new title, 'India'. *Billboard* remarked that the opening went without a hitch, the smoothest in ten years, but relegated the story to page three. The implication was that the Big One and circuses in general were considered somewhat passé in the entertainment world.[12]

Ringling-Barnum was entering a period of stress. Audience receipts had recovered from depression, but the cost structure of the circus was in tatters with the rise in labour costs, and circus morale was poor. The humiliating death of John Ringling, and no doubt the news of Gumpertz's manoeuvring over Taibosh, left a bad taste in the mouth for performers in the Big Show. Tension between managers and circus workers was reflected in the class resentment that the handlers of workhorses in the circus (under threat from motor vehicles and hoists) meted out on pampered 'dude' ring-performance horses. Unskilled roustabouts were also beginning to unionize.

The Ringling-Barnum circus was reported to be 'near 100% union' by the end of May 1937. A Union of Circus Workmen was set up under the auspices of the American Federation of Actors, an upstart union headed by a Shakespearian actor called Ralph Whitehead. Ringling-Barnum management did their best to discredit Whitehead by digging into his private life. But, at least in the summer of 1937, Ringling-Barnum under Gumpertz could afford to cover wage hikes, as audiences were good with plentiful straw houses, putting 'piles of green bills back in the red wagon's coffers', while continued agricultural depression kept food and transport costs down.

Another mark of the old order passing was that 1937 was the last year of the great circus publicist or 'advance man' Dexter Fellowes, who died in November. But the really sensational event of the year's end was the deposition of Sam Gumpertz. John Ringling North (eldest son of Ida Ringling) had been elected president of the Ringling Brothers corporation after the death of his uncle John in December 1936. A year later he organized a buy-out of Gumpertz's New York banker friends, wiping out the inheritance of Uncle John's debts. Sam Gumpertz yielded the general management to Johnny North and his brother Henry, and gracefully retired to his holdings on Coney Island.[13] The door was now open for Franz Taibosh's return to Ringling-Barnum.

California Interlude

CLICKO'S FORTUNE was now tied once again to that of the Big One. The Ringling-Barnum circus boasted a restoration under the management of the Ringling family, in the form of Ringling nephews Johnny North and Henry North. They had kicked out wily old Sam Gumpertz. Back in his Coney Island fairground holdings, Gumpertz promised a complete revamp of the resort with new attractions imported from Europe. In March 1938 he announced plans to build a new pier into the sea at Philadelphia, in collaboration with the circus proprietor George A. Hamib. Many years later, band-leader Merle Evans looked back on the Gumpertz period of the Ringling-Barnum show and said: 'I guess he was a pretty good manager even if he wasn't well liked, specially among the old timers. They called him "The Gump." He had poor eyesight, but nothing much escaped him. If something in the spec looked shabby, he saw it … [But] I was glad when a Ringling was back in the office again.'

The two North brothers were full of enthusiasm, regardless of show-business news from Europe that 'War clouds hurt bookings'. They made a big deal about a new attraction in the form of a facially disfigured gorilla that they renamed Gargantua. (The previous owner was no little old lady, as they claimed, but the female proprietor of a commercial menagerie.) But these were difficult times for greenhorns to take over circus management. Newly unionized circus workers, who had just won wage concessions from Gumpertz, saw the North brothers as a soft target.[1]

John North was in everyday charge of the show while his brother Henry, who considered himself something of a musician and composer, took care of public relations. The brothers decided to add more sex and music to the circus in the style of the Ziegfeld Follies and Busby Berkeley films, and to dispense with the stentorian announcements of Clyde Ingalls. The April 1938 opening repackaged the old prewar-style 'India' pageant as 'Nepal', with show-girls in sexy costumes, outsize walkaround figures of Walt Disney's Seven Dwarfs, and the animal procurer Frank Buck in pith helmet—a poor substitute for the tiger-training Clyde Beatty, whom Gumpertz had driven out of the show. Gargantua was dragged around the hippodrome track in an air-conditioned glass box, and had been credited in pre-show publicity with mauling new owner Johnny North. Equestrian director Fred Bradna was on crutches with a broken leg in plaster when he blew his magic silver whistle to open the show.

The annual splash given to Ringling-Barnum on the front page of an April *Billboard* was nearly back to normal: 'R-B bows to near capacity. Audience astounded ...' But *Billboard* was more interested in the fact that the film star Gary Cooper was in the audience, in the royal box, than in listing Ringling-Barnum performers. Display 6, the Parade of Freaks, in which Clicko was back after a year's absence, was criticized as somewhat passé and dismissed peremptorily in the following paragraph: 'Almost all the queer people in Ingalls's menage seem to feel that they need not sell the arena crowds on their right to a place in the freak procession; that Mother Nature speaks eloquently for them. No new faces observed in this year's freak parade.' One should recall that Clyde Ingalls had been gagged that year from boosting the 'freaks' with his usual grand spiel.[2]

The season was stricken from the start by strife between the new North management and the show's four hundred roustabout workers. They demanded a minimum wage of $45 a month for the Madison Square Garden and Boston indoor stands, plus board, and were pushing to literally double their $30 monthly wage on the road under canvas. The roustabouts staged a series of lightning strikes at New York and Boston; clowns were pictured in the press, at Henry North's prompting, doing the roustabouts' work of hauling ropes. An editorial in the *New York Times* remarked that circus owners must face up to the modernization ('streamlining', to use the current buzzword) of labour relations, with unionization even embracing artists. 'Collectivism had laid hand on the most individualistic and most irresponsible of all professions ... a tribe of playboys in a serious world. But even their make-believe world is now being systematized and planned and regimented. Laugh, clown, laugh! The old, strolling, joyous and carefree *commedia* of the mummer *strade* is pretty much *finita*.'[3]

In early June 1938 the Ringling–Barnum circus travelled on to Ohio and Indiana—first Columbus, and then Dayton, Lima, Sandusky, Toledo and Fort Wayne. But John North found that business everywhere was bad that year. When the circus reached Dayton, Ohio, he 'offered' the roustabouts of the American Federation of Actors (AFA) a twenty-five per cent wage cut, so that they could continue to play to unfilled houses in the depressed Mid-West. Not surprisingly, the union turned down the request. The circus responded by sacking up to two hundred workers at Lima, and forty at Fort Wayne. At Toledo, there was such chaos and delay in setting up the matinée and evening performances that Gargantua the gorilla attacked its keeper. Circus morale was low. This is confirmed by reports of increased numbers of injuries among performers, who depended on the more skilled roustabouts to set up equipment safely.

John North decided to cut out the stand at depressed Cleveland, Ohio, and to confine future stands to the more prosperous East. The circus proceeded to Newark in New Jersey and Harrisburg in Pennsylvania. (For similar reasons, all the other US railroad circuses headed for Canada.)

On Monday, 16 June 1938, at Pittsburgh, John North addressed his assembled workers 'at the Monday dinner hour from a raised platform in the center of the big top, flanked by crew bosses and circus officials'. He announced that a pay cut was inevitable to cover the increased costs of materials that the circus had to buy. This had to be negotiated now, in order to turn round the circus's finances by the end of the month. Here he quoted an old maxim of circus business economics that if a show did not make a profit by 1 July, it would never make a profit over the rest of the summer season. (Thus circuses always headed for the best territories first, and left the less profitable stands for later.) North suggested that the Big Show always had to carry the losses of all the Ringling little shows, which explained why 'Uncle John' had had to run to the banks (and had been taken to the cleaners by Gumpertz). Gumpertz had increased circus workers' pay by a hundred per cent before he left at the end of 1937. Now that pay must come down to a more realistic level.

Class war continued. While he was talking to his labour, North was ordering new diesel-powered tractors from Philadelphia to replace human and elephant muscle in getting trains loaded. At Erie, Pennsylvania, sixty-seven baggage stock workers walked out, and air-brake lines were sabotaged on twelve Ringling–Barnum rail-cars. Pinkerton private security agents were called in to guard the trains. Matters cannot have been improved by news that lawyers for John Ringling's divorced widow, Emily Buck, were scrambling for a bigger piece of the Ringling Brothers cake.

Showdown came at Scranton, Pennsylvania, on Saturday, 25 June 1938. Workers finally turned down North's 'offer' of a twenty-five per cent pay cut. Old Edith ('Mrs Charlie') Ringling came and delivered a futile appeal for everyone to pull together as members of the 'circus family'. The voting at the meeting, by open acclamation, turned her down, despite the trapeze artiste Art Concello collecting the signatures of two hundred and fifty performers willing to take a pay cut, so that 'the show must go on'. The AFA officially announced it was on strike when four thousand spectators were sitting under the big top, awaiting the evening performance.

Rowdy customers mobbed the box offices to get their money back. AFA delegates sat with John North till 11.30 that night, but the meeting ended in complete deadlock. Only animal keepers continued to work on site, while cast and crew retired to their tents and rail-cars to listen to a radio broadcast of that night's historic big fight between American 'brown bomber' Joe Louis and Nazi Germany's 'white hope' Max Schmeling.

John North announced that Ringling-Barnum would pack up and return to winter quarters in Florida, and was roundly denounced by the AFA for a 'squeeze-out'. The next day, Sunday, North cancelled the 1938 contracts of all workers *and* performers. Ralph Whitehead of the AFA called Ringling-Barnum managers 'mules', 'butchers' and 'half-baked'. In return he was called a '(blank) Bolshevik'. The AFA demanded full payment of all outstanding pay for its members before they left the lot. This delayed the trains leaving for Florida until Monday and Tuesday.

The president of the Circus Fans Association of America watched as the circus trains left the marshalling yards after a long stop at Washington DC, and revealed his prejudices. 'I am sick at heart ... At the Potomac yards, I watched the train leave for Sarasota. Words cannot begin to describe the sadness of the picture. It is very difficult for me, too, to understand why an actors' union should be controlled by roustabouts who seldom know what it is to serve even one circus season.'

The remains of the Ringling-Barnum circus crept back into Sarasota early on the morning of Friday, 1 July. An Indiana newspaper, the *Evansville Courier*, carried a cartoon of the circus disappearing in a cyclone, with a small elephant standing by and saying, 'Have to pinch myself to be sure I'm not dreaming.'

On Saturday, 2 July, President F.D. Roosevelt visited the site of the upcoming New York World's Fair on Flushing Meadow, to lay the cornerstone of the US federal exhibit building. Striking workers, protesting a demarcation dispute between workers and managers over who should lay telephone cables, temporarily suspended picketing out of respect for the Chief Executive.[4]

◎

Some Ringling-Barnum performers were re-engaged in Idaho on the next biggest Ringling show, the Al G. Barnes–Sells–Floto circus, which was duly picketed by members of the AFA. Other performers such as Franz Taibosh were simply offered rail tickets back home.

But Franz by this time had no home to go to, at least in New York City. Costs or opportunities had induced Evelyn Cook to buy a roadster and to drive westwards with her daughter Barbara in May 1938. They were now somewhere in Iowa—was it really Dubuque?—on their way eventually to the West Coast. Evelyn had the idea of linking up with her friend Dorothy Herbert in Hollywood, where Dorothy had become a minor film star in Westerns, as a glamorous young woman adept at trick-riding with horses. Who knew what breaks there might be for other trained equestriennes?

Ringling-Barnum management made contact with Evelyn Cook as Franz's *de facto* guardian. Franz took a train to Chicago. There, in either the mainline train station or the Ringling offices, he waited for Evelyn and Barbara to arrive in their new car. Then began what Barbara would later recall as the great adventure of her young life. Evelyn drove the car westwards, with Franz and Barbara as passengers. From Iowa they started on the long journey across the plains, stopping at hotels or the modish new 'motels' (motor hotels) on the way.

Evelyn was still a little embarrassed by her charge, and attempted to smuggle him into a hotel. Barbara and Franz were about the same size, and a subterfuge was attempted, with Franz under an overcoat entering the hotel as if he were little Barbara returning from the car to the room. It is hardly surprising that the hotel management tumbled to the wheeze, given the considerable differences in the anatomies of child and man, and there was considerable explaining to be done.

In the rarified world of the far Mid-West and the Rockies, Franz could not be convincingly explained away as some kind of grand paterfamilias. The explanation that he was a circus 'freak' would scarcely have given more comfort to rural innkeepers. Franz Taibosh therefore reverted to his old ploy, from his days with Frank Cook, of announcing himself as a grand potentate. He adopted the persona of some exotic prince or pasha, and even once presented himself to a startled hotel clerk as Haile Selassie, exiled Emperor

Barbara and Evelyn Cook with Franz at Pike's Peak, Colorado,
29 July 1938. (Barbara Cook de Romain)

Barbara and Franz stare at what Evelyn claimed was Lake Tahoe,
August 1938. (Barbara Cook de Romain)

of Abyssinia. (The real Haile Selassie had fled to live in Weston-super-Mare, England, after the Italian invasion of 1936.)

In hotel after hotel, or motel after motel, Franz swept up to the reception desk, in silk hat and tie and formal evening dress, puffing on one of his long cigars, and announced in his strange-sounding English that he would be staying the night, with this young woman and her child. The young woman was extremely glamorous, and the child cute with curls like Shirley Temple. The explanation that they were on their way to Hollywood seems to have convinced sceptical hoteliers.

The journey via Denver and Colorado Springs across the Rocky Mountains is recorded in snapshots taken on the way. Three photographs show an ancient and battered-looking Franz around Pike's Peak (inspiration for the song 'America the beautiful') on 29 July 1938. Franz stands proudly by the car on a mountain pass, next to a road sign that marks an elevation of 12,310 ft above sea level. In another photo he sits on a pile of rocks, calmly ready for a portrait with his suit jacket buttoned up, looking somewhat sternly into the camera. In a third photo, taken at the same spot, the elegant young widow Evelyn Cook stands with her hands on the shoulders of her smiling daughter Barbara on one side and a smirking Franz on the other side. (Barbara Cook remarks that she was eight at the time, but her mother was presenting herself professionally as only eighteen!) A fourth photo taken the same day, captioned 'Near Colorado Springs 1938' on the back, shows Barbara and Franz sitting on a rock next to a small lake with boats in the background.

Standing in front of snow-dusted mountains and breathing the sharp mountain air, Franz recalled his childhood in South Africa. Barbara asked him if he missed Africa, and whether he wanted to return home. 'Ag heck, no,' was something like his reply. 'Africa is a dump. America is my home.'

Evelyn drove north through Cheyenne into Wyoming, and from there across Nevada into northern California. A photo shows the front of the car parked at a viewpoint overlooking an apparently small lake, with the backs of Barbara in a swimsuit and Franz in shirtsleeves and suspenders, standing at a chain-link barrier and staring at the view. The back of the photo is captioned:

> I had just told Barbara that was Lake Tahoe. Bush asks Barbara 'What place Mama Cook say?'
>
> *Barbara*: 'Bushie, that is Lake Tahoe.'
> *Bushman*: 'Ye b'lieve dat Bobby?'

Lake Tahoe is, of course, a very large lake, and this was surely one of the many small lakes in Nevada that preceded it near the highway. Franz, who had travelled the States for so many years, probably knew this. This little snippet is particularly interesting as it reveals that while Franz was addressing Evelyn respectfully as 'Mama Cook' and Barbara familiarly as 'Bobby', Evelyn affectionately called Franz 'Bush' and Barbara called him 'Bushie'.

The transcontinental adventures of the trio ended in the Los Angeles suburb of Glendale, where they rented a house, 1442 Montgomery Street, to last out the winter of 1938–9. Glendale was in the vicinity of Hollywood, where Dorothy Herbert worked. In later years Barbara assumed that her mother had hoped to develop profitable social connections there, maybe a new husband, rather than seeking employment. If so, she was to be disappointed. But what was to be a relatively short period in Franz Taibosh's life was, for Barbara, redolent with childhood memories as one of the happiest times of her life.

Evelyn Cook told Laurens van der Post many years later that blacks in those days were subject to a curfew of 6 pm in this all-white suburb. She had to keep Franz secretly in the house at night until they gained the confidence of the neighbours. The trio continued to live in the extravagant style to which Evelyn and indeed Franz had become accustomed. The suburban villa was maybe not as large as Evelyn had wanted, but there was no question of doing without domestic help.

Barbara later recalled that the 'maid' was a pleasant, slim African American woman, not quite the sort of plump woman whom Franz might refer to as the 'mama' that he wished to marry. Franz pursued her relentlessly round the house, interrupting her duties with playful pinches on the bottom. She appeared to tolerate this at first, but one day was heard screaming from the living-room that she would put up with this no more. Evelyn and Barbara rushed in to find the maid on top of the grand piano, staving off Franz with a broom. She then gave notice and quit, saying that the old man was an incorrigible pest who could not be trusted.

The story brings to mind the mouse with the stereotypical Negro maid in a *Tom and Jerry* cartoon. It amused Barbara at the time, and it took many years for her to realize that it also underlined a lack of sexual and emotional fulfilment on Franz's part. There was no question of Evelyn allowing or arranging, like her late husband, for Franz to enjoy the services of a brothel. For all her glamour and extravagance, and annoying inconsistencies that grated on Barbara as she grew older, Evelyn was a prude.

Franz gave Barbara's childhood an edge of daring and excitement. Franz's customary expletives, the sacrilegious 'Jeezus' and other words obscene or scatological that are common in the vulgar Afrikaans variant of English spoken by Franz, were taboos for Barbara, which her mother allowed only Franz to break.

Franz and Barbara were constant companions for those months in California. Practically the same height as each other, they ate their meals next to each other and played together. Barbara recalled how one day Franz tried to wriggle under a chair during hide-and-seek and got stuck by his protruding bottom, which he referred to as his 'step' ('stoep' or verandah). In a strange town, where she was not going to school, Barbara met few other children. Instead she lived happily in a household that she considered entirely normal, and subsequently could hardly understand why other children did not also have a jolly little old man to play with.

Franz spent much of his time gardening. He became very aware of the flutter of lace curtains in the next-door house, where two single elderly women lived. For their benefit he danced and let out blood-curdling yells and did his whole sideshow routine of the menacing Wild Man. They may have responded in terror at first, but soon became good friends. They appreciated Franz's skill in growing roses, and he was frequently to be seen in their yard planting and pruning.

Presumably Franz stayed up after Barbara went to bed, smoking and consuming such alcohol as was strictly rationed by Evelyn, and listening to the radio. Barbara remembered that Franz always had difficulty in getting up in the morning. He would appear reluctantly at breakfast, in a woollen dressing-gown, facing a boiled egg or fried bacon and refusing to speak until he had drunk a whole cup of really strong coffee. Until that moment he sat silent and glowering, with his elbows on the table, the tip of his left-hand pinkie (small finger) holding up the lid of the eye left lazy by his stroke a decade earlier.

Glendale may have been Elysium for Barbara, but life without greater company and activity became boring for Franz, and Evelyn did not achieve the social or professional advantage she sought in Hollywood circles. There was no reason to stay out west beyond the end of the mild California winter. Evelyn was anxious to return to the greater social swim of New York. No doubt Franz also wanted to return to summer employment back east. He had, after all, been employed for only half his expected summer engagement with a sideshow in 1937.

Photographs of Franz in California include Barbara and Franz, in a ten-

Evelyn Cook, Mrs Johnnie Baker (Buffalo Bill's niece), Maud W., Barbara Cook, Franz and his dog 'Boots' at Glendale, California. (Barbara Cook de Romain)

gallon hat, in front of Evelyn and two men friends playing table tennis in the yard outside the Glendale house. In another photograph, Franz has his arms around Barbara and another little girl. (According to Evelyn's note on the back of the photo, the little girl was an illegitimate daughter of the film actor Walter Pidgeon and 'lived across the street from us in Hollywood'.) The three are standing next to the guy ropes of a circus tent, and Franz is dressed in his leopard-skin costume. Presumably he was making a guest appearance at the circus as Clicko the Bushman. (The most likely circus was Al G. Barnes–Sells-Floto, which had taken on some Ringling-Barnum performers and was covering the western half of the States, giving the North brothers a whopping profit of $400,000 at the end of their otherwise troubled first season.)

A group portrait, taken on the edge of woodland, shows Franz smoking a cigarette and patting his German shepherd dog, Boots. Next to them stand

*Barbara, Franz in costume, and Walter Pidgeon's daughter outside
a circus tent at Los Angeles (probably Ringling Brothers' Al G.
Barnes–Sells–Floto Circus). (Barbara Cook de Romain)*

Barbara, a middle-aged woman called Maud W., and an even older woman,
Buffalo Bill's niece Mrs Johnnie Baker, who is holding a smiling Evelyn
around the waist.[5]

There was a further photograph, reported by Van der Post in *A Mantis
Carol*, of Franz sitting on a toboggan in the snows of Colorado. Franz had
become a little old man with a heavy muffler round his throat, and a balaclava
on his head. He looks cold but undefeated. The photo could have been taken
on their summer transit through Pike's Peak; alternatively it was taken on a
final holiday out of Glendale, on the winter slopes of Colorado, before the
odd little Cook–Taibosh family returned east.[6]

Back in New York City, an interviewer from the WPA Federal Writers' Project
tracked down a certain Mrs Tommie Clicko on 14 September 1938, at 272

Manhattan Avenue, in a middle-class African American and Puerto Rican community. Described as a spry and presentable, chain-smoking fifty-nine-year-old with 'beautiful warm brown skin', and blessed with a dry sense of humour, she prattled on fairly inconsequentially about her life, interrupted periodically by her married daughter and neighbours.

From the interview, we gather that Mrs Tommie Clicko had been born at Atlanta, Georgia, in 1879, but had got married to her first husband and left for St Louis in 1898. Following the classic jazz route of northward migration, she and her first husband, described as a 'music-writer', moved on from St Louis to Chicago and then arrived in New York, via Ohio, in about 1918. She made her living as a dressmaker but had obviously seen better times because not only did she wear gold earrings but she had a story about having once lost a diamond necklace set in platinum. She also expressed bourgeois disparagement of poor people who did not wash. Presumably she had a classic smoker's cough. The interviewer suggests that she was suffering from tuberculosis.

Her second husband, presumably Mr Tommie Clicko, was barely mentioned except to say that he was in Sea View sanatorium suffering from tuberculosis. On the face of things this precludes Franz Taibosh being Tommie Clicko, but the extraordinary name 'Clicko' suggests some link. Was this the American 'mama' that Franz had always desired, but had now perhaps discarded? Her age, location and situation, and her previous show-business marriage, are all persuasive. But the most likely explanation must surely be that the woman wished, quite understandably, to cover her true identity from the intrusive interviewer, and had plucked Franz's stage-name, with which she was familiar, out of the blue.[7]

18

THE GREAT
TERMINAL DANCE

He would ... stand there in his bare feet, with only his trousers firmly belted round his peculiar little middle. He would put out his hands wide in front of him, give a kind of a lion-like growl, and begin stamping his feet. Then, in the centre of his stomach, we would see all his muscles coming together in a sort of ball and jerk to the left side of his body.

FRANCES PATTERSON—apparently a niece of the sculptor Malvina Hoffman—had known Franz Taibosh in a New York hotel during her 1930s childhood. She recalled Franz Taibosh's dancing when she was interviewed by Laurens van der Post in 1959. She added that the muscular ball in Franz's belly danced round in rhythm with his stamping feet. Sometimes he thrust his neck forward, with his eyes closed, his hands grasping downwards. At other times he leaned his neck backwards, with his hands stretched outwards and a look of great longing on his face.

Van der Post interpreted the former as being 'the dance of the little hunger', and the latter as 'the dance of the great hunger'. The former was a plea to Mother Earth for food; the latter was a plea to Grandma Sky (the constellation Sirius) for eternity, and the raising of dust from the earth to cover his footsteps when he finally disappeared from the world. Both dances were individual rather than group dances, and were 'the great terminal dances of Bushman life'. Van der Post surmised that Franz Taibosh had been 'singularly lonely and exiled' in New York, like the Bushman convict longing for open spaces who withers and dies in the confinement of a jail. Frances Patterson countered: 'But he always appeared so happy that one didn't suspect there could be anything important lacking in his life.' The children for whom Franz danced were entranced by him: 'There was not a child who entered the family who did not instantly become his friend.'[1]

@

Evelyn Cook, writing from California, began looking for work back east for herself as well as Franz in the middle of January 1939. She wrote to J.W. Conklin of the Conklin Shows in Hamilton, Ontario, asking for work that summer in Canada as an equestrian alongside Franz working in the Lewiston sideshow. Conklin's reply was mildly welcoming but cautioned her that he would not be re-engaging the Lewistons that year. He would instead be organizing his own sideshow, which Clicko could join at 'the very lowest salary you would take for him for a season of five months starting on April 29th'.

'Personally, I like Harry very much,' Conklin said of Lewiston, but Harry had overstepped the mark 'with the Blow Off attraction he presented in the annexe of his sideshow during 1938'. Evidently he meant the exposures in an extra tent—before they were replaced by a flea-circus—of either Leo-Leona the hermaphrodite or the nudity of Stella Card Rogan, the tattooed lady.

Conklin was to visit Los Angeles in February, but negotiations were inconclusive. Evelyn, Franz and Barbara returned east by train to New York City, evidently to stay once again at the Hôtel des Artistes. But Franz was bored with the social round, and eager to work again with Harry Lewiston's Fair Freaks. He enjoyed being with Harry and Rose, who were kind to him. No doubt he also preferred their show's slower pace of moving from place to place, once every one to three weeks, rather than once every one to three days as he had done for twenty-odd years with the Big Show.

Evelyn Cook as 'guardian of Franz Taibosh' made the arrangements for him to rejoin Lewiston's World's Fair Freaks at Chicago from 13 April 1939 until February 1940, for $30 a week in summer and $15 in winter, plus 'food, transportation, and laundry to be paid for by Harry and Rose Lewiston'. The contract was signed and sworn on 17 March 1939.[2]

Harry and Rose Lewiston, with a small son in tow, ran a small group of artists almost as a family affair, recruiting only their friends such as Kongee, a quiet Indian Muslim, who silently jabbed pins into himself and was billed as 'the human pincushion'. The Lewistons had made good money the previous summer during their second year attached to the Conklin carnival, especially at the annual Canadian National Exposition in Toronto, with attractions such as the microcephalic Negro 'pinheads' Kiko and Sulu. They had been able to buy a spanking new aluminium trailer for themselves to live in on the road; but after breaking with Conklin, over the issue of the blow-off, they had done less well as an independent show over the rest of 1938. Now, in 1939, Harry

Lewiston hoped to repeat his previous success at the 1933 Chicago World's Fair, at the 1939 New York World's Fair.

The initial appearance of the World's Fair Freaks in April 1939 was in combination with the Dee Aldrich sideshow attached to the Barnes-Carruthers circus at the Chicago Stadium. The combined show was advertised as featuring not only 'the Television Girl, the Girl in the Gold Fishbowl; Elma Von Linn, three-legged woman; Eldo Clark, anatomical marvel', but also 'Bushman and the Pinheads'.[3]

From April until November 1939, Franz toured once more with the World's Fair Freaks, but Harry Lewiston failed to get an official stand at the New York World's Fair. Instead, individual performers were loaned to other shows there, such as to the midget village. Rose Lewiston's fortune-tellers found employment at the fair, while Harry went off by himself touring with his snake act, attached to the William Glick shows. As for Franz Taibosh, he divided his time between staying with Rose at the World's Fair and touring in the aluminium trailer with Harry.

The New York World's Fair opened at Flushing Meadow on Long Island at the beginning of May 1939. War fever was raging across the Atlantic, but the organizers trusted that there would be no depression in the amusement industry. They were duly gratified when up to six hundred thousand people came to the fair on the day it opened.

We do not know exactly where Franz performed. Likely venues include the Miracle Town of midgets, the John Hix Odditorium that paraded body-contortionists and bearded ladies, and the 'Strange As It Seems' show. Colleagues from the Ringling-Barnum circus made guest appearances at the fair in shows such as Bull Burns's Canary circus. Other midway attractions included the Snapper cuddle-up tub, the Laff-in-the-Dark, a midget auto speed-race and 180-ft-high Sky Ride, plus a giant roller-coaster and the Fun House. There was also a Cuban village, Seminole and Hopi villages, and a Merrie England village, as well as plentiful vaudeville, musical talent and girlie shows. Merrie England offered zippy forty-five-minute stage versions of *The Comedy of Errors*, *A Midsummer Night's Dream*, *As You Like It* and *The Taming of the Shrew*. A sketch company called Philip Lord's Gang Busters staged anti-crime and anti-drug shows. The latest dance craze was jiving to the jitterbug. *Billboard* ran a headline in the style of *Variety*: 'Phooey on jitterbugs: campus raps rhythm-maniacs as neurotic jive peasants'.

But the New York World's Fair was a commercial flop. The circus man Frank Hamib had to turn his menagerie of wild African animals into a 'Zulu show' with black American actors, but that failed after just one week. Buck's

Wild West show first turned itself into Jungleland and then collapsed. Even the mechanical model of the Victoria Falls in the British official pavilion had to be closed down after problems in spouting. John North's Wild West show, called 'Cavalcade of the Centaurs', only took prime spot because it proffered both 'steers and sex'—stampeding cattle and no less than sixteen naked Lady Godivas on horseback. The favourite nightspot was the Cuban village, which gained notoriety after two women were arrested for indecent exposure during a nudist competition.

Business was so bad by the beginning of July that many shows closed, and the downturn in fair attendance continued into August. War depression had after all crossed the Atlantic, and with it came other European hostilities. Around this time, Jews like Harry Lewiston were beaten up by Fascist thugs.[4]

In August 1939 'Old Billy', the redoubtable showbiz weekly *Billboard*, gave recognition to Clicko as something of an institution in the world of show business. It carried a photograph of Clicko together with Harry Lewiston at Rochester, upstate New York. Franz is shown cupping a hand to his ear as if rather deaf. The story on the World's Fair Freaks gave him star billing, with his name immediately after Harry Lewiston's and before that of the show's master of ceremonies.

It is not known exactly where the World's Fair Freaks appeared in and around Rochester that August. Possibilities in the vicinity included Dreamland (former Breeze) Park at Rochester—with 'Jay-Dee the Ape Man' and free aerial gymnastics—and the 26th annual Caledonian fair at Watertown, the 99th Lake Ontario county fair in the Bristol hills, and—not so far away—the Niagara county fair at Lockport.

Events in Europe proceeded apace, with their reverberations in America. The *Rochester Democrat and Chronicle* of 3 August 1939 reported that Hollywood planned to make a movie about Pastor Niemöller, now in a German concentration camp. On 16 August the newspaper featured a story about the Hitlerite leader of the German-American Bund who had been summoned to appear before the House of Representatives' committee on Un-American Activities, and its cartoonist noted: 'Hitler keeps *five astrologers!*' and 'that, in their combined reading of the stars, the climax of the fuehrer's career is seen to be coming *this September*'. (He obliged by invading Poland two weeks later.)

Harry Lewiston was relieved that he had not invested in his own show at the New York World's Fair. He and Rose prepared themselves to take their show on the road again for the winter season, with their 'advance man' fixing up venues in empty city-centre stores. On its 'Museums' page, *Billboard* tells us that Lewiston's World's Fair Freaks opened in the old Woolworth's store building at Danville, Virginia, for a ten-day stint on 26 October 1939. Heavy attendance was reported because of spot ads on local radio. The show was said to have greatly improved since 1938, with new scenery and lighting. Apart from Franz, his stage-name consistently spelt 'Cliko', featuring as the lead attraction, there were musicians, the sword-swallower, the fire-eater, the chimpanzee, Harry's giant python—and precious few real 'freaks'.

A subsequent headline in *Billboard* reads: 'World's Fair Freaks clicks in Danville; Lewiston hurt'. Harry Lewiston had been injured while unpacking the giant python but was fit enough for the little show to move on to 407 Market Street in Parkersburg, West Virginia. Business was again good there, and the show then proceeded to reasonable (rather than good) business at 205 Main Street in Zanesville. By the latter part of November the show went on from Zanesville to Pittsburgh, where it was set up on the corner of Wood Street and Liberty Avenue, for an indefinite period.[5]

Cook family tradition says that Franz fell ill in November 1939 and had to be collected by Frances Sullivan. This was to be confirmed nine months later by the Sullivan family's physician, who stated that Franz Taibosh had been suffering from a congestive heart condition for nine months—though family tradition is almost certainly wrong in suggesting that Frances collected Franz from Toronto, rather than Pittsburgh or a previous stop. No doubt stressed by the onset of cold weather and long nights, he was complaining of tiredness and possibly influenza. Hence Franz spent three unusually cold months including Christmas with Frances and her husband at Claverack— before returning to the Lewistons' show in the latter part of February 1940.

It is possible that Franz was still present when the Lewistons celebrated Thanksgiving on 20 November at Pittsburgh. Lewiston's World's Fair Freaks appears to have gone on to Minneapolis, where it closed on 24 December for a party, and was featured in a radio broadcast. In January 1940 the show reached Ohio, where it met sub-zero weather at Youngstown and many performers caught chills, before passing on to 211 South High Street at Columbus, Ohio, where the temperature dropped to four degrees below freezing at eleven on the morning of 18 January. The show was so short of attractions by mid-January that it had to advertise in *Billboard* once again: 'Harry Lewiston wants outstanding side show features'.

On 22 January 1940, the Lewiston show opened at Vine Street in Cincinnati. Unusually cold weather continued, and the show moved south to Lexington, Kentucky, where once again it featured on local radio and entertained a local police chief. After thirteen days in Lexington, where the show brought in fifteen thousand people, it opened at Knoxville, Tennessee. On Sunday, 18 February 1940, the *Knoxville Journal* reported 'World's Fair Freaks will be shown here', from the following day at the Old Sentinel Building, Gay Street and Church Avenue. Twenty-eight people would appear from Monday to Saturday with continuous performances from 11 am to 11 pm, but there was no mention of Franz Taibosh.

Franz's heart never fully recovered from his winter illness, but he rejoined the Lewiston tour when it moved to the warmer South. An item in *Billboard*, datelined Knoxville, Tennessee, 24 February 1940, tells us that Franz was interviewed by his fellow artiste Earl Hall on a local radio programme, 'Merry-go-round', on station WNOX.

Billboard claimed that there had been good local newspaper coverage for the Lewiston show at Knoxville, but only the above item has been located. There was little other news in the papers: the Second World War was still in its 'phoney' stage in Europe. *Gone with the Wind* was breaking all audience records. Leon Trotsky was quoted from his Mexican exile as predicting that one day 'the United States would rule supreme [but] over a "desolate and miserable planet."'

Franz Taibosh presumably lasted out the rest of the Lewistons' winter tour up to March 1940. The Lewistons drew up a new contract for the summer season, dated March 1940 (though the actual day was not filled in), repeating the same terms as the previous contract of March 1939. But the contract was never witnessed and sworn before a notary public. Nor was 'Cliko the African Dancing Bushman' actually advertised as part of the Lewistons' summer tour beginning April 1940. Lewiston had decided to concentrate that summer—not very successfully as it turned out—on the exhibition of freak farm animals.

Franz had a reputation in sideshow circles for being so lively and robust that he had never taken a sick day off. But even a good trouper cannot troupe for ever. He was old and exhausted, and weakened by the winter's illness, and had reached the limit of his ability.[6]

Franz stayed out the spring and summer in retirement with Frances and Pat Sullivan at Claverack near Hudson. There, in the intense heat and humidity of July and August, he faced what *Billboard* called 'The final curtain'. Another old trouper, 'Doc' Alstone, referred to retirement in old age from the circus as being like standing in the 'connection'—the tented tube where performers enter the big top—waiting for the ringmaster's whistle to call the artist to perform on the other side.

August 1940 saw momentous events across the Atlantic. In the words of the *Washington Post*: 'Beginning August 8, the mighty German air force, the spearhead of all Hitler's victories, began to visit total war on Britain. A thousand raiders a day is now a daily occurrence. This great battle is … the Battle of Britain.'

The last photograph of Franz Taibosh (as shown by Frances Patterson to Laurens van der Post in 1959) may be from 1940. It portrayed him sitting indoors, in heavy carpet slippers and a thick dressing-gown. His skin was wrinkled, his hair white, his cheeks sunken. He was apparently toothless and his dry lips were tightly drawn. But there was a look of endearment on his face for someone out of shot. Frances Patterson said that Franz had been induced to come out of bed when very weak. The account in *A Mantis Carol* claims that she had sat at the bedside of Franz, holding his hand for a long time. He held her hand tight but lay still. Then he stirred, opened his eyes, and smiled—'not as an old man but as he smiled when I first met him in the prime of his life.'

Franz was not a man given to profound utterances about life and death, but as he was dying his thoughts turned in that direction. He was baptized and received into the faith by the parish priest at St Mary's Church in Hudson, the Sullivans' Roman Catholic parish church.

The priest was subsequently most insistent that it was a genuine conversion, rather than a panicky deathbed repentance, and denied that Franz Taibosh was in any way unable to grasp what he was doing. Frances and Patrick Sullivan were devout and observant Catholics, and no doubt over the years had often taken Franz with them to church, as an enquirer unto the faith. Franz would have grasped the meaning of the sacraments and of the proximity of God to Man through Love and through Christ's Resurrection from the dead, and could now savour the fulfilment of repentance and the joy of true faith. In the words of the Psalm (71: 7–8): 'I am become as it were a *monster* unto many: but my sure trust is in thee. O let my mouth be filled with thy praise: that I may sing of thy glory and honour all the day long. Cast me not away in the time of [old] age: forsake me not when my strength faileth me.'[7]

There was of course no need to give Franz an extra baptismal name:

'Franz' was perfectly adequate, as a version of the same saint's name carried by both Frank Cook and Frances Cook Sullivan. Barbara Cook believes that Franz Taibosh felt closer to her sister Frances than to any other person in the world. Frances had had no children of her own. She was a good woman, a much better 'mother' to her half-sister than Evelyn Joyce Cook.

A couple of days after his baptism, Franz Taibosh died at the home of Frances and Patrick Sullivan, at Claverack, on Saturday, 31 August 1940. He must have been at least seventy years old, but not more than eighty— hardly the hundred and fifteen years credited in his obituaries. The death was certified by Lawrence J. Early, MD. The cause of death was said to be congestive heart failure, from which he had been suffering for nine months, and hypertensive heart and arterial diseases from which he had been suffering for nine years.

After a funeral service at St Mary's in Hudson, the casket of Franz Taibosh was carried by the undertaker (Neal M. Anderson) and buried in Cedar Park Cemetery. Franz Taibosh's death certificate described him as single, aged about 115, *Occupation*: 'Showman—Retired—Circus Ringling Bros.', *Birthplace*: South Africa, *Father's Name*: Haus Taibosh [an obvious slip for 'Hans'], *Mother's Maiden Name*: Unknown.[8]

A couple of days after Franz died, Nazi Germany celebrated one year of its 'revolutionary history' in creating the New Europe. There was only one significant enemy left: an offshore island. The Sunday edition of the *New York Times* for 1 September reproduced a cartoon from the *Christian Science Monitor*, showing Great Britain springing back from Nazism—while Austria, Poland, Belgium, France and Norway all fell down before it.[9]

*Sullivan family gravestone including Franz Taibosh,
Cedar Park, Hudson, N.Y.*

◉

Franz Taibosh was buried in section 14-H, in the Roman Catholic section of Cedar Park Cemetery. In November 1947, when Patrick Sullivan died, Franz's casket was disinterred and reburied next to Pat's in Plot 85 of the family section 9-H in the south-eastern corner of Cedar Park. When Frances Cook Sullivan eventually died, aged eighty-one, in 1981, she was buried next to them. A new headstone for the Sullivan family plot, with all three names on it, was unveiled in 1993.

Visitors may find the sturdy grey headstone of the Sullivan family among rows of identically shaped headstones on a green lawn. Under the heading of Sullivan, three names are appended: 'Franz Taibosh died 1940/ Patrick K. 1900 1947/ Frances C. 1900 1981'.[10]

CONCLUSION
A MANTIS CAROL?

WHEN FRANZ TAIBOSH DIED in 1940, an obituary in the *New York Times* called him 'the only African bushman ever exhibited in this country'.[1] Two decades later, the traveller and storyteller Laurens van der Post came across memories of Taibosh living in New York, and incorporated the tale some years later in his fact-based novel *A Mantis Carol*. Van der Post confessed that he had failed to establish where in Africa the Bushman came from, or how he had arrived in America.

Franz can be seen as a motherless child who discovered that he could transcend bullying by humour and ecstatic dancing. He eventually found a nest with the motherly, sisterly and daughterly women of the Cook-cum-Sullivan family, and died in the arms of Mother Church as a baptized Catholic. A less charitable view might see him as a failure in life and love, reduced to a bottom-pinching old pest: his grabbing and pestering of women was obviously sexually aggressive, rather than just a longing for feminine solace.

My initial view of Franz Taibosh was as a passive victim, meekly led into purgatory by Paddy Hepston. The picture that emerges from Franz Taibosh's later career in America is more complex. He was perfectly capable of making vital decisions, notably his decision not to go back to Africa, but to stay on with the Cook–Sullivan family.

However, the significance of the life of Franz Taibosh is greater than that of one individual: it highlights strands of interlinked history on three continents. It raises questions about the rise and fall of 'scientific racism', and about the repression and simulated expression of 'wildness' in popular entertainment. It shows how Africa and Africans were perceived by early-twentieth-century Westerners, and fills the gap in explaining how the Western image of African Bushmen has evolved from dangerous wildness to their being seen as benevolent universal ancestors.

◎

Franz Taibosh was almost the last Wild Man in captivity, but there were still others touring in the race exhibits of Nazi Germany. Franz died at the height of the Battle of Britain, a pivotal moment when the most advanced technology combined with the most vicious racial terrorism was first turned back from world domination.

Scientific racism—the nineteenth-century equation between technological mastery and biological mastery—had reached its peak by the 1920–1930s.[2] Positivistic belief in science as the inevitable advance of discovery of absolute universal truths—during a century when technological and moral progress could be equated—was beginning to be questioned. Another Franz, the German-born American anthropologist Franz Boas, the same man who had organized the demeaning racial exhibits at the 1904 St Louis World's Fair, now concluded that there was no necessary connection between race and culture or personality. Individuals and cultures should be judged in their own lights.

A persistent theme in this book has been the dichotomy and tension between the wild and the tame, the savage and the civilized, the impulsive and the intentional. Clicko represented the former but, in order to do so in performance, he had to finely tune such emotions through the application of intellect.

The 'paradox of acting' in both naturalistic theatre and the more pantomimic expressions of dance and opera—how to impose technique on spontaneity—has long been recognized. Early-nineteenth-century actors like Edmund Kean and Edwin Forrest were credited with channelling 'fitful impulse' or elemental forces through 'nice calculation': evoking the ravening beast within them without losing control. The performance scholar Jane R. Goodall has given the name 'beast actors' to such performers. Franz Taibosh played perfectly on the anxieties over 'resurgence of primitive and animal tendencies' and 'barely submerged savagery' that have kept audiences on the edge of their seats during the acts of uncaged panthers, like Henry Irving and Laurence Olivier, prowling the stage.[3]

In America, Franz Taibosh was known for acting out parodies of great and pompous people. Dance-drama could be a safety valve from political oppression as well as a Dionysian release from psychological suppression. Jean Rouch's 1954 documentary film *Les Maîtres fous* showed Gold Coast migrant workers ridiculing the absurd manners of their colonial masters. Terence Ranger has shown this extensively in his pioneering historical study of *Dance and Society in Eastern Africa*.[4] But the fact that Franz had previously been noted for his wonderful imitations of wild animals in dance reminds us that sincere tribute to the gods might be fused or confused with mockery.

Dancing, specifically folk or traditional dancing, is an assertion of cultural identity. With the disappearance of actual opportunities for hunting, trance-dancing in search of the spirits of wild animals became the particular marker of Khoesan hunter ideology and identity.[5] What was perceived as an epileptic fit on the part of Franz Taibosh dancing in a Cambridge theatre in 1914 was in all probability the beginnings of a trance, journeying back from present individual realities to an imaginary communal past.

As a showman, Franz Taibosh must bear some responsibility for the propagation by popular entertainment acts in the West, and particularly in America, of freakish racist ideas. In his memoirs, Franz's friend the freak-show manager Harry Lewiston pondered on the lies and distortions about Africa and Africans he had planted in the minds of millions of Americans by his sideshow and midway lectures: 'Since that time I've often wondered how many arguments my "facts" generated. Even those who didn't pay to see our show were exposed to some of this so-called African lore which was pure hokum.'

We can make excuses for Franz Taibosh. But we do not need to go as far as Ben Shephard and argue that it is 'absurd and censorious' to condemn early-twentieth-century black performers for going along with 'what the market wanted'. Franz Taibosh was just an ordinary person and the tide of racism was in full flood; he did not raise his head above the tide and swim against it. Off stage he proved his humanity in many small ways, and attracted the devotion of many. But on stage, his act was a libel on a continent and its peoples.[6]

Franz Taibosh both presaged and then posthumously played a direct part in what Ben Shephard has called the mutation—'in the supple hands of Laurens van der Post'—of the image of Bushmen from 'bestial savages' into 'unspoiled children of nature, to be envied by degraded and industrialized Westerners'. (We may object that P.T. Barnum and others had begun this 'mutation' many years earlier by portraying previously repulsive Bushmen as adorable Earthmen.) Transformation of the Bushman image has also been fed in recent years by the increased militancy of so-called First Nations throughout the world, and by the rise of advocacy groups in the West such as Survival International campaigning on behalf of indigenous peoples. The struggle of some Bushmen to establish rights of permanent residence in a Kalahari game reserve in Botswana has shot into the world headlines since 2000.

Clicko the Wild Dancing Bushman was seen by millions of people in North America between 1917 and 1940, and must have affected the consciousness of a considerable number. They were taught that Clicko was an authentic representative of his 'race', and that Bushmen were remnant people from the Stone Age. But they would also have seen that Clicko's savagery could be tamed. In much the same way as Walt Disney turned previously repulsive dwarfs into darlings for Snow White, children in particular came to see Clicko the Bushman as a lovable character. Cuddly rather than cruel.

Ten years after the death of Franz Taibosh, the Marshall family from Massachusetts ventured into the Kalahari and began the first really systematic ethnography of Bushmen since Dorothea Bleek and Lucy Lloyd. (As Robert Gordon has shown, the Denver Museum expedition of 1929–30 dashed through Namibia to confirm crude old stereotypes rather than living with and observing and talking with Bushmen.) The Marshalls reflected post-war disillusionment with modern industrial society threatened with atomic suicide, and wished to rediscover pristine hunter-gatherer roots.[7] Young John Marshall began to experiment with making ethnographic documentary films, increasingly allowing subjects to speak for themselves. Meanwhile, a documentary of the old newsreel-type with sententious over-voice, titled *Remnants of a Stone Age People*, made by Louis Knobel for the South African government, was nominated for best short film at the Cannes film festival of 1953.[8]

The travel writer Colonel Laurens van der Post was then commissioned by the BBC to produce a documentary series for television. Born in the Orange Free State of South Africa, Van der Post had affectionate memories of a nursemaid (transmuted from Coloured to Bushman in his various memoirs) and guilty memories of horrific tales his grandfather told of going out to hunt and shoot Bushmen as vermin. Van der Post's *The Lost World of the Kalahari* (BBC-tv, June 1956) was a hit television series in Britain and America and was then a book published in paperback. Their powerful combination of curiosity, affection and guilt has coloured Western perceptions of the Bushmen of the Kalahari ever since.

It was *The Lost World of the Kalahari* that led Laurens van der Post to the story of Franz Taibosh, though he called him 'Hans Taaibosch'. On a visit to publicize the book and film in New York in December 1959, he was approached by a woman troubled by her dreams of a praying mantis. This led him in turn to meet 'an attractive woman whom I took to be in her mid-thirties', who came to his hotel room and showed him photographs—one of a bronze sculpture which he assumed she had made—and who recounted at length her memories of the Bushman, while he made notes.

Van der Post was intrigued by the idea of a Bushman from the Kalahari surviving in the canyons of New York City. But he wrote nothing about 'Hans Taaibosch' until fifteen years later, and then somewhat in a hurry without his wife's usual sub-editing. It was a semi-mystical biographical novel titled *A Mantis Carol* (1975). The book was more a novel rather than a biography because it contained so many speculations and factual guesses, though it did catch some of the spirit of the man.

The *Mantis* of the book's title was the insect god that Southern San people danced for—Van der Post's sources for Bushman culture being invariably the literary collections made by Dorothea Bleek and Lucy Lloyd. The *Carol* was a Christmas song for the Christ child, who was to die but who was to rise again from the dead. The book worked its way towards the resolution of Khoesan and Christian beliefs. Dance was seen as the way to assuage the 'great hunger' within us, which is the hunger for Love—the reconciliation of the great paradox of 'history, time and space transcended in terms of its one great and for ever Now'. Hans Taaibosch was portrayed as a victim, as an innocent abroad, or as a sort of extra-terrestrial being at large in New York but wanting to go back home to the Kalahari, and now after death recruiting his last best hope—Laurens van der Post himself—to get him back.

Laurens van der Post's fascination with Bushmen may partly be attributed to the influence of the philosopher-psychologist Carl Jung, searching for the 'primitive shadow', though Van der Post never made any explicit connection between Hans Taaibosch and the small brown man of Jung's *Memories, Dreams and Reflections*.

The book *A Mantis Carol* marks a signpost on Van der Post's journey of self-discovery that was to result in him calling himself a White Bushman.[9] It is a journey that other white South Africans have since claimed to be following. The identification of white suburbanites with Bushmen in the wilds was popularized by *The Gods Must Be Crazy* films of the 1980s. It was reinforced in the 1990s by the assertion of a common Afrikaans language identity and hunting heritage between Bushmen and Boers, facing the supposedly common threat of Black African empowerment.

There is a further intriguing twist. If indeed, as his biographer claims, Laurens van der Post was descended from Krotoa (Eva the Hottentot) of the 1650s, then Laurens and Franz Taibosh were distant cousins![10]

What he had actually been told by his hotel visitor in 1959 is not clear, but Laurens van der Post exercised great poetic licence in *A Mantis Carol*. He wrote a scene in which the sculptor is modelling Hans Taaibosch's head with wet clay, while Hans continually jumps off his chair to stand beside her. 'Every time he noticed how like his own likeness the clay was growing under her hands, he would do a little dance of acknowledgement for her, before bounding gaily back to his chair.' When the clay head was finished, he came up and greeted it with 'You, Hans Taaibosch, you child of …'—here he gave the clicking name of some ancestral figure.

> 'What are you doing there with my face but without my body?'
> He then laughed a deep, low laugh of content from the pit of his stomach. Then solemn as I had never known him, he put his hand on my shoulder, to ask, 'Did you really do that just for old Taaibosch—just for him?'
> I said, why yes, of course. And do you know, he sat down on the studio floor, wept for the one and only time I've ever seen him weep and then, just as suddenly, jumped up and did a dance all round the studio that shook the furniture.

The sculpture acted like a mirror in restoring Hans's vision of himself. The 'mirror of our time' has cracked, added Van der Post, 'and indeed for Taaibosch must have been utterly shattered, until on that day … the clay still warm between her fingers was fulfilled.' He quotes the sculptor as saying, 'from that day on, I believe he was happier than ever, and somehow more confident'.

According to *A Mantis Carol*, Hans Taaibosch on his deathbed in a New York skyscraper asked 'Dolly'—his name for the sculptor, or was it her niece?—to dance for him. 'Dolly, dance for me, please. Please dance for me, Dolly, I have so often danced for you.' She got up to dance, kicking off her shoes, and began to dance the dance of the great hunger with heavy stamping of her feet, with her back to him. But, even as she began, she heard the death rattle in Taaibosch's throat expelling the air from his lungs. 'I instantly whirled about, and Taaibosch had gone … on a great long walkabout of the universe.' (Once again, Van der Post uses Australian imagery of the dreamtime and walkabouts.) A doctor was summoned, who confirmed Taaibosch's death.[11]

We now know the name of the young woman who brought photographs to show to Laurens van der Post in a New York hotel penthouse in December 1959. Frances Patterson—described by Barbara Cook many years later as 'a talented, sensitive and very fragile person'—was a few years older than Barbara, and had lived in the same hotel as Evelyn and Barbara and Franz Taibosh in New York City during the later 1930s. But Van der Post deliberately confused or conflated Frances Patterson with the distinguished sculptor Malvina Hoffman, who appears to have been her aunt.

The photograph of Franz Taibosh's head in bronze, which Frances Patterson showed to Laurens van der Post, was a sculpture by Malvina Hoffman, owned by the Field Museum in Chicago. It was somewhat inferior in composition to Hoffman's other sculptures, and appears to be a study towards her exhibition in the Hall of Man at the Field Museum in 1933. It is not a good likeness but is obviously based on a fine 1931 photograph of Franz Taibosh's head and shoulders still held by the museum. Hence we may suggest that Malvina Hoffman worked from the photograph, and may doubt whether Franz ever sat for her. If he did indeed sit, then the sitting can be dated from a reference in *A Mantis Carol* to October–November 1932, when Franklin D. Roosevelt was elected with the disapproval of Frank Cook. A later date is ruled out by Malvina Hoffman's statement that the only sculptures that she added to the Hall of Man exhibition after its 1933 opening were those of American Indians.[12]

In Britain, publication of *A Mantis Carol* was timed to catch the Christmas market of 1975, with American publication following in early 1976. Reviews in the British and American press were 'cool, sparse and rather baffled'. But Laurens van der Post's otherwise very critical biographer, J.D.F. Jones, believes it to be 'one of Laurens's most interesting, infuriating, least known books'.[13]

Van der Post's books about the Kalahari Bushmen, including *A Mantis Carol*, have received a mauling at the hands of recent writers. Mathias Guenther's *Tricksters and Trancers: Bushman Religion and Society* dismissed Van der Post's knowledge of Bushman religion as bogus, twisted out of nineteenth-century literary sources without 'the protocol of ethnographic data gathering'. Guenther was particularly scathing about Van der Post's equation of the Mantis with Jesus Christ, both seen as divine tricksters arbitrarily dispensing life and death. Edwin Wilmsen, on the other hand, has mocked Van der Post's latter-day self-identification as a White Bushman.[14]

To be fair to the late Sir Laurens, having learned that I had traced the previously unknown career of Franz Taibosh in Europe, he was most gracious in wishing me success in tracing Franz's origins in Africa—or, as he put it in *A Mantis Carol*, to 'find a place in the record of his people'.[15]

Frances Cook Sullivan, Evelyn Joyce Cook and Barbara Cook were somewhat hurt by the publication of *A Mantis Carol*. They felt that Franz Taibosh had been 'stolen' from them in distorted form, and that maybe Frances Patterson had not had the right to possess the photographs that she showed to Van der Post. According to J.D.F. Jones, Evelyn Joyce Cook wrote to Van der Post in May 1978 to reproach him for 'so much mis-information in your book'. In later years, Barbara Cook would dismiss *A Mantis Carol* as 'sheer fantasy'.

Evelyn Joyce Cook set out to write her own true account of the life of Franz Taibosh. She enrolled in an evening class for aspirant writers at a New York City college. Barbara, at that time living in the Bahamas and working for the *Nassau Guardian*, assisted her by writing to a journalist contact in South Africa, while Evelyn corresponded directly with Van der Post. But these enquiries produced no hard facts in reply about Franz Taibosh's African (and European) origins. The biography became a partial memoir of Franz's life in America. By 1980 Evelyn Joyce Cook had produced two versions of an introduction, and a number of draft chapters of a typescript she entitled 'I inherited a Bushman'.

In a letter of October 1980, Evelyn's friend the old circus lawyer F.B. Kelley (living in St Louis, Missouri), author of *The Great Circus Street Parade*, helpfully provided a list of contacts at possible publishers—Doubleday, Elsevier-Nelson, Morrow and Academy. Evelyn had already contacted Avon without success, though they thought that the story had charm. But the trail went dead; even Kelley could not find a publisher for his book on the circus tiger-tamer Mabel Stark. However, ten years later in January 1990 'the old Circus Gal' reportedly sent Laurens van der Post 'all sorts of fascinating information' (presumably a complete draft of the memoir). Circus historian Fred Pfening, Jr., then asked for a chapter from 'I inherited a Bushman' to be published in *Bandwagon: The Journal of the Circus Historical Society Inc.*, which he edited. 'This little pig went nightclubbing' was published as a *Bandwagon* article in January 1992.[16]

The author interviewing Barbara Cook de Romain near Oneonta, NY. (Prof. Robert J. Gordon)

I first bumped into the 'Wild Dancing Bushman' in a file of the Anti-Slavery and Aborigines' Protection Society papers, in Rhodes House Library at Oxford in 1967, but more or less forgot about him until about 1990. Then, thanks to Professor Bernth Lindfors of the University of Texas, I learned that the man I had read about dancing on stage in England had gone on to America to perform in the Ringling Brothers and Barnum & Bailey circus.

But where did Franz Taibosh originate from in Africa? I could find no trace of him around the Kalahari, from which that Oxford file said he had come. Laurens van der Post before his death told me that he had given up the quest for Taibosh's origins. But I was put in contact with Evelyn Cook before her death, and learned from Barbara Cook de Romain that Franz had been brought up on the farm of one Christian Roberts or Roberts Christian. While living and working in Botswana, I visited South Africa periodically and searched fruitlessly in old directories in libraries and archives. But I found no one who matched the details, until one day in the Cape Town archives when I was almost ready to catch a flight back home.

In one part of the archives there was a scatter of large leather-bound books that were eagerly consulted by amateur genealogists, while I sat in another part of the reading-room consulting documents brought from the vaults. In the hour I had remaining before leaving for the airport, I walked over and inspected the heavy volumes, which turned out to be handwritten registers of Cape Colony and Cape Province wills and estates from the 1870s to the early 1940s. I inspected each year under both *C* and *R* and there, towards the end of the last volume, I came across Christiaan Willem Roberts. He was the same man I had seen recorded in electoral rolls as plain Willem Roberts. After locating and talking with his son in Pretoria on the telephone, at last I had the key to rounding off this biography with the origins of Franz Taibosh.

There is at least one Taibos or Taaibosch family still living today in the town of Middelburg, close to Heydon on the northern edge of the Sneeubergen. The names Franz and Hans are commonplace among their relatives, some of whom live on the Camdeboo plains around the town of Aberdeen. An uncle with the name of Hans is recalled who worked for Boswell-Wilkie's circus in South Africa between the two world wars. But there is no memory of any uncle called Franz who disappeared just before the First World War.[17]

APPENDIX

1918–38 Circus Stands by
US State & Canadian Province

	1918	1919	1920	1921	1922	1923	1924	1925	1926	1927	1928	1929	1930	1931	1932	1933	1934	1935	1936	1937	1938
Alabama	-	3	3	-	2	1	3	3	1	2	1	1	4	-	1	3	-	3	6	4	(3)
Arizona	3	-	-	-	3	-	-	1	-	1	-	2	-	-	-	-	2	-	-	-	-
California	12	-	-	-	14	16	-	14	-	13	-	13	-	-	-	-	13	-	-	-	-
Colorado	4	3	-	-	1	1	-	-	-	-	-	-	-	-	-	1	1	-	3	-	-
Connecticut	6	5	5	4	2	4	5	4	4	3	3	3	5	2	5	5	6	6	6	4	-
Delaware	-	1	1	1	-	-	-	1	1	1	1	1	1	1	1	1	1	1	1	1	1
District of Columbia	1	1	1	1	1	1	1	1	1	1	1	1	1	1	1	1	1	1	1	1	
Florida	-	3	-	-	-	-	-	-	-	4	4	2	-	-	6	2	2	3	3	3	(11)
Georgia	-	7	2	-	5	-	1	-	1	2	3	4	-	1	-	1	5	3	3	3	(3)
Idaho	1	-	-	-	-	-	-	-	-	-	-	-	-	-	-	-	-	-	-	-	-
Illinois	5	2	6	11	1	2	1-	1	2	1	4	3	6	7	3	6	5	5	6	4	(5)
Indiana	1	4	3	5	1	-	4	1	2	2	3	3	1	3	3	4	4	2	2	2	1(1)
Iowa	-	1	3	6	-	9	-	7	7	7	-	1-	1-	1	6	4	3	9	9	7	(4)
Kansas	12	7	3	-	3	1-	3	8	8	5	5	-	3	1	1	2	2	9	9	3	(4)
Kentucky	-	-	-	2	-	-	-	-	1	-	1	1	-	-	-	1	1	2	2	-	-
Louisiana	-	1	2	-	7	2	-	1	2	5	2	5	5	2	2	4	5	5	2	4	(6)
Maine	-	-	-	-	3	-	1	1	1	1	1	1	1	-	1	1	3	3	-	3	-
Maryland	1	1	1	1	1	1	1	1	1	1	1	1	1	1	1	1	1	1	1	1	1
Massachusetts	10	7	8	7	4	5	3	3	4	2	3	3	5	4	5	6	8	4	4	4	1
Michigan	-	7	9	1	5	5	4	7	5	3	5	-	-	3	5	10	-	3	3	1	(3)
Minnesota	-	2	2	3	5	4	5	4	-	7	4	4	1	6	3	4	-	-	1	3	(7)
Mississippi	-	-	4	-	1	-	-	-	3	3	1	1	1	-	-	2	-	-	-	2	
Missouri	6	4	-	5	2	3	4	4	4	2	-	-	10	5	5	3	5	3	3	2	(5)
Montana	2	-	-	-	3	-	-	-	-	-	5	5	-	-	-	-	-	-	-	-	-
Nebraska	-	2	2	4	4	-	-	4	-	6	-	2	2	2	3	1	-	2	-	-	(1)
Nevada	-	-	-	-	-	-	-	-	-	-	-	-	-	-	-	1	1	-	-	-	-
New Hampshire	-	-	-	-	-	-	-	1	1	-	-	-	1	1	1	1	1	-	-	-	-
New Jersey	7	2	2	1	1	2	1	1	2	4	3	4	4	1	2	2	4	4	1	3	2
New Mexico	-	-	-	2	2	-	2	-	2	-	-	-	-	-	3	-	-	-	-	2	-

	1918	1919	1920	1921	1922	1923	1924	1925	1926	1927	1928	1929	1930	1931	1932	1933	1934	1935	1936	1937	1938
New York	12	12	11	14	9	9	10	9	6	12	10	8	15	12	16	8	13	11	10	10	7
North Carolina	-	4	2	7	2	5	1	8	-	5	-	5	-	-	-	6	2	3	6	5	(5)
North Dakota	-	-	-	-	2	1	-	4	-	3	5	5	-	-	-	-	-	-	-	-	(3)
Ohio	5	11	10	7	1	8	10	3	10	6	3	7	7	8	6	10	7	7	9	8	5
Oklahoma	3	9	2	-	-	2	11	-	15	-	10	-	4	-4	4	4	2	6	7	7	(9)
Oregon	1	-	-	-	2	3	-	2	-	2	-	4	-	-	-	-	-	-	-	-	-
Pennsylvania	2	14	9	11	6	8	14	7	8	7	8	5	8	9	9	3	15	10	6	10	5
Rhode Island	1	1	-	1	1	1	1	1	1	1	1	1	1	1	1	1	1	1	1	1	-
South Carolina	-	3	2	-	3	1	-	1	-	1	-	1	-	3	-	2	1	2	1	1	(1)
South Dakota	0	1	0	1	-	-	1	4	-	5	-	-	1	-	1	-	-	-	-	-	(7)
Tennessee	0	5	4	3	-	4	1	2	-	6	4	4	-	3	-	3	5	6	6	6	(5)
Texas	10	15	11	-	9	8	18	6	16	11	13	5	13	-	9	8	11	10	11	13	(18)
Utah	2	-	-	-	-	3	-	-	-	-	-	-	-	-	-	-	2	-	-	-	-
Vermont	-	-	-	-	-	-	-	-	-	-	-	-	-	-	-	-	-	-	-	-	-
Virginia	-	4	3	2	-	1	-	-	-	4	-	-	-	-	-	3	-	4	1	1	-
Washington State	6	-	-	-	5	3	-	4	-	4	6	-	-	-	-	-	-	-	-	-	-
West Virginia	-	4	4	-	-	-	4	-	-	1	-	-	-	4	-	1	1	1	-	-	1
Wisconsin	-	2	3	7	3	4	4	5	5	5	7	6	2	6	6	4	-	7	7	9	(1-)
Wyoming	1	-	-	-	-	-	-	-	-	-	-	-	-	-	-	-	-	-	-	-	-
CANADA																					
Alberta	-	-	-	-	4	3	-	-	-	3	-	-	-	-	-	-	-	-	-	-	-
British Columbia	-	-	-	-	-	-	-	-	-	2	-	-	-	-	-	-	-	-	-	-	-
Manitoba	-	-	-	-	2	1	-	-	-	1	-	-	-	-	-	-	-	-	-	-	-
Ontario	-	-	-	-	6	-	-	4	8	-	4	5	2	6	6	-	-	-	-	-	-
Quebec	-	-	-	-	3	-	-	2	-	1	1	1	-	-	-	-	-	-	-	-	-
Saskatchewan	-	-	-	-	2	5	-	-	-	4	-	-	-	-	-	-	-	-	-	-	-

Note: *1918: Barnum & Bailey; 1919–38: Ringling Brothers and Barnum & Bailey (1938 figures in brackets: from July, Al G. Barnes–Sells Floto). Based on locations listed in 1954 Ringling Brothers and Barnum & Bailey Circus Route Book, link available from Circus Historical Society main web-page <www.circushistory.org>. These figures do not always exactly correlate with other sources, e.g. Billboard.*

NOTES

Introduction

1. Jung (1967: 204); Samuels (1995: 4–5); McGuire (1991: 299–3); Van der Post 1976b: 53 (1976: 53 & 197).
2. The term 'Coloured' is more fully defined in Adhikari (2005).
3. *Oxford English Dictionary*, 2nd edn (hereafter *OED–2*), vol. 2, p. 691, entry on 'Bushman'.

Chapter 1

1. Prof. Anthony Traill (University of Witwatersrand) wrote to this author, email 29 June 2002, that *koo–rang* is 'very much like' the Korana word /*oo–da–s* (its opening click–consonant marked as / on a typewriter), citing Nienaber (1963: 382) that the same word was recorded as *t'oodas* by the traveller P.B. Borcherds in 1861, and adding, 'The –ng is a mystery. It may represent nasalization of the preceding vowel but there are no nasal vowels in the above form.'
2. Field Museum (Chicago) photo no. 67644 caption. Taibos is *Rhus burchelli* in Latin, *mogodiri* in Setswana. See Ferreira (1929: 354). For uses of taibos see *South African Commercial Advertiser*, 23 March 1831; for place names see Defense Intelligence Agency (1992); Maingard (1962: vii).
3. British Parliamentary Papers (BPP), no. 69 of September 1837: 'Papers Relative to the Wesleyan Missions and to the State of Heathen Countries'; M.R. Taaibosch 1869 quoted in Maingard (1932: 109 & 113). Confirmation that the Korana 'had inhabited the site of Cape Town and the vicinity when the Dutch took possession of the colony' can be found in Arbousset & Daumas (1836) cited by Strauss (1979: 2); also Backhouse (1839) cited by Engelbrecht (1936: 4); Stow (1905: 110); Maingard (1932: 110); Schapera (1953: 25); Penn (1995).
4. Rev. Edward Terry, *A Voyage to East India*, 1655, as quoted in Edwards & Walvin (1983: 11–12): the 'guts' were dried animal intestines regarded as a medicinal necklace; Theal (1927/1964: 374–6). See also Cope (1967); Edwards & Walvin (1983: 3–4 & 10).
5. Fairbridge (1931: 23–38); Heap (1993: 17–26); Nienaber & Raper (1983: 142); E. Raper (1987: 69–70). Until the mid-nineteenth century the lower Orange River and its Vaal tributary were considered to be one Great River or Gei-Gariep. Above the Vaal confluence, the upper Orange was considered to be a separate river, the Nu-Gariep or Black River,

known to the English as the Cradock.

6. Breutz (1955–6: 30–1); Breutz (1968: 28).
7. Willcox (1986); Penn (1999); Halford (c.1930s).
8. Sanders (1975: 43, 50–2 & 196–7); Mears (1970: 21–2).
9. BBP reprint of C. 4275 of February 1885: 'Further Correspondence re ... Transvaal and Adjacent Territories', 71/57.
10. Breutz (1968: 17–21); Shillington (1985). *Cape Argus*, 3 Dec. 1885, 2; 4 Dec., 4; 8 Dec., 3; 10 Dec., 3; 12 Dec., 3; 24 Dec., 3; Van Onselen (1996).
11. State of New York, County Court, County of Columbia: 'In the matter of ... Franz Taibosh, alias Clicko, an alleged incompetent person', Order & Petition, filed 12 April 1937 by Attorney Lewis E. McNamee (copies in Cook Family Papers); Barbara Cook de Raczynska (*Nassau Guardian*, Bahamas) to Richard Lytton (*Cape Argus*, Cape Town), 29 Dec. 1958; Evelyn Joyce Cook (New York) to Lytton, 11 Jan. 1959 (in possession of South African Museum, Cape Town; copies courtesy of Rob Gordon).
12. Neville et al. (1994: 65–9); Gutsche (1968); Cape Town Deeds Office: Deeds vol. 4/B.56.A (Middelburg, Eastern Cape), Farms Middelburg 141–143; Cape Town Archives, MOCC 89146/1943: Estate of Christiaan Willem Roberts. As well as those bearing the surnames Christian and Christiani, there are Robarts, Robberts, Robertse and Robertze families in South Africa.
13. Palmer (1990: 283).
14. Southey (1990: 117 & 119–20); Cape Town Deeds Office, vol. 4/B.56.A: Middelburg (Eastern Cape), Farms Mid. 142/1, 143/1, 143/1/1, 144/1.
15. South African Museum, Cape Town: Correspondence of Evelyn Joyce Cook & Barbara Cook de Raczynska [later de Romain] addressed to Richard Lytton (*Cape Argus*), Dec. 1958 – Jan. 1959 (photocopy courtesy of Robert J. Gordon).
16. Palmer (1990: 33–4); Peires (1989); Mandela (1994); Kirby (1968).
17. Hewitt (1931). I am grateful to Sven Ouzman of the National Museum at Bloemfontein for this interpretation and a photocopy of Hewitt (1931).
18. *The Star* (Johannesburg), 8 Oct. 1913, 10c; BBP, reprint of C. 4275 of February 1885, 71/57. I have not followed the suggestion that Franz was referring to 'half a century ago ... early wars in the Cape' fought by Cape colonial rather than British imperial troops.
19. Palmer (1990: 283).
20. Cape Voters' List 1899. See Burchell (1882–4/1953), vol. 2, 126.
21. Author's telephone interview with Christiaan Willem Roberts (grandson, 1938–), Pretoria, 21 June 1999; Amery (1907), vol. 5, 129; Maurice (1910), vol. 4, 71, 238 & 463–5; Southey (1990: 119). See also Aucamp typescript (n.d.: 26–8).
22. Southey (1990: 115 & 118–19); Amery (1907), vol. 6, 379–529; Cape Town Archives, CCP 11/1/43 1903, Cape of Good Hope Voters' Roll, Electoral District of Middelburg, Field-cornetcy no. 2 Naauwpoort; Mafikeng Museum photographic collection: copy seen courtesy of Otsile Ntoane, Nov. 1999; plus quote in 'Tsala ea batho: Solomon Tshekesho Plaatje 1876–1932, the friend of the people', supplement to *Diamond Fields Advertiser (DFA)*, 17 Oct. 2001, 6.
23. Cape Town Archives, 1905, 1907 & 1909, Cape Voters' Rolls, Field-cornetcy of Rhenosterburg.
24. Palmer (1990: 283); Archer (2000); cf. Van Onselen (1996); *DFA*, 5 Sept. 1912, 7d, citing

Graaff-Reinet Advertiser.

25. Telephone interview with C.W. Roberts, Pretoria, 21 June 1999.

26. *Daily Chronicle*, 4 Oct. 1913, 5; State of New York, County Court, County of Columbia: 'In the matter of ... Franz Taibosh ... filed 12 April 1937'; Cape Town Archives, Cape Voters' Roll; *South African Almanack and Reference Book 1911–1912* (1911: 393, 704 & 795).

27. Martin (1999: 97–103); Lott (1995: 42); Katz (1982); Kirby (1968).

28. Lindfors (1996a & 1999).

29. Altick (1978: 38, 279–80 & 290); Lindfors (1983a: 2 & 5, 1985 & 1996a); Strother (1999); Skotnes (1996: 42, 48, 69, 70 & 72); Myers (1913). For illustrations see *Illustrated London News*, vol. 7, 13 Sept. 1845, 160 & vol. 21, 6 Nov. 1852, 372; for 1853 illustrations see Skotnes (1996: 46 & 71).

30. Adams (1997); Peacock (1990 & 1995); Bogdan (1988: 190, fig. 53); Skotnes (1996: 41 illus.); Poignant (2004: 191–3); Landau (1996); Lagden (1924: 6–7).

Chapter 2

1. *Rand Daily Mail*, 6 Oct. 1913.

2. *DFA*, April–July 1911, esp. 11 July, 2c; author's telephone interview with C.W. Roberts, Pretoria, 21 June 1999.

3. *DFA*, 10 Oct. 1911, 2; 1 April 1912, 8b; Racster (1951: 107).

4. *DFA*, 3 July 1911, 2c & 8d; 4 July, 7f; 5 July, 8d; 6 July, 7g; 8 July, 2c & 7e; 12 July, 8c; 12 July, 7c; 12 Feb. 1912, 7a; 13 Feb, 7g.

5. Author's interview with Barbara Cook de Romain, Oneonta NY, 8 May 1994; *Rand Daily Mail*, 6 Oct. 1913; 30 May 1912, 7g; *DFA*, 28 May 1912, 7b; 30 May, 7g; 1 June, 7d.

6. *DFA*, 10 Oct. 1913, 6g; Barbara Cook de Romain notes seen by author, 22 March 1996; *Daily Chronicle*, 4 Oct. 1913, 5.

7. *DFA*, 30 May 1912, 7g.

8. Kimberley Pass for WDB, 25 July 1912, as referred to in copy of legal proceedings in Fairfield County court, Bridgeport Conn., Sept. 1919 – Dec.1930 re. Franz Taibosh alias 'The Wild Dancing Bushman', as supplied by clerk of court to Mrs Frank A. Cook, Hotel Park Plaza, New York, Nov. 1958 (Cook Family Papers).

9. *DFA*, 25 July 1912, 8e; 26 July 1912, 8e.

10. Maria Willman Papers, McGregor Memorial Museum, Kimberley, MMKD 2591/1, 2592/1, 2593, 2644—thanks to Fiona Barbour; *DFA*, 22 Dec. 1911, 8c; 27 Dec. 1911, 5f; 6 March 1912, 7b–e.

11. *DFA*, 8 July 1911, 6d; *Evening Chronicle* (Johannesburg), 2 Oct. 1913, 5g.

Chapter 3

1. Birth certificate in Dublin Registry of Births & Deaths; Hyman (1972), appendix 4, register of Dublin Hebrew congregation births and deaths 1820–79, 256.

2. Engelman (1990: 189 & 175); Twitchell (1992: 55).

3. See note 1 above.

4. Engelman (1990: 170).

5. Hyman (1972: 18–24); Engelman (1990: 163 & 170); 'Ireland' in *Encyclopaedia Judaica* (Jerusalem: Keter Publishing, 1972), vol. 8: 1463

6. *Thom's Irish Almanac and Official Directory, 1887–1904*; Hyman (1972: 169–72); Prunty

(1999: 152–7 & 167).

7. Hyman (1972: 173–4, 190–1 & 333 n.89).

8. Cook family tradition according to Barbara Cook de Romain interview, 8 May 1994.

9. There is no record of Hepston/Epstein in Rae (1898).

10. *DFA*, 6 Sept. 1912, 7e re Von Wouw sculpture.

11. *The Kimberley Year Book and Directory for 1906–7*, 159 (copy in McGregor Memorial Museum Library); Province of Cape of Good Hope (1910), *List of Persons in the Electoral Division of Kimberley, whose names have been registered in the year 1909* (copy in Kimberley Africana Library, NR 4334), 26, voter 775; Roberts (1976); E.J. Africa (1992), fig. 4.

12. *The Kimberley Year Book and Directory for 1914–15*, 67, 158 & 233.

13. *The Star* (Johannesburg), 8 Oct. 1913, 10c; Manifest for ship *Philadelphia*, sailed Liverpool, arrived New York 3 May 1917: <www.ellisisland.org/search>.

Chapter 4

1. Pretoria Archives Depository, BNS 1/7/37–2633: typed copy of Acting Consul-General New York to Foreign Office London, 22 April 1919 (copy courtesy of Robert Gordon); Birkby (1948: 91–5 & 103); Malherbe (1981: 97–102); Jim Stockley email on Boswell family, 15 July 2002, on Leicester & Rutland Family History website <www.lrfhs.net>.

2. Gutsche (1972: 109 n.36); Gutsche Papers C9 109.

3. Waterhouse (1990: xiii); Russell (1987: 181 & 185); *Table Talk* (Melbourne), 31 Oct. 1912, 21; 23 Oct. 1913, 27; Brisbane (1991: 143–4); Waterhouse (1995: 53 & 63); *West Australian*, 13 & 30 Sept. 1912, 8.

4. Richard Waterhouse, personal communication re student research; Broome & Jackomos (1998: 16–18, 26 & 83–91); Mark St Leon emails; St Leon (1981: 215–29, 233; 1992: 119–21); Ramsland & St Leon (1993: 11); *West Australian*, 1 Aug. 1912, 8; Brisbane (1991: 177); Fogarty (2000: 23); *Newcastle Morning Herald*, 22 March 1912, 5; *Melbourne Argus*, 8 Nov. 1911, 13–14; Broome & Jacomos (1998); St Leon (1981).

5. Waterhouse (1990: 110–19; 1995: 71–3 & 86); *World's Fair*, 11 July 1914, 14; *The Theatre* (Sydney), x 10, Oct. 28; Russell (1987: 82); St Leon (1990: 4).

6. Scott (1946: 39 & 216); Kilgarriff (1998); Disher (1938: 74); *Douglass's Directory* (1907: passim; 1913: 217–19); biography of Ketelbey on <musicweb.uk.net/garlands/ketelbey. htm> accessed 3 March 2002.

Chapter 5

1. *The Era*, 18 June 1913, 92; *Encore*, 19 June 1913, 14.

2. *The Performer*, 10 July 1913, 20; *The Referee*, 13 July 1913, 4; *The Era*, 14 Dec. 1912, 34; Slide (1994: 311–12); Melbourne Performing Arts Museum Library, Programmes for 1913 & 1914, London editions of *Hullo Rag–time!*

3. Hewison (1983: 40); 'A ragtime army!', *The Standard* (London), 10 Oct. 1913, 7f; *The Era*, 23 Nov. 1912, 20; 25 Dec., 13.

4. Merriman–Labor (n.d.: 31–93, 116–18, 149–67, 176–230).

5. *The Era*, 22 June 1912, 20 & 34; 27 Nov., 3.

6. *The Encore*, 26 June 1913, 24; 3 July, 5; 10 July, 5; *The Era*, 25 June 1913, 9; *The Performer*, 3 July 1913, 4; Pickering (1993: 159–60).

7. Slide (1994: 494–5); *The Encore*, 26 June 1913, 14; *The Era*, 12 Oct. 1913, 20; 'The tango

on trial', *Evening News* (London), 19 Nov. 1913, 6e; Kilgarriff (1998: 203).

8. *The Era*, 15 June 1912, 22; 27 Nov., 4; 21 Jan. 1913, 18; *The Performer*, 6 Nov. 1913, 25; *The Encore*, 10 July 1913, 20; 24 July, 18; 19 June, 6.

9. *The Performer*, 10 July 1913, 13 & 22; 25 June 1914, 14; 2 July, 23; Gilbert (1963: 24).

10. *The Performer*, 10 July 1913, 25; personal communication from John Winckler via John Aldridge, July 2005, re 1913 transport links including tramways.

11. *The Performer*, 10 July 1913, 25; 17 July, 6 & 9; Mander & Mitchenson (1974: illus. 252); Scott (1946: 216); Kilgarriff (1998: 38).

12. *The Encore*, 24 July 1913, 21.

13. *Daily Chronicle*, 4 Oct. 1913; *The Encore*, 17 July 1913, 24; *Billboard*, 27 Jan. 1917.

14. *The Encore*, 24 July 1913, 24; Kilgarriff (1998: 143–4).

15. *Rand Daily Mail*, 6 Oct. 1913; Yarmouth photograph in Duckworth Laboratory, Cambridge; *East Anglian Daily Times*, 5 Aug. 1913, 5c; *Yarmouth and East Norfolk Standard*, 8 Aug. 1913, 5.

Chapter 6

1. W.L.H. Duckworth, letter to *The Times* (London), 2 Oct.1913, 4d & 5d.

2. *The Standard*, 8 Oct. 1913, 10c; Duckworth (1916).

3. *The [Oxford] Dictionary of National Biography* (1971: 316–17); Taylor (1965: 571); *Who Was Who 1851–1960* (1961: 571).

4. *Pretoria News*, 2 Oct. 1913, 5b; 4 Oct., 5g–h; *DFA*, 3 Oct. 1913, 5e.

5. *Cape Times*, 3 Oct. 1913; 6 Oct.

6. *Rand Daily Mail*, 6 Oct. 1913.

7. *The Star* (Johannesburg), 8 Oct. 1913, 10c; *DFA*, 4 Oct. 1913, 5f; 10 Oct., 6g.

8. *South Africa*, 10 (1293), 4 Oct. 1913, 31–2.

9. Cochran (1946: 46–7); Toole-Stott (1962), vol. 3: 222, entry 7821.

10. 'African bushman. Savage who may be 110 years old. Now doing dancing turn in Paris circus' by Our Correspondent, Paris, 3 October, *Daily Chronicle*, 4 Oct. 1913, 5.

11. *South Africa*, 10 (1294), 11 Oct. 1913, 82; *Rand Daily Mail*, 6 Oct. 1913, 8h; *Straits Times* (Singapore), 2 Dec. 1913, 9g.

12. *South Africa*, as note 11 above; Evans (1981: 446).

13. *South Africa*, as note 11 above; Duckworth (1916); *Cambridge Daily News*, 18 Nov. 1913, 4d.

14. *The Times*, 11 Nov. 1913, 7c; Duckworth (1916).

15. *Cambridge Daily News*, 8 Nov. 1913, 3e; 10 Nov., 3e & 4f; 11 Nov., 3a & 3f; *Cambridge Independent Press*, 14 Nov. 1913, 3f; Slide (1994), 460.

16. Duckworth (1916); *The Magnet*, 12 July 1913; *World's Fair*, 12 July 1913, 8; *Evening News* (London), 21 Nov. 1913, 10.

17. *The Times*, 20 Nov. 1913, 11; State of New York, County Court, County of Columbia, Order & Petition, filed 12 April 1937 (Cook Family Papers).

18. For *Shimmyshauen* I have been referred, by an informant in Namibia whose identity I have mislaid, to A. Selmeci & D. Henrichsen (1995), *Das Schwartzkommando*, Bielefeld: Aisthesis.

Chapter 7

1. *Cambridge Daily News*, 20 April 1914, 3; 25 April, 1a (advertisement); 28 April, 4; *Cambridgeshire Weekly News and Express*, 24 April 1914, 6d & 7h; 1 May, 3 & 12; *Cambridge*

Independent Press, 8 May 1914, 5.
2. *Cambridge Daily News*, 28 April 1914, 4.
3. R. Douglass Vernon to APS, 25 May 1914 (Rhodes House Library (RHL), Oxford, MSS. Brit. Emp. s.22/G.125 'Bushman, Ill–treatment of Wild Dancing'); personal communication from Janet Morris, Assistant Archivist, Emmanuel College, email, 22 June 2003.
4. R. Douglass Vernon to APS, 25 May 1914 (RHL);'Kaffir Boys' (1911) in RHL: MSS. Brit.Emp. s.22/G.126; Copland (1979: 150); Coan & Wright (1955: 58–9 & 111–25); Shepherd (1986); Public Record Office (London), CO 879/574, 150.
5. *South Eastern Gazette*, 28 April 1914, 1a; 12 May, 5a.
6. L. Norley, Maidstone, to APS, 15 May 1914 & 20 May (RHL 'Bushman, Ill-treatment').
7. *Gravesend and Dartford Reporter*, 16 May 1914, 8d.
8. *The Performer*, 3 July 1913, 28; 30 Oct., 16; London Metropolitan Police Commissioner to APS, 18 June; Fanny Haddon to APS, 23 June 1914; W.L.H. Duckworth to APS, 3 July 1914; Chairman Variety Artistes' Federation to APS, 6 July 1914 (RHL).
9. *Manchester Guardian*, 6 Oct. 1913, 9d; *Cambridge Independent Press*, 31 Oct. 1913, 7a; *Evening Telegraph* (Dublin), 27 July 1914, 3; *World's Fair*, 8 Aug. 1914, 21; *Evening Telegraph* (Dublin), 3 Aug. 1914, 6a; 19 Sept., 5g & 8.
10. *Daily Express* (Dublin), 11 Aug. 1914, 3g.

Chapter 8
1. Disher (1942: 14 & 16). See also *World's Fair*, 16 May 1914, 1 & 5; 23 May, 2; Pertwee (1979: 71).
2. *Clapham Observer*, 11 July 1913, 3a.
3. *Evening Telegraph* (Dublin), 5 Aug. 1914, 3.
4. *Margate Advertiser*, 22 May 1915, 8c–d; *Cambridge Daily News*, 9 Sept. 1915, 3b.
5. *Thanet Times*, 21 May 1915, 1f; *Margate Advertiser*, 22 May 1915, 5e.
6. *Margate Advertiser*, 22 May 1915, 1d.
7. *Thanet Times*, 28 May 1915, 5b.
8. *Margate Advertiser*, 5 June 1915, 1f & 2c.
9. *Margate Advertiser*, 7 Aug. 1915, 1d, 1g, 2b; 14 Aug., 7b.
10. *Margate Advertiser*, 24 July 1915, 6.
11. Burke (1941: 136–7).
12. *Cambridge Daily News*, 3 Sept. 1915, 7d.
13. *The Herald* (Melbourne), 3 Oct. 1913, 7d.
14. J. Goddard to E.D. Morel, 12 July 1915 (RHL 'Bushmen, Ill-treatment'); APS to Goddard, 15 July 1915; Report by Detective Department to Chief Commissioner's Office, Margate Police, 27 July 1915, encl. in Chief Constable's Office to APS, 27 July 1915.
15. W. Schreiner to APS, 29 July 1915; H.H. Johnston to APS, 1 Aug.1915 (RHL 'Bushmen, Ill-treatment').
16. Willan (1990: 174–80).
17. H.H. Johnston to APS, 1 Aug.1915 (RHL); APS to Vernon, 10 Sept. 1915 (RHL 'Bushmen, Ill-treatment').
18. Venn (1947); *The Times*, 18 Nov. 1913, 5d; 19 Nov., 10d; 'The new dentistry. Dr Cunningham in London', *Cambridge Independent Press*, 21 Nov. 1913, 2f; *The Performer*, 3 July 1913, 25; *East Anglian Daily Times*, 4 Aug. 1913, 5f; Zangwill (2001).

19. *The Era*, 17 Aug.1912, 23; 27 Aug. 1913, 29; *World's Fair*, 9 May 1914, 13; Low (1950: 19–23 & 31–4); Cameron (1994: 45).
20. Cunningham to Harris, 17, 19–20 & 20 Sept. 1915 (RHL); APS to Schreiner, 13 Sept. 1915 (RHL 'Bushmen, Ill-treatment').
21. Goddard to APS, 3 Oct. 1915 (RHL 'Bushmen, Ill-treatment').
22. Zangwill (2001).

Chapter 9

1. State of New York, County Court, County of Columbia, Order & Petition, filed 12 April 1937 (Cook Family Papers).
2. *Cork Weekly News*, 9 Oct. 1915, 7g.
3. Ensor (1936: 475); Coogan (1991/1990: 475); O'Donnell & Clifford (1992: 11 & 16); *Havana Post*, 2 May 1916, 1.
4. Public Record Office (London), FO 116/24, Passport Index of Names, Aug. 1915 – June 1916; FO 610/130, Passports Register, Feb.–May 1916 (five shillings fee); passport details also noted in Cook Family Papers.
5. *Havana Post*, 10 May – 29 Oct. 1916; 'History of the Royal Hanneford Circus' on <sahibshrine.org/circus/hanneford.htm> accessed 3 April 2002.
6. *Billboard*, 8 July 1916, 3 & 22; 15 July 1916, 27; 12 Aug.1916, 24–5.
7. *Billboard*, 15 July 1916, 27; 22 July., 23; 26 Aug., 23; 9 Sept., 22; 30 Sept., 24; 6 Jan. 1917, 237; *Havana Post*, 9 Dec. 1916; McCulloch (2000: 8).
8. Van der Post (1976a: 67-9).
9. *Havana Post*, 2 Jan. 1917, 6; 'Liberal revolt in Cuba 1917' on <www.onwar.com/aced/nation/cat/cuba/fcuba1917.htm> accessed 3 April 2003; *New York Clipper*, 21 Feb. 1917, 14; *Daily Gleaner*, 5 March 1917, 1.
10. *Billboard*, 24 March 1917, 58.
11. *Billboard*, 13 Jan. 1917, 29; Kasson (1978: 109); 'Gumpertz back from Cuba', *Billboard*, 24 March 1917, 91.
12. Interview with Sam Gumpertz, *Billboard*, 24 Feb. 1917, 26; Kasson (1978); McCulloch (2000: 199 & 258–67).
13. *New York Clipper*, 14 March 1917, 14; 21 March, 14; 28 March, 14; Interview with Sam Gumpertz, *Billboard*, 24 Feb. 1917, 30; 24 March, 72.

Chapter 10

1. *Billboard*, 24 March 1917, 36, 69, 72, 101, 103, 194 & 218; 14 April, 9; 23 March 1918, 18; Manifest for ship *Philadelphia*, sailed Liverpool, arrived New York, 3 May 1917: <www.ellisisland.org/search.>
2. Author's interview with Barbara Cook de Romain, Oneonta NY, 22 March 1996; *New York Clipper*, 16 May 1917, 14; May (1963: 308–9).
3. *Billboard*, 10 Feb. 1917, 25; 7 April, 1 & 79; 30 June, 50; *Billboard*, 2 June 1917, 24; 9 June, 69; 'Gumpertz game', 21 July, 66–7.
4. *Billboard*, 2 June 1917, 24 & 69; 23 June, 30; Jeffery Stanton, 'Coney island–freaks' on <naid.sppsr.ucla.edu/coneyisland/articles/freaks.htm> accessed 7 March 2003; *Billboard*, 9 June 1917, 69; 7 July, 75.
5. *Billboard*, 22 Dec.1917, 11 & 60; *Havana Post*, 13 Nov. 1917, 5; 14 Nov., 5; Bradna

(1952: 192); Passenger 008 in manifest of *Carillo* arrived New York, 8 Jan. 1918: <www. ellisisland.org/search>.

6. Barbara Cook de Romain interview; W.M. Mann & L.Q. Mann Papers, Smithsonian Institution Archives & Special Collections, record unit 7293. Ref. 'Wilson is Victor' in *Havana Post*, 10 Nov. 1916, 1.

7. *Billboard*, 6 April 1918, 29; Bradna (1952: 93); 'Sam Gumpertz. A searcher for human eccentricities—interestingly described in New York Herald', *Billboard*, 27 Aug. 1921, 73 & 96.

8. *Billboard*, 31 Aug. 1929, 68; 23 Jan. 1937, 'The final curtain', 37–9.

9. Van der Post (1976a: 67–9).

10. Van der Post (1976: 70–1); Bouissac (1976: 152–4).

Chapter 11

1. American Museum of Natural History, NYC, 1996, body cast in the attic seen courtesy of Belinda Kaye, archivist, & Thomas R. Miller & Enid Schildkraut, anthropologists.

2. *Billboard*, 6 April 1918, 29; Passengers 007 and 008 in Manifest for the *New York* arrived New York, 5 April 1918: <wwww.ellisisland.org/search>. The entry for Frantz Taaibosh is marked with additional signed entries dated 11/1/20, 12/1/24, and 11 Nov. 1927.

3. Dulles (1952: 131); May (1932: 1); Fletcher Smith, 'Future of circus business in doubt', *New York Clipper*, 19 Dec. 1917, 33; Ogden (1993: 47).

4. Bradna (1952).

5. Bradna (1952); Kline (2001: 18 & 27).

6. *Billboard*, 9 March 1918, 28; 30 March, 1, 29 & 61; 20 April, 29; Bradna (1952: 86).

7. Ramsland & St Leon (1993: ix) quoting Robert C. Toll but with no source; Kline (2001); Bradna (1952: 17–20 & 40–1).

8. Bradna (1952: 234); *Billboard*, 6 April 1918, 30; 11 May 1918, 44.

9. Hilliar (1918: 18); Braathen (1973: 25).

10. *Billboard*, 3 April 1920, 5 & 87; Johnston (1934).

11. Bradna (1952: 242); Drimmer (1973: 355); Bakner (1973: 35–6); Lindfors (1983b); Goodall (2002: 53–7); Mark Sceurman, 'In search of Zip What Is It?', <weirdnj.com/_localheroes/ zihtml> accessed 7 March 2003; *Billboard*, 27 Aug. 1921, 73 & 96; Cook (1996: 144).

12. Bradna (1952: 119–20, 316 & 321); contract signed by Gumpertz & Hepston, 18 May 1918—copy in Cook Family Papers.

13. *Billboard*, 11 May 1918, 36, 44 & 63; 18 May, 29; 26 May, 28; 8 June, 27; 29 June, 3 & 26; 6 July, 3 & 54; 21 Sept., 24; 28 Sept., 30 & 54; 12 Oct., 26–7; 19 Oct., 54; *Oakland Tribune*, 1 Sept. 1918, 24; *San Francisco Chronicle*, 6 Sept., 14; 7 Sept., 4; 9 Sept., 6; 'Among ιs mortals' [sketches] by W.E. Hill in *San Francisco Chronicle*, 8 Sept. 1918, supplement 5 ['de' and 'dat' here substituted for 'the' and 'that'].

14. *Los Angeles Times*, 14 Sept. 1918, 3; 17 Sept., 3; 18 Sept., 3.

15. *Los Angeles Times*, 16 Sept. 1918, 2; 17 Sept., 1; 19 Sept., 1; *San Francisco Chronicle*, 8 Sept. 1918, 8.

16. Anon., *The Life History of Clicko* (1922).

17. Bradna (1952: 95); Braathen (1973); *Billboard*, 19 Oct. 1918, 3, 4, 20, 26 & 54; 2 Nov., 26; 28 Dec., 53–4; Blume (1999: 192).

18. Willson (1932: 198).

19. See note 18.

Chapter 12

1. *Bridgeport Post*, 12 Dec. 1918, 2.
2. *Bridgeport Post*, 2 Dec. 1930, 1 & 19.
3. Willson (1932: 199).
4. Barbara Cook de Romain interview.
5. Willson (1932: 199-200).
6. State of New York, County Court, County of Columbia, Order & Petition, filed 12 April 1937 (Cook Family Papers); PRO London, open-shelf index to British Consul New York correspondence.
7. Copies in Cook Family Papers.
8. *Billboard*, 29 March 1919.
9. St Leon (1990: 4 & 10; 1991: 35); Jando (1991: 19–20); Ogden (1993: 94–5, 106, 136–7, 190, 230–1, 248, 267 & 375); Lewiston (1968: 199); *Billboard*, 18 Oct. 1919, 47; 19 March 1921, 17 & 219; 5 March 1921, 61 (Circus Solly); Lentz (1988: 22–3).
10. *Billboard*, 5 April 1919; 25 April, 34.
11. Obituary of Tiny Doll (Elly Ann Schneider), 1914–2004, *Weekly Telegraph* (London), 22 Sept. 2004, 38.
12. Russ Simonton, 'All freaks but us, say side-show freak folk', clipping from unknown newspaper (marked 'NEA May 00'), Circus World Museum, Baraboo: Chindahl Papers, Box 05, Folder 43.
13. *Billboard*, 14 June 1918, 44; Bakner (1973), 36.
14. *Billboard*, 31 Aug. 1929, 68; 23 Jan.1937, 'The final curtain', 37–9; Sonnenberg (2002: 16). I have not located a copy of Frank A. Cook, 'Queer tricks that people try to play on the circus', *American Magazine*, Feb. 1923.
15. *Billboard*, 21 June 1919, 45 & 82; 28 June, 43 & 46; 5 July, 42; 12 July, 41 & 45.
16. *Bridgeport Post*, 27 June 1919 ('West end in uproar when Clicco runs') & 29 June ('Steinke makes a clown of himself before huge mobs'), copy courtesy of Paul Landau & Roger Levine.
17. *Billboard*, 12 July 1919, 32; 19 July, 41 & 43; 2 Aug., 42–3 & 86.
18. *Billboard*, 16 Aug. 1919, 86; 30 Aug., 102; *Chicago Tribune*, 1 Aug. 1919, 4–7; 3 Aug., 1 & 8; 7 Aug., 11 & 17; 8 Aug., 1; 9 Aug., 4; 10 Aug., 5; 10 Aug., 2; 11 Aug., 5; 15 Aug., 6.
19. *Billboard*, 6 Sept. 1919, 43; 13 Sept., 116; 20 Sept., 5 & 38; 11 Oct., 44; 18 Oct., 46; 25 Oct., 46–7; 1 Nov., 76 & 96; 15 Nov., 56; 22 Nov., 54; 29 Nov., 56.
20. Interview with Barbara Cook de Romain & her notes in Cook Family Papers; Ogden (1993: 85–6); Davis (2001: 49).
21. *Billboard*, 22 Nov. 1919, 80; 6 Dec., 80; 7 Feb., 90; 13 March, 36; Lentz (1988), 22; St Leon (1990: 10).

Chapter 13

1. State of New York, County Court, County of Columbia, Order & Petition, filed 12 April 1937 (Cook Family Papers).
2. Manifest for *The Majestic* arrived at New York 21 Nov. 1923: <www.ellisisland.org/search>.
3. *Chicago Tribune*, 17 June 1920, 7; 19 June, 1; 21 June, 1 & 3; 22 June, 1; *Billboard*, 26 June 1920, 73 & 102; 3 July, 55 & 57; 19 March 1921, 'Spring special', 17 & 219; Ogden (1993).

4. Cochran (1946: 29–30); *World's Fair*, 27 June 1914, 6; *Billboard*, 23 March 1918, 166.
5. Willson (1932: 200–1).
6. *Billboard*, 7 Aug. 1920, 55; 21 Aug., 57; 28 Aug., 5; 18 Sept., 55; 2 Oct. 1920, 57.
7. Personal communication with the late Prof. Isaac Schapera, who knew Lestrade well; University of Cape Town administration archives; personal communication from Peabody Library, Harvard University.
8. Bradna (1952: 284 & 298).
9. Green (1986: 236–7) quoting Charlie Chaplin autobiography; Durant (1957: 204, photo of LA publicity); Bradna (1952: 29-30, 116–17 & 321); *Billboard*, 12 Aug. 1922, 101; 26 Aug., 79; 2 Sept., 5 & 103; 9 Sept., 106; 16 Sept., 66; 23 Sept., 70; Townsend Walsh, 'From the cradle to the sawdust ring' [interview with Fred Stelling], *Billboard*, 14 June 1923, 72.
10. *Billboard*, 17 March 1923, 13 & 245; 24 March, 7; 5 May, 78 & 121; 12 May, 92; 13 Oct. 1923, 80; 20 Oct., 82; 3 Nov., 81 & 127.
11. Bakner (1973: 36); *Billboard*, 5 April 1924, 5–6; 19 April, 75; 10 May, 7; 24 May, 70; 5 July, 68, 71 & 111; 2 Aug., 70; 16 Aug., 130.
12. *Billboard*, 2 April 1921, 7, 17 & 94–6.
13. *Billboard*, Easter 1922; Barbara Cook de Romain, personal communication.
14. Bradna (1952: 236 & 240–2).
15. Ogden (1993: 242); May (1963: 284); Culhane (1990: 169–70); Tucker (1973: 2–3); *Billboard*, 5 April 1924, 6; 12 April, 12.
16. *Billboard*, 30 July 1921, 84; 3 Sept., 64; 17 Sept., 5; 8 Oct., 47 & 57; 15 Oct., 188; 29 Oct., 67; 19 Nov., 68; Davis (2002: 72) citing Allan Harding, 'The joys and sorrows of a circus fat lady', *American Magazine*, n.d.
17. Notes from Barbara Cook de Romain; Van der Post (1976a: 79); *Billboard*, 10 Dec. 1921, 25; 24 Dec., 67; 7 Jan. 1922, 66.
18. Stanley F. Dawson's jottings in *Billboard*, 11 Nov. 1922, 74; *Billboard*, 23 Jan.1937, 39.
19. State of New York (1937) as in note 1; notes from Barbara Cook de Romain dated 1995; Van der Post (1976a: 80–1).
20. Van der Post (1976a: 74–5).
21. Hammarstrom (1992); Van der Post (1976a: 83). Rastafarians make a similar case for smoking.
22. Drimmer (1973: 354–5); interview with Barbara de Romain.
23. *Knickerbocker Press*, c. 2 Aug. 1925 (photocopy courtesy of Prof. Bernth Lindfors). See also Gordon (1997).

Chapter 14

1. Dunkle (1926: 5 & 9); Bradna (1952).
2. Bakner (1973: 36); Drimmer (1973: 355); Mark Sceurman, 'In search of Zip What Is It?', <weirdnj.com/_localheroes/zihtml> accessed 7 March 2003; Dunkle (1926: 59); *Billboard*, 25 April 1926, 75.
3. *Billboard*, 20 March 1926, 37; 27 March, 66; 10 April, 5 & 10–11; 16 April 1927, 906; Barbara Cook de Romain notes.
4. North & Hatch (1960: 243); Ogden (1993); Hammarstrom (1992: 27 & 44); Bradna (1952: 131); Barbara Cook de Romain notes.

5. Bradna (1952: 96–7, 136); Braathen (1973: 26).
6. *Billboard*, 7 April 1928, 5; 14 April, 5 & 85; 21 April, 56 & 67; 15 July 1928, 15; 16 July, 9; 18 July, 2, 76; 6 Oct. 1928, 60; 13 Oct., 62; 20 Oct., 13; 3 Nov., 62; 17 Nov., 60; *Chicago Tribune*, 14 July 1928, 1.
7. Lentz (1988: 21); Bogdan (1988: fig. 54).
8. Barbara Cook de Romain, personal communication; *Billboard*, 30 March 1930, 85; Herbert (1989: part 2, 19).
9. Hammarstrom (1992: 29); Plowden (1967: 110 & 137).
10. *Billboard*, 22 June 1929, 52; 20 July, 54; 31 Aug., 68; 7 Sept., 122.
11. Barbara Cook de Romain chronology notes; *Billboard*, 14 Sept. 1929, 50; 21 Sept., 3, 52 & 54; 28 Sept., 93; 26 Oct., 1.
12. *Billboard*, 12 Oct. 1929, 54; 26 Oct., 56 & 60 (also referring to it as the Clowns Club); Barbara Cook de Romain interview.
13. *Billboard*, 2 Nov. 1929, 58 & 61; 9 Nov., 59; 16 Nov., 58; 21 Dec., 57; Ogden (1993: 150–2); *Billboard*, 5 Oct. 1929, 62.
14. *New York Sun*, 8 April 1930; Bradna (1952: 243–51); Tucker (1973: 3); *New York World*, 1 April 1930; Johnston (1934); *Billboard*, 2 Nov. 1929, 65; 30 Nov. 1929, 97; 4 Jan. 1930, 89; 1 Feb., 79; 8 Feb., 56; 15 Feb., 69; Braathen (1973: 26); State of New York, County Court, County of Columbia, Order & Petition, filed 12 April 1937 (Cook Family Papers).
15. *Billboard*, 5 April 1930, 3, 90, 92 & 93; 27 June 1931, 42 [punctuation modified]; Sonnenberg (2002: 16); *World-Herald* (Omaha), 8 Aug. 1930, 30; 10 Aug., 4; 12 Aug., 6 & 8; 17 Aug., section 2; 24 Aug., section 25; 25 Aug., 1 & 4; *Omaha Bee-News*, 24 Aug. 1930, section c3; 26 Aug., 6.
16. Tucker (1973: 2–3); *Billboard*, 12 April 1930, 96; 3 May, 84; 17 May, 83; 28 June, 100; 9 Aug., 84; 23 Aug., 86; 6 Sept., 84; 11 Oct., 86; 25 Oct., 57.
17. *Bridgeport Post*, 2 Dec. 1930, 1 ('Wild man to testify here in court suit: now civilized, former Barnum freak will take stand').
18. *Bridgeport Post*, 2 Dec., 1 & 19 (Wild man's manager dead, circus men say'); 3 Dec. ('Wild man suit taken off docket: freak's manager believed dead, lawyer withdrawn case against circus'); Register of Births, Marriages & Deaths for England & Wales, Deaths October–December 1925: Epstein, Morris, at Whitechapel (London), aged 50.
19. *Billboard*, 11 April 1931, 3, 75 & 78.
20. Barbara Cook de Romain notes.
21. Culhane (1990: 205); Weeks (1993: 218–41); Hammarstrom (1992: 29–32); Braathen (1973: 24); *Billboard*, 12 Sept. 1931, 60.
22. Hasson (1980: 22).
23. Barbara Cook de Romain interview; Jones (2001: 315).
24. Barbara Cook de Romain interview; *Billboard*, 16 April 1932, 3 & 61–2; 23 April, 53; North & Hatch (1960: 353–4); Durant (1957: 128–9).
25. *Billboard*, 23 April 1932, 53 & 61; *Billboard*, 30 March 1929, 3 & 84–6; *Billboard*, 27 June 1931, 42; McCulloch (2000: 199); Lewiston (1968).
26. Bogdan (1988: 190–2 & 280); Barbara Cook de Romain interview.

Chapter 15

1. Slide (1994: 410–11); Barbara Cook de Romain interview.

2. *Billboard*, 25 March 1933, 26; 8 April, 26; 15 April, 5 & 11; Floyd L. Bell, 'S.W. Gumpertz: superlative showman', *Billboard*, 29 April 1933, 26; 22 July, 26 & 35.
3. *Billboard*, 24 June 1933, 21, 31 & 48; 1 July, 31 & 37; 8 July, 36; 15 July, 25; 22 July, 37; 29 July, 3 & 34; 5 Aug., 38; 12 Aug., 38; 19 Aug., 30; Slide (1994: 411–12).
4. Lewiston (1968: 185–90).
5. Malherbe (1981: 229–30); Malherbe to 'Darling Girlie', 10 Oct. 1933 in File 327 & entries in his copy of *Walker's Diary (South African edition) for 1933* in File 569, both in E.G. Malherbe Manuscript Collection, Killie Campbell Africana Library, Campbell Collection, University of KwaZulu-Natal, Durban.
6. *Chicago Tribune*, 2 June 1933, 4; 6 June, 9 & 19; 7 June, 5 & 38; 9 June, 8 & 14; Hoffman (1936: 155–6 & plates 134ff); Hoffman (1965: 115–29, 215–19 & 254–76); *Current Biography* (1966–7: 466), entry for 'Hoffman, Malvina (15 June 1887–10 July 1966)'.
7. Cook (1992: 42); *Billboard*, 23 Jan. 1937, 39.
8. Sarasota RBBB Press Clippings: *New York Sun*, 31 March 1934, 15; *New York Post*, 12 April 1934, 3; *Billboard*, 7 April 1934, 1, 3 & 55; clipping from *New York Evening Post*, 14 April 1934, in Chindahl Papers, Box 05/Folder 42, Circus World Museum, Baraboo.
9. Cook (1992: 42–5).
10. *Billboard*, 30 June 1934, 46.
11. *Billboard*, 19 May 1934, 37; 23 June, 36; 21 July, 34; 28 July, 43; 4 Aug., 34; 18 Aug., 35; Durant (1957: 218–19); Bradna (1952: 316); *Oshkosh Northwestern*, 2 Aug. 1934, 1 & 13; 3 Aug., 9; 6 Aug., 4; *Capital Times* (Madison), 2 Aug. 4 & 9; 3 Aug. 1934, 4 & 11; 4 Aug., 3; 5 Aug., 1 & 4; 6 Aug., 1 & 4; 7 Aug., 11.
12. *Billboard*, 25 Aug. 1934, 65 & 67; 15 Sept., 40; 22 Sept., 34 & 46.
13. Wood (1980: 19); Lewiston (1968: 195–6 & 99–105).
14. *Billboard*, 29 Sept. 1934, 63; 20 Oct., 37; 27 Oct., 38; 3 Nov., 1; 10 Nov., 38; 29 Dec., 233.
15. *Billboard*, 2 Feb. 1935, 38, 56 & 57; 23 Feb., 40 & 41; 2 March, 36; 16 March, 1 & 38; 23 March, 38 & 43.
16. *Billboard*, 13 April 1935, 89; 20 April, 1–2 & 57–60; McKennon (1979: 427).
17. Lewiston (1968: 198); interview with Barbara Cook de Romain; Wood (1980: 17–19).
18. Braathen (1973: 25); *Billboard*, 2 March 1935, 1; 2 Nov., 36; 16 Nov., 9, 11 & 13; 27 Nov., 36; 14 March 1936, 1; 28 March, 1; 4 April, 1; 23 Jan. 1937, 1; 16 Nov. 1935, 35; 27 Nov. 1935, 34 & 37.
19. *Billboard*, 2 Feb. 1935, picture on 38; 7 Dec., 35–6; 7 March 1936, 34; 21 March, 1 & 37; 11 April, 44; 18 April, 1, 34 & 49; 25 April, 36 & 61; Hammarstrom (1992: 34).
20. Herbert (1989: part 2, 19); *Billboard*, 21 Dec. 1935, 34–5; 8 Feb. 1936, 36; 15 Feb., 38.
21. *Billboard*, 30 Nov. 1935, 47; 4 Jan. 1936, 32; 11 Jan., 32; 8 Feb., 34; 22 Feb., 1 & 22; 18 Jan. 1936, 36.
22. Hammarstrom (1992: 34).
23. *Billboard*, 14 March 1936, 1; 28 March, 1; 4 April, 1; Mayer (1936).
24. Sarasota RBBB Press Clippings: *New York Post*, 14 & 15 April 1937.
25. Ward (1998: 60); *Billboard*, 23 Jan. 1937, 'The final curtain', 36–40.

Chapter 16

1. Barbara Cook de Romain interview.
2. *Billboard*, 27 March 1937, 36.

3. State of New York, County Court, County of Columbia, Order & Petition, filed 12 April 1937 (Cook Family Papers).
4. Barbara Cook de Romain interview; internet sites <cafedesartistesnyc.com> & <letsgo. com> accessed 7 March 2003.
5. Lewiston (1968: 220).
6. Letters in possession of Barbara Cook de Romain.
7. *Leader-Post* (Regina), 13 July 1937, 16; 14 July, 1; 15 July, 1 & 10.
8. *Calgary Daily Herald*, 17 July 1937, 23; 19 July, 2; 20 July, 1; 21 July, 1 & 4.
9. Barbara Cook de Romain notes dated 1995; *Billboard*, 1 Jan. 1938, 94.
10. Lewiston (1968: 230–1, 237–56).
11. Hynd (1945). I am grateful to Bernth Lindfors for notes on this.
12. *Billboard*, 17 April 1937, 3 & 40–1; Sarasota RBBB Press Clippings: 'Dexter Fellows: expansive press agent of the "greatest show on earth"', *New York Woman*, c. April 1937; 'Gumpertz all set for Big Show at Madison Sq. Garden', *Jewish Examiner*, 2 April 1937, 7.
13. Sarasota RBBB Press Clippings: *New York Post*, 13 April 1937, 13; *Billboard*, 22 May 1937, 3; 5 June, 3; 12 June, 43; 16 June, 3.

Chapter 17

1. *Billboard*, 1 Jan. 1938; 2 April, 1; 26 April, 1; Lentz (1988: 22).
2. Sarasota RBBB Press Clippings: George Ross, 'New York' column, *Sentinel* (Norwalk, Conn.), 1 April 1938; *Telegram* (Elmira NY), 3 April; *News Tribune* (Rome, Georgia) and *Star* (Aniston, Alabama), 4 April; *Billboard*, 16 April 1938, 1 & 74–5.
3. *Billboard*, 16 April 1938, 1 & 74–5; Sarasota RBBB Press Clippings: *Boston Sunday Post*, 20 March 1938, 2; *Variety* (New York), 14 April 1938; *Leader* (Lowell, Mass.), 14 April 1938; *New York World-Telegram*, 14 April 1938; *Sun* (Binghampton NY), 15 April 1939; *New York Times*, 14 April 1938, 7; *Times-Herald* (Dallas), 14 April 1938.
4. *Billboard*, April–July 1938, *passim*, esp. 9 July, 1, 23 & 63; Hammarstrom (1992: 53).
5. See Herbert (1988–9); interview with Barbara de Romain plus letter with address; Jones (2001: 315); copies of photographs courtesy of Barbara Cook de Romain.
6. Van der Post (1976a: 84–5) mentions 1937 but 1938 is more likely.
7. 'Interview with Mrs. Tommie Clicko' by Dorothy West, New York, 14 Sept. 1938, Library of Congress, American Life Histories: Manuscripts from the Federal Writers' Project, 1936–40. <http://memory.loc.gov/ammem/wpaintro/wpahome.html> accessed 26 April 2006.

Chapter 18

1. Van der Post (1976a: 48, 71 & 112-14).
2. Contract between Evelyn Joyce Cook and Rose Lewiston, signed 17 March 1939, on Hotel Anthony Wayne, Akron, Ohio, letterhead, in Cook Family Papers.
3. Barbara Cook de Romain interview; Lewiston (1968); *Billboard*, 22 April 1939, 64.
4. *Billboard*, 9 July 1938, 61; 6 May 1939, 30 & 83; 11 March 1939, 31; 22 April, 3; 6 May, 30; 13 May, 69; Lewiston (1968).
5. *Billboard*, Aug. 1939; *Rochester Democrat and Chronicle*, 2 Aug. 1939, 11 & 14; 2 Aug., 11 & 15; 8 Aug., 12 & 14; 16 Aug., 1 & 12.

6. *Columbus Dispatch*, 18 Jan. 1940, 1; *Billboard*, 2 March 1940, 49; *Knoxville Journal*, 18 Feb. 1940, 7; 25 Feb., 5; Tucker (1973: 2); draft contract between Evelyn Joyce Cook and Rose Lewiston, signed March 1939, on Tod Hotel, Youngstown, Ohio, letterhead, in Cook Family Papers.

7. Psalm 71, as translated in the Episcopalian/Anglican *Book of Common Prayer* (1549/1662).

8. Interview with W.E. 'Doc' Alstone, July 1938, in Library of Congress WPA (same source as Chapter 17 note 7 above); *Washington Post*, 1 Sept. 1940; Van der Post (1975: 117); interview with Barbara Cook de Romain; *Billboard*, Sept. 1940; transcript from the Register of Death, Franz Taibosh, 31 August 1940 (Register no. 32, Town of Claverack, County of Columbia, State of New York, copy dated at Philmont, 16 April 1979), in Cook Family Papers.

9. *Washington Post*, 2 Sept. 1940, 5; *New York Times*, 1 Sept. 1940, e3; *Chicago Tribune*, 1 Sept. 1940, 1–3.

10. Barbara Cook de Romain interview, & site inspection by this author courtesy of Robert J. Gordon.

Conclusion

1. *New York Times*, 1 Sept. 1940, E3.
2. Barkan (1992).
3. Goodall (2002: 11–15, 166–84).
4. Ranger (1975).
5. Van Vuuren (2006: 229).
6. Lewiston (1968: 190); Shephard (2003: 227–8).
7. Shephard (2003: 227–8); Gordon (1997).
8. Personal communication from Lauren van Vuuren, University of Cape Town, 18 Sept. 2002.
9. Van der Post (1975/1976a); Jones (2001: 313–19), Chapter 29, 'A Mantis Carol'; Jung (1967).
10. Van der Post's 'Hottentot' Descent in Jones (2001: xv).
11. Van der Post (1975: 73).
12. Barbara Cook de Romain interview; Hoffman (1965: 276–88).
13. Jones (2001: 313).
14. Guenther (1999); Wilmsen (1989 & 1990).
15. Letter from Laurens van der Post to this author, 10 Feb. 1992.
16. Interview with Barbara Cook de Romain; F.B. Kelley to Evelyn Cook, 19 Oct. 1980, in Cook Family papers; Cook (1992).
17. Telephone interview with Dibora Taibos (Middelburg, E. Cape), by Jan-Bart Gewald, 10 Dec. 2001.

BIBLIOGRAPHY

1. *Archival sources*
1A: *Private collections*
Aucamp Papers (in private possession, Middelburg, E. Cape):
  'Die Geveg op The Willows' [The Skirmish at The Willows], typescript based on research at the University of Orange Free State by Leon Vorster, grandson of A.D. Koekemoer; original donated to War Museum, Bloemfontein
Author's possession:
  Correspondence with Evelyn Joyce Cook (New York), 1992
  Correspondence with Barbara de Romain (Oneonta and Paris), 1995, 1996, 2003, 2005
  Correspondence with Sir Laurens van der Post (London), 6 and 10 February 1992
  Interview with Frikkie Aucamp (Kruger Street, Middelburg), interpreted by Emlitia Bezuidenhout Loock, 5 July 1999
  Interview with Mr Joubert (Heydon, near Middelburg), 4 July 1999
  Interviews with Carl Loock (Sunny Dell, near Middelburg), 4–5 July 1999
  Interviews with Barbara Cook de Romain (Maryland, near Oneonta NY), 8 May 1994 and 24 March 1996
  Telephone interviews in Afrikaans by Liesel Hubbard with Mrs Taaibos (Kimberley), April 1996
  Telephone interview with C.W. Roberts, East Lynne, Pretoria, 21 June 1999
  Telephone interview in Afrikaans by Jan-Bart Gewald with Mrs Dibora Taibos (Middelburg), December 2001
Bernth Lindfors Papers (in private possession, University of Texas at Austin):
  Miscellaneous photocopies
  Copies of Grand Palace Clapham poster and photo-postcard signed Wild Dancing Bushman, 1913
Cook Family Papers (in possession of Barbara Cook de Romain, Maryland near Oneonta NY, March 1996):
  Chronology of Franz Taaibosch's life, by Barbara Cook de Romain, 1993
  Correspondence Evelyn Cook with F.B. Kelley, October .1980
  Correspondence Evelyn Cook with Harry Lewiston, June–October 1937, January–March 1939, March 1940
  'I inherited a Bushman', partial manuscript by Evelyn Joyce Cook, undated

'I inherited a Manuscript', essay by Barbara de Romain, dated 19 March 1996

Copy of legal proceedings in Fairfield County court, Bridgeport, Conn., September 1919 – December 1930 re Franz Taibosh alias 'The Wild Dancing Bushman', as supplied by clerk of court to Mrs Frank A. Cook, Hotel Park Plaza, New York, November 1958

Copy of legal proceedings in Columbia County court, City of Hudson, NY, April–June 1937 re Franz Taibosh, alias Clicko, an alleged Incompetent Person. Petition of Frances Cook Sullivan, &c.

News clippings of Paris newspapers, October 1913 re 'l'Homme sauvage': photocopies from Bibliothèque Nationale, Paris, 1996

Notes on Taaibosh and Hepston passports, 1916 and 1918

Photographs of Franz Taibosh, 1918, originals held by American Natural History Museum, New York

Photograph of bronze head of Franz Taibosh by Malvina Hoffman (Chauncey Memorial Hall, Field Museum, Chicago)

Photographs of Evelyn Cook, Franz Taibosh, and Barbara Cook in Rockies and California, 1938–9

Verified transcript of death, April 1979: Franz Taibosh d. 31 August 1940

1B: *Public collections*

Austin, Texas: *Harry L. Ransome Library, University of Texas:*
Miscellaneous photographs of sideshow entertainers

Baraboo, Wisconsin: *Circus World Museum:*
Index and documents relating to Franz Taibosh

Cambridge, England: *Duckworth Laboratory, University of Cambridge:*
Photographs of Franz Taaibosh, dated 1913

Cambridge, England: *Jesus College Library, University of Cambridge:*
W.L.H. Duckworth Papers, boxes 1–2

Cape Town: *Archives Depository:*
CCP 11/1/30 – 11/1/58: *Cape of Good Hope Voters' Rolls*, 1893, 1895, 1899, 1903, 1905, 1907, 1909
CCS 3/1/5: Cape of Good Hope Census 1904, Returns, vol. ii
MOCC 89146/1943, Index of Estates (1872–1943/44): File 89146, Estate of Christiaan Willem Roberts, died Pretoria, 11 September 1943. Death certificate signed by Christofel Johan Roberts, East Lynne, Pretoria
General Directory of (United) South Africa, 1898–9, 1911, 1912, 1913, 1914

Cape Town: *Deeds Office (90 Plein Street):*
Deeds Volume 4/B.56.A (Middelburg, Eastern Cape), Farms Middelburg 141–143

Cape Town: *University of Cape Town, Administration Archives:*
Personal file of G.P. Lestrade, including curriculum vitae
University of Cape Town Council Minutes vol. 24, 24 February 1920 – 13 December 1921

Cape Town: *University of Cape Town, African Studies Library, Manuscripts and Archives Department*:
G.P. Lestrade Papers (microform BCZA 91/9944-10007 BU)

Cape Town: *South African Museum*:

Correspondence Barbara Cook de Raczynska [later de Romain] and Evelyn Joyce Cook with Richard Lytton (*Cape Argus*), December 1958 – January 1959 (photocopy courtesy of Robert J. Gordon)

Chicago: *Field Museum of Natural History*

Photographs of Bushman (Franz Taibosh)

Bronze head of Franz Taibosh by Malvina Hoffman in Chauncey Memorial Hall

Photographs: Malvina Hoffman, 'Races of Man', negatives 3 and 3A ('Bushman Man: Negroid-Mongoloid Mixture: Kalahari Desert, South Africa')

Dublin: *National Archives of Ireland*:

Census of Ireland for the Year 1881, Preliminary Report (Dublin: Alex Thom and Co., 1881)

Thom's Irish Almanac and Official Directory, annual volumes for 1887–1904

Dublin: *Registrar of Births and Deaths*:

Birth certificate of Morris Hepston, 1877

Durban: *Killie Campbell Africa Library, Campbell Collection, University of KwaZulu-Natal*:

E.G. Malherbe Manuscript Collection

Kimberley, South Africa: *McGregor Memorial Museum*:

Maria Willman Papers, MMKD

London: *General Register Office for England and Wales (Births, Marriages and Deaths)*

Entry of death: October–December 1925, Whitechapel, County of London, No. 272: 14 December 1925, London Hospital, Morris Epstein, aged 50

London: *Public Record Office (in National Archives of England and Wales), Kew*:

CO 879/574: Colonial Office Confidential Print, Africa (South), 1899

FO 6: Passport Records

FO 115/2493: Consular Reports, New York etc., 1919, nos. 1–20

FO 116/24: Passport Index of Names, August 1915 – June 1916

FO 278/10: Consular Correspondence Register, Havana, 1917–18

FO 278/11: Consular Correspondence Register, Havana, 1919–20

FO 369/124: Consular Class Correspeondence, USA

FO 610/130: Passports Register, February–May 1916

Melbourne: *Performing Arts Museum Library, St Kilda Street Art Centre*:

Colleano Family Collection (ACCN 208)

Theatre Scrapbook Australia 1909–1914 (045/14/2.3093)

Theatre Scrapbook Melbourne 1910–1916 (024/1.3029.B6)

Scrapbook Collection Melbourne 1908–1916 (B3.1991.123.1)

New York: *American Museum of Natural History, Central Park West*:

'Races of Man', photo negatives of Bushman [Franz Taibosh], 1918

Oxford: *Rhodes House Library, Anti-Slavery and Aborigines' Protection Society Papers*:

Mss. Brit. Emp. s.22/G.125: re 'Bushman, Ill-treatment of Wild Dancing', 1914

Mss. Brit. Emp. s.22/5.126: re Rev. Balmer's 'Kafir Singing Boys', 1911

Pretoria: *Archives Depository*:

BNS 1/7/37 – 2633: correspondence re Franz Taaibosch 'Wild Dancing Bushman', 1919 (photocopy courtesy of Robert J. Gordon)

San Antonio, Texas: Public Library, Hertzberg Circus Collection

Copy of c.1922 publicity pamphlet, Anon. *The Life History of Clicko: The Dancing*

Bushman of Africa
Sarasota, Florida: *John and Mable Ringling Museum Library:*
 Press clippings re 1930s Circus News
Washington, DC: *Smithsonian Natural History Museum, National Anthropological Archives:*
 William M. Mann and Lucille Quarry Mann Papers, c.1885–1981, boxes 2–20; catalogue
 entry 282 (RU 7293)

2. Published primary sources
2A. Africa
Boonzaier, D.C. 1923. 'My playgoing days: 30 years in the history of the Cape Town stage'.
 South Africa Review, 9 March – 24 August (reprinted in F.C.L. Bosman, *Drama en Toneel
 in Suid-Afrika. Part 2: 1856–1912*. Pretoria: Van Schaik, 1980)
British Parliamentary Papers. 1971. Shannon: Irish Universities Press Series reprints:
 Colonies (Africa) vol. 20 (1826–36): Cape of Good Hope
Hodgson, T.L., ed. Richard Cope. 1977. *The Journals of the Rev. T.L. Hodgson, Missionary to the
 Seleka-Rolong and the Griquas 1821-1831*. Johannesburg: Witwatersrand University Press
Maingard, L.F. 1932. 'Studies in Korana history, customs and language'. *Bantu Studies*, 6 (2,
 June): 103–62
Maingard, L.F. 1962. *Korana Folktales: Grammar and Texts*. Johannesburg: Witwatersrand
 University Press
Malherbe, Ernst Gideon (III). 1981. *Never a Dull Moment*. Cape Town: Howard Timmins
Mandela, Nelson R. 1994. *Long Walk to Freedom: The Autobiography of Nelson Mandela*.
 Boston: Little, Brown
Rae, Colin. 1898. *Malaboch or Notes from My Diary on the Boer Campaign against the Chief Malaboch
 of Blaauwberg District Zoutpansberg, South African Republic, to Which is Appended a Synopsis of
 the Johannesburg Crisis of 1896*. London: Sampson, Low, Marston; and Cape Town: Juta
Schapera, Isaac, ed. 1953. *The Early Cape Hottentots, Described in the Writings of Olfert Dapper
 (1668), Willen ten Rhyne (1686) and Johannes Gulidmus de Grevenbroek (1695)*. Cape
 Town: Van Riebeeck Society

2B. Europe
Buchan, John, intro. by Robin W. Winks. 1988. *The Four Adventures of Richard Hannay: The
 Thirty-nine Steps* [1915], *Greenmantle* [1916], *Mr Standfast* [1919], and *The Three Hostages*
 [1924]. Boston: David R. Goodie
Cochran, Charles B. 1946. *Showman Looks On*. London: J.M. Dent
Duckworth, Wynfrid Laurence Henry. 1913a. Letter to *The Times* (London), 2 October 1913,
 5d ('Imperial and Foreign Intelligence' page)
Duckworth, W.L.H. 1913b. Further letter on 'A Bushman in England' to *The Times*, 11
 November 1913, 7c
Duckworth, W.H. 1916. *Descrizione di un Boscimano del Sud Africa*. Roma: Presso la Sede della
 Società Romana di Anthropologia (Revista di Anthropologia, volume 20). [I am grateful to
 the Duckworth Laboratory at Cambridge for a copy, and to Karim Sadr for a translation.]
Jung, C.G. 1967. *Memories, Dreams, Reflections*. London: Collins 'Fontana Library'
McGuire, William, ed. 1991. *The Freud–Jung Letters: The Correspondence between Sigmund
 Freud and C.G. Jung*. Harmondsworth: Penguin Books [1st edn, 1974]

Muir, Frank. 1997. *A Kentish Lad: The Autobiography of Frank Muir*. London: Corgi Books (Bantam Books)

Myers, Lindo S. 1913. Letter on 'Mysterious Bushman' to *Daily Chronicle* (London), 4 October 1913, 4

2C. America

American Life Histories: Manuscripts from the Federal Writers' Project, 1936–1940, on Library of Congress, Washington DC, website <http://memory.loc.gov/ammem/wpaintro/wpahome.html>, accessed 26 April 2006, incl. interviews with W.E. 'Doc' Alstine, Portland, Oregon, July 1938 ('Circus days and ways'); Mrs Tommie Clicko, 272 Manhattan Ave., New York City, 14 September 1938; Maude Cromwell. Long Island, NY, 6 January 1939 ('Circus people is [*sic*] like other human beings'); Alfred O Philipp, Chicago, 14 June 1939 ('Chicago folkstuff: vaudeville')

Anon. c.1922. *The Life History of Clicko: The Dancing Bushman of Africa* [pamphlet in the Hertzberg Circus Collection, San Antonio, Texas]

Bradna, Fred, with Hartnell Spence. 1952. *The Big Top: My Forty Years with The Greatest Show on Earth, including A Circus Hall of Fame*. New York: Simon and Schuster

Cook, Evelyn. 'This little pig went nightclubbing'. *Bandwagon*, 36 (January–February 1992): 42–8

Culhane, John. 1990. *The American Circus: An Illustrated History*. New York: Henry Holt

Herbert, Dorothy. 1988–89. 'Herbert's horses' [draft autobiography]. *Bandwagon*, 'Part one', 32 (6, November–December 1988); 'Part two,' 33 (1, January–February 1989): 19–30; 'Part three' (2, March–April); 'Part four' (3, May–June): 14–25; 'Part five' (4, July–August): 26–8; 'Part six' (5, September–October): 22–32; 'Part seven' (6, November–December)

Kline, Tiny. 2001. 'Showground bound where caste is observed according to rank and rating'. *Bandwagon* (Columbus, Ohio), 45 (23, May–June): 9–18 and 27

Lentz, John. 1988. 'Merle Evans: his final interview'. *Bandwagon*, 32 (1, January–February): 21–3

Lewiston, Harry, with Jerry Holtman. 1968. *Freak Show Man: The Autobiography of Harry Lewiston as Told to Jerry Holtman*. Los Angeles: Holloway House

Malherbe, Ernst Gideon. 1981. *Never a Dull Moment* [autobiography, incl. US]. Cape Town: Howard Timmins

Mann, William M. 1948. *Ant Hill Odyssey* [i.e. autobiography to 1917]. Boston: Little, Brown (Atlantic Monthly Press Book)

North, Henry Ringling, and Alden Hatch. 1960. *The Circus Kings: Our Ringling Family Story*. New York: Doubleday

Sonneberg, C.A. 'Red'. 2002. 'Oldtime circus fixers: legal adjusters'. *Bandwagon*, 46 (5, September–October): 14–16

Tucker, Albert. 1973. 'The strangest people on earth'. *Sarasota Sentinel*, 7 July: 2–3 [photocopy from J.and M. Ringling Museum, Sarasota, Florida]

Van der Post, Laurens. 1975. *A Mantis Carol*. London: Hogarth Press

Van der Post, Laurens. 1976a. *A Mantis Carol*. New York: W. Morrow

Willson, Dixie. 1932. *Where the World Folds Up at Night*. New York and London: D. Appleton

Wisconsin Circus Lore. 1937. Madison, Wisconsin: Folklore Section , Women's and Professional Projects, Federal Writers' Projects (Wisconsin), Works Progress Administration [mimeo, copy in University of California Library, Berkeley]

Wood, Warren H. 1980a. 'This way please' [i.e. RBBB in 1934]. *Bandwagon*, 24 (3, May–June): 27–30

Wood, Warren H. 1980b. 'With Ringling-Barnum in 1935'. *Bandwagon*, 24 (5, September–October): 17–19

3. *Newspaper and periodical stories*

3A. Africa

Cape Times (Cape Town), Thurs., 3 December 1885, 2e: 'Massouw and the Boers'

Cape Times, Fri., 3 October. 1913, 7b: 'Bushman in the Kalahari: an "interesting anthropological problem"'

Cape Times, Mon., 6 October 1913, 6h: 'That Kalahari Bushman: interview with Miss Bleek'

Diamond Fields Advertiser, Fri., 3 October 1913, 5e: 'Scientist and Bushman: farmer's interesting find in the Kalahari'

Diamond Fields Advertiser, Wed., 8 October 1913, 5f: 'The dancing Bushman: has the professor been spoofed?'

Rand Daily Mail (Johannesburg), Fri., 3 October 1913, 8f: 'Dancing Bushman: farmer's discovery in the Kalahari' (Reuter's/SA Press Agency cable)

Rand Daily Mail, Mon., 6 October 1913, 8h: 'That dancing Bushman: has the professor been spoofed?: sidelights on a London story'

The Star (Johannesburg), Thurs., 2 October 1913, 9b: 'Dancing Bushman: found in the Kalahari' (Reuter's South African Service)

The Star, Wed., 8 October 1913, 10c: 'The dancing Bushman'

Transvaal Leader (Johannesburg), Sat., 4 October 1913, 10b: 'Exported Bushman'

3B. Asia and Australasia

Straits Times (Singapore), Fri., 31 October 1913, 2b: 'African Bushman savage may be 110 years old. Now dancing in Paris circus'

3C. Europe

Cambridge Daily News (Cambridge), Tues., 18 November 1913, 4d: 'The little legpuller: South African Bushman's visit; university reception'

Cambridge Daily News, Tues., 28 April 1914, 4e: 'A link with the past: wild dancing Bushman's visit' (with photograph 'The last of his race')

Daily Chronicle (London), Fri., 3 October 1913, 7: 'Mysterious Bushman in London'

Daily Chronicle, Sat., 4 October 1913, 5: 'African Bushman: savage who may be 110 years old: now doing dancing turn in Paris circus'

Illustrated Magazine of Art (London), 1853: 445: 'Flora and Martinus, children of the Earthmen tribe' [copy in Killie Campbell Collection, University of Natal, Durban]

South Africa (London), 100 (1293, 4 October 1913): 31–2: leaderette (short editorial) on 'The Bushman and the bunny-hug'

South Africa, 100 (1294, 11 Ocober .1913): 81–2: leaderette on 'Another "black dwarf" tale'

South Africa, 100 (1297, 1 November 1913): 'That Kalahari Bushman: the view of an authority' [i.e. Dorothea Bleek]

South Eastern Gazette (Maidstone, Kent), Tues., 12 May 1914, 5a: theatrical review of programme at Palace Theatre, Maidstone

3D. America

Billboard (Cincinnati, Ohio), 29 (8, 24 February 1917): 26 and 30: interview with Samuel W. Gumpertz

Billboard, 34 (28 October 1922): 'Laughter and thrills still the biggest forces to draw crowd' (reprinted from *San Antonio Express*, 15 October 1922)

Billboard, 35 (14 June 1923): 72: 'From the cradle to the sawdust ring' [interview with Fred Stelling] by Townsend Walsh

Billboard, 39 (1 May 1926): 45 and 59: 'Visiting the Big One in New York' by W.W. Dunkle

Billboard, 49 (4, 23 January 1937): 33 and 38–9: obituary ('The final curtain') for Frank A. Cook

Billboard, 51 (34, 26 August 1939): 66: photograph of 'Clico' with Harry Lewiston

Billboard, 52 (37, 14 September 1940): 28: obituary ('The final curtain') for 'Taibosh – Franz, African Bushman known as Cliko'

Bridgeport Post (Bridgeport, Connecticut), Thurs., 12 December 1918: 1c: 'African Bushman remains abducted'

Bridgeport Post, 27 June 1919: 'West end in uproar when Clicco runs'

Bridgeport Post, Tues., 2 December 1930, 1 centre-page, 'Wild man's manager dead circus men say' and photograph '"Wild man" and two friends'

Knickerbocker Press (Albany, New York), Mon. [c. 4 August 1925]: 'Savants off on African hunt for mate to Albany Bushman: only native of Bocheana land [*sic*] desert in U.S., Frank Tarbosh [*sic*] lives in North Pine Avenue with circus man' and photographs 'Franz Tarbosh [*sic*], the only African bushman in America, garbed as savage of the desert, and in store clothes' (photocopy courtesy of Circus World Museum, Baraboo)

New York Times (New York), Mon., 2 September 1940, 15c: obituary for 'Franz Taibosh: African Bushman, a midget, had been with Ringlings'

4. *Newspaper and periodical runs consulted*
4A. Africa

Bloemfontein Post (Bloemfontein), October–November 1913 [hard copy in Kimberley Africana Library]

Cape Argus (Cape Town), Dec. 1885 [microform in University of Cape Town African Studies Library]

Cape Times (Cape Town), August 1912; October 1913 [ditto]

Diamond Fields Advertiser (Kimberley), June–July 1911; October 1911 – April 1913; September–October 1913 [hard copy in McGregor Memorial Museum and Kimberley Public Library]

Evening Chronicle (Johannesburg), October 1913 [microform in Africana Library, Johannesburg]

The Friend (Bloemfontein), October 1913 [hard copy in British Newspaper Library]

Kimberley Evening Star (Kimberley), July–November 1913 [hard copy in Kimberley Africana Library]

Pretoria News (Pretoria), October 1913 [microform in Africana Library, Johannesburg]

Rand Daily Mail (Johannesburg), October–November 1913 [ditto and British Newspaper Library, Colindale, London]

The Star (Johannesburg), December 1911 – January 1912; October 1913 [British Newspaper Library]

Transvaal Leader, October 1913 [ditto]

Sunday Times (Johannesburg), October 1913 [ditto]

4B. Asia and Australasia

The Advertiser (Adelaide), October 1913 [microform in Australian National Library, Canberra]

Daily Telegraph (Sydney), October 1913 [ditto]

The Herald (Melbourne), October 1913 [microform in Victoria State Library, Melbourne]

Kalgoorie Miner (Kalgoorie, W. Australia), July–May 1913 [microform in Australian National Library]

Melbourne Argus (Melbourne), November 1911 [microform in British Newspaper Library]

Straits Times (Singapore), August–December 1912; October 1913 [microform in Singapore National Library]

Sydney Morning Herald (Sydney), October–November 1913 [microform in Australian National Library]

Table Talk (Melbourne), July 1912 – February 1913; October–November 1913 [ditto and Victoria State Library]

The Theatre (Sydney), August 1912 – March 1913 [ditto]

West Australian (Perth), August–October 1912 [microform in West Australia State Library]

4C. Europe

The Bioscope (London), November 1913 [hard copy at British Newspaper Library, Colindale, transferred to Westminster Public Library, Leicester Square branch]

Cambridge Daily News (Cambridge), August–November 1913; April 1914; May 1915; September 1915 [hard copy at Colindale]

Cambridge Independent Press (Cambridge), October–November 1913; April–May 1914 [ditto]

Cambridgeshire Weekly News and Express (Cambridge), April–May 1914 [ditto]

Clapham Observer, Tooting and Balham Times (London), July 1913 [ditto]

Cork Weekly News and Cork County People (Cork), September–November 1915 [ditto]

Croydon Times (Croydon, Surrey), May 1913 [ditto]

Daily Chronicle (London), October 1913 [microform at Colindale]

Daily News and Leader (London), November 1913 [ditto]

East London Advertiser (London), July 1913 [hard copy at Colindale]

The Era, incl. *The Wednesday Era, a Mid-Week Edition of 'The Era'* [theatrical trade journal] (London), June 1911 – June 1914 [hard copy at Colindale; microform in Westminster Public Library, Leicester Square branch]

Daily Express (Dublin), August 1914 [hardcopy at Colindale]

Evening News (London), Nov. 1913 [microform at Colindale]

Evening Telegraph (Dublin), July–October 1914 [ditto]

Gazette des Théatres (Paris), 19 Oct. 1913 [consulted by Barbara Cook de Romain in Bibliothèque Nationale, Paris]

Gravesend and Dartford Reporter (Gravesend, Kent), May–June 1913; May 1914 [hardcopy at Colindale]

Gravesend and Northfleet Standard (Gravesend), May–June 1913 [ditto]

Holborn and Finsbury Guardian (London), July 1913 [ditto]

Islington Daily Gazette and North London Tribune (London), July 1913 [ditto]

Kent Messenger and Gravesend Telegraph (Gravesend), June 1913; May–June 1914 [ditto]

Kent Messenger and Maidstone Telegraph (Maidstone, Kent), May–June 1914 [ditto]

The Magnet: A Journal Devoted to the Interests of the Music Hall, Theatrical and Equestrian Professions, May–September 1913 [ditto]

Manchester Guardian (Manchester), October 1913 [microform at Colindale]

Margate, Ramsgate and Isle of Thanet Gazette (Margate, Kent), May–October 1915 [hardcopy at Colindale]

The Performer: The Official Organ of the Variety Artistes Federation (otherwise *The VAF Performer*), July–November 1913; June–July 1914 [ditto]

Putney Newsletter (London), June 1913 [ditto]

The Referee, Founded by Pendragon (London), June–July 1913 [ditto]

Shepherd's Bush and Hammersmith Gazette (London), April–July 1913 [ditto]

South Africa (London), October–November 1913 [hard copy in Kimberley Africana Library]

South-Eastern Gazette (Maidstone), April–June 1914 [ditto]

The Standard (London), October 1913 [ditto]

Thanet Times (Margate), May–July 1915 [ditto]

The Times (London), October–November 1913 [hard copies in Edinburgh and Witwatersrand University libraries]

West London Observer (London), July 1913 [hard copy at Colindale]

World's Fair (Oldham, Greater Manchester) [fairground entertainment journal], July–September 1913; April–August 1914 [ditto]

4D. America

Billboard (various subtitles, incl. *Indispensable to the Professional Entertainer and Allied Interests*, later *The World's Foremost Amusement Weekly*) (Cincinnati, Ohio), July 1916 – September 1940 [microform in British Newspaper Library; University of Wisconsin Library, Madison; hard copy in University of Texas Library, Austin]

Calgary Daily Herald (Calgary, Alberta), July 1937 [microform in British Columbia Archives]

Capital Times (Madison, Wisconsin), August 1934 [microform in University of Wisconsin Library, Madison]

Chicago Tribune (Chicago), August 1919; June 1920; July 1928; June 1933; September 1940 [microform in University of California Library, Berkeley; University of Wisconsin Library, Madison]

Columbus Dispatch (Columbus, Ohio), January 1940 [microform in Library of Congress]

Daily Gleaner (Kingston, Jamaica), January 1916 – April 1917 [microform in British Newspaper Library]

The Enquirer (Cincinnati, Ohio), January 1940 [microform in Library of Congress]

Havana Post, April 1916 – December 1917 [microform in British Newspaper Library and University of Vermont Library]

Knickerbocker News (Albany, New York), August–September 1940 [microform in Library of Congress]

Knoxville Journal (Knoxville, Tennessee), February 1940 [ditto]

The Leader-Post (Regina, Saskatchewan), July 1937 [microform in British Columbia Archives]

La Lucha: Edicione la Habana (Havana, includes *The Lucha: Latin America's Pioneer Afternoon News Paper in English*), November 1917 [microform in British Newspaper Library]

Los Angeles Times (Los Angeles), September 1918 [microform in University of California Library, Berkeley]

Morning Oregonian (Portland, Oregon), August 1922 [microform in British Columbia Archives]

New York Times (New York), September 1940 [microform in British Newspaper Library]

New York Clipper: The Oldest Theatrical Publication in America (New York), February–December 1917 [microform in Library of Congress]

Oakland Tribune (Oakland, California), September 1918 [microform in University of California Library, Berkeley]

Omaha Bee-News (Omaha, Nebraska), August 1930 [microform in Nebraska State Historical Society]

Oshkosh Northwestern (Oshkosh, Wisconsin), August 1934 [microform in University of Wisconsin Library, Madison]

Rochester Democrat and Chronicle (Rochester, New York), August 1939 [microform in Library of Congress]

St Paul Pioneer Press (St Paul, Minnesota), December 1939 [microform in University of Wisconsin Library, Madison]

San Francisco Chronicle (San Francisco), September 1918 [microform in University of California Library, Berkeley]

Variety (New York), June 1926; September 1940 [microform in University of Wisconsin Library, Madison]

Washington Post (Washington, DC), July–September 1940 [microform in British Newspaper Library]

Winnipeg Free Press (Winnipeg, Manitoba), September 1937 [microform in British Columbia Archives]

World-Herald (Omaha), August 1930 [microform in Nebraska State Historical Society]

5. *Unpublished secondary sources*

Africa, Edward John. 1992. 'Die Maleierkamp van Kimberley 1882–1957'. University of the Orange Free State, Bloemfontein: MA thesis

Van Vuuren, Lauren. 2006. 'The Great Dance: Myth, History and Identity in Documentary Film Representation of the Bushmen'. University of Cape Town, Department of Historical Studies: PhD

6. *Published secondary sources*
6A. **General**

Barkan, Elazar. 1992. *The Retreat of Scientific Racism: Changing Concepts of Race in Britain and the United States between the Two World Wars*. Cambridge: Cambridge University Press

Bouissac, Paul. 1976. *Circus and Culture: A Semiotic Approach*. Bloomington, Indiana: Indiana University Press

Croft-Cooke, Rupert, and Peter Coates. 1977. *Circus: A World History*. New York: Macmillan [London, 1976]

Debord, Guy, transl. Donald Nicholson-Smith. 1994. *The Society of the Spectacle*. New York:

Zone Books

Dubow, Saul. 1995. *Scientific Racism in Modern South Africa.* Cambridge: Cambridge University Press

Dudley, Edward, and Maximillian E. Novak. 1972. *The Wild Man Within: An Image in Western Thought from the Renaissance to Romanticism.* Pittsburgh: University of Pittsburgh Press

Goodall, Jane R. 2002. *Performance and Evolution in the Age of Darwin: Out of the Natural Order.* London: Routledge

Jung, C.G. 1967. *Memories, Dreams, Reflections.* London: Collins 'Fontana Library'

Kirby, E.T. 1974. 'The shamanistic origins of popular entertainments'. *Drama Review,* 18 (1, March): 5–15

Lindfors, Bernth. 1996a. 'Ethnological show business: footlighting the dark continent' in Thomson (1999), 207–18

Lindfors, Bernth, ed. 1999. *Africans on Stage: Studies in Ethnographic Show Business.* Bloomington and Indianapolis: Indiana University Press; and Cape Town: David Philip

Parsons, Neil. 1999. 'Clicko or Franz Taaibosch: South African Bushman entertainer in Britain, France, Cuba, and the U.S.A.' in Lindfors (1999), pp. 203–27

Petty, Sheila. 1999. 'Africans on display: the problematics of human exhibition', review of Lindfors (1999) on <H-AfrLitCine@h-net.msu.edu>, November 1999

Rydell, Robert W. and Nancy E. Gwinn. 1994. *Fair Representation: World's Fairs and the Modern World.* Amsterdam: Free University of Amsterdam Press

Savigliano, Marta E. 1995. *Tango and the Political Economy of Passion.* Boulder: Westview Press

Schechter, Richard, and Willa Appel, eds. 1990. *By Means of Performance: Intercultural Studies of Theatre and Ritual.* Cambridge: Cambridge University Press

Stoddart, Helen. 2000. *Rings of Desire: Circus History and Representation.* Manchester: Manchester University Press; and New York: St Martin's Press

Thomson, Rosemarie Garland, ed. 1996. *Freakery: Cultural Spectacles of the Extraordinary Body.* New York: New York University Press

Van der Post, Laurens. 1976b. *Jung and the Story of Our Time.* Harmondsworth: Penguin

Young, Robert J.C. 1995. *Colonial Desire: Hybridity in Theory, Culture and Race.* London and New York: Routledge

6B. Africa

Adhikari, Mohamed. 2005. *Not White Enough, Not Black Enough: Racial Identity in the South African Coloured Community.* Cape Town: Double Storey/Juta; and Athens, Ohio: Ohio University Press

Amery, Leopold S., general ed. 1907. *The Times History of the War in South Africa 1899–1902,* Volume 5. London: Sampson Low, Marston

Archer, Sean. 2000. 'Technology and ecology in the Karoo: a century of windmills, wire and changing farming practices'. *Journal of Southern African Studies,* 26 (4, December): 675–96

Bank, Andrew. 2006. *Bushmen in the Victorian World: The Remarkable Story of the Bleek-Lloyd Collection of Bushman Folklore.* Cape Town: Double Storey/Juta

Bergh, J.S., and J.C. Visagie. 1985. *The Eastern Cape Frontier Zone 1660–1980.* Durban: Butterworth

Breutz, Paul-Lambert. 1968. *The Tribes of the Districts of Taung and Herbert*. Pretoria: Department of Bantu Administration and Development (Ethnological Publications 51)

Breutz, Paul-Lambert. 1955–6. *The Tribes of Mafeking District*. Pretoria: Native Affairs Department (Ethnological Publications 32)

Cameron, Kenneth M. 1994. *Africa on Film: Beyond Black and White*. New York: Continuum, 1994

Coan, Josephus R. and Charlotte Crogman Wright. 1955. *Beneath the Southern Cross: The Story of an American Bishop's Wife in South Africa*. New York: Exposition Press

Cope, John. 1967. *King of the Hottentots* [life of Corey]. Cape Town: Howard Timmins

Copland, David. 1979. 'The African musician and the development of the Johannesburg entertainment industry, 1900–1960'. *Journal of Southern African Studies*, 5 (2, April): 135–64

Engelbrecht, J.A. 1936. *The Korana: An Account of their Customs and their History, with Texts*. Cape Town: Maskew Miller (with Carnegie Corporation)

Fairbridge, Dorothea. 1931. *Historic Farms of South Africa: The Wool, the Wheat, and the Wine of the 17th and 18th Centuries*. London: Oxford University Press

Ferreira, F.H. 1929. 'Setlhapi nomenclature and uses of the indigenous trees of Griqualand West'. *Bantu Studies*, 3 (3): 349–56

Gordon, Robert J. 1997. *Picturing Bushmen: The Denver African Expedition of 1925*. Athens, Ohio: Ohio University Press; Cape Town: David Philip; and Windhoek: Namibia Scientific Society

Gordon, Robert J. 1999. '"Bain's Bushmen": scenes at the [Johannesburg] Empire Exhibition, 1936', in Lindfors (1999), pp. 266–89

Guenther, Mathias. 1999. *Tricksters and Trancers: Bushman Religion and Society*. Bloomington: Indiana University Press

Gutsche, Thelma. 1968. *The Microcosm* [a history of the Colesberg area]. Cape Town: Howard Timmins

Gutsche, Thelma. 1972. *The History and Social Significance of Motion Pictures in South Africa 1895–1940*. Cape Town: Howard Timmins

Halford, Samuel James. c.1930. *The Griquas of Griqualand: A Historical Narrative of the Griqua People: Their Rise, Progress, and Decline*. Cape Town: Juta

Hastings, Macdonald. 1956. *The Search for the Little Yellow Men*. New York: Alfred A. Knopf

Heap, Peggy. 1993. *The Story of Hottentots Holland: Social History of Somerset West, the Strand, Gordon's Bay and Sir Lowry's Pass over Three Centuries*. Somerset West: Author [1st edn, A.A. Balkema, 1970]

Hewitt, John. 1931. 'Discoveries in a Bushman cave at Tafelberg Hall'. *Transactions of the Royal Society of South Africa*, 29 (2): 185–96 + xvi [photocopy courtesy of Sven Ouzman]

Jones, J.D.F. 2001. *Storyteller: The Many Lives of Laurens van der Post*. London: John Murray

Katz, Richard. 1982. *Boiling Energy: Community Healing among the Kalahari !Kung*. Cambridge, Mass.: Harvard University Press

Kirby, Percival R. 1968. *The Musical Instruments of the Native Races of South Africa*. Johannesburg: Witwatersrand University Press [2nd edn].

Lagden, Godfrey. 1924. *The Native Races of the Empire*. London: W. Collins (The British

Empire series, 10)

Landau, Paul Stuart. 1996. 'With camera and gun in southern Africa: inventing the image of Bushmen c. 1880 to 1935' in Skotnes (1996), pp. 128-41

Lindfors, Bernth. 1996b. 'Hottentot, bushmen, kaffir: taxonomic tendencies in nineteenth-century iconography'. *Nordic Journal of African Studies*, 5 (2), 1-28

Maingard. Louis F. 1932. 'Studies in Korana history, customs and language'. *Bantu Studies* (Johannesburg), 6 (2): 103–62

Martin, Denis-Constant. 1999. *Coon Carnival: New Year in Cape Town, Past and Present*. Cape Town: David Philip

Maurice, Frederick, et al. 1910. *History of the War in South Africa 1899–1902. Compiled by Direction of His Majesty's Government*. London: Hurst and Blackett, vol. 4

Mears, W.G.A. 1970. *Wesleyan Baralong [Barolong] Mission in Trans-Orangia 1821–1884*. Cape Town: C. Struik

Morel, Edmund Dene. 1907. *Red Rubber: The Story of the Rubber Trade Flourishing in the Congo in the Year of Grace 1906*. London: T. Fisher Unwin

Neville, Dennis, Beatrix E. Sampson and C. Garth Sampson. 1994. 'The frontier wagon track system in the Seacow valley, north-eastern Cape'. *South African Archaeological Bulletin*, 49 (160, December): 65–72

Nienaber, G.S. 1963. *Hottentots*. Pretoria: J.L. van Schaik

Palmer, Eve. 1990. *The Plains of Camdeboo*. Johannesburg: Jonathan Ball (1st edn, London: Collins, 1966)

Peires, Jeff B. 1989. *The Dead Will Arise: Nongqawuse and the Great Xhosa Cattle-Killing Movement of 1856–7*. Johannesburg: Ravan

Penn, Nigel. 1995. 'The Orange river frontier zone, c.1700–1805', in A.B. Smith (1995), pp. 21–109

Penn, Nigel. 1999. *Rogues, Rebels and Runaways: Eighteenth-century Cape Characters*. Cape Town: David Philip

Racster, Olga. 1951. *Curtain Up! The Story of Cape Theatre*. Cape Town: Juta

Ranger, Terence Osborn. 1975. *Dance and Society in Eastern Africa 1890–1970: The Beni Ngoma*. London: Heinemann

Roberts, Brian. 1976. *Kimberley: Turbulent City*. Cape Town: David Philip; and Kimberley: Historical Society of Kimberley and the Northern Cape

Sanders, Peter. 1975. *Moshoeshoe Chief of the Sotho*. London: Heinemann; and Cape Town: David Philip

Schapera, Isaac, ed. 1930. *The Khoisan Peoples of South Africa: Bushmen and Hottentots*. London: Routledge and Kegan Paul

Shillington, Kevin. 1985. *The Colonisation of the Southern Tswana 1870–1900*. Johannesburg: Ravan

Smith, Andrew B., ed. 1995. *Einqualand: Studies of the Orange River Frontier*. Cape Town: University of Cape Town Press

Southey, Joan. 1990. *Footprints in the Karoo: A Story of Farming Life*. Johannesburg: Jonathan Ball

Stow, George W., ed. by George McCall Theal. 1905. *The Native Races of South Africa: A History of the Intrusion of the Hottentots and Bantu into the Hunting Grounds of the Bushmen, the Aborigines of the Country*. London: Swan Sonnenschein; and New York: Macmillan

[Theal edition with source references removed]

Strauss, Teresa. 1979. *War along the Orange: The Korana and the Northern Border Wars of 1868–9 and 1878–9*. Cape: Town: University of Cape Town, Centre for African Studies (Communications No. 1)

Theal, George McCall. 1907. *The Portuguese in South Africa from 1505 to 1795*. London: George Allen and Unwin, reprinted as 'History of South Africa', vol. 2, 3rd edn 1916 and 4th edn 1927 (facsimile reprint, Cape Town: C. Struik, 1964)

Van Onselen, Charles. 1996. *The Seed is Mine: The Life of Kas Maine, a South African Sharecropper, 1894–1965*. New York: Hill and Wang

Vossen, Rainer. 1998. 'Historical classification of Khoe (Central Khoisan) of Southern Africa'. *African Studies* (Johannesburg), 57 (1): 93–106

Willan, Brian. 1990. *Sol Plaatje: South African Nationalist 1876–1932*. London: James Currey [1st edn, London: Heinemann, 1984]

Willcox, A.R. 1986. *Great River: The Story of the Orange River*. Winterton, Natal: Drakensberg Publications

6C. Asia and Australasia

Brisbane, Katharine, ed. 1991. *Entertaining Australia: An Illustrated History*. Sydney: Currency Press

Broome, Richard and Alick Jackomos. 1998. *Sideshow Alley*. St Leonard's, NSW: Allen and Unwin

Fogarty, Jim. 2000. *The Wonders of Wirths: Wirths' Australian Circus 1880–1963*. Oak Flats, NSW: J.B. Books

Poignant, Roslyn. 2004. *Professional Savages: Captive Lives and Western Spectacle* [19th century Aboriginal Australians exhibited overseas]. New Haven: Yale University Press

Ramsland, John, with Mark St Leon. 1993. *Children of the Circus: The Australian Experience*. Springwood, NSW: Butterfly Books

St Leon, Mark. 1981. *The Circus in Australia 1842–1921*. Wahroonga, NSW: Author

St Leon, Mark. 1990. 'An unbelievable lady bareback rider: May Wirth'. *Bandwagon*, 34 (3, May–June): 4–13

St Leon, Mark. 1992. *Index of Australian Show Movements Principally of Circus and Allied Arts 1933–1956*. Glebe, NSW: Author

Waterhouse, Richard. 1990. *From Minstrel Show to Vaudeville: The Australian Popular Stage 1788–1914*. Kensington, NSW: New South Wales University Press

Waterhouse, Richard. 1995. *Private Pleasures, Public Leisure: A History of Australian Popular Culture since 1788*. South Melbourne: Longman Australia

6D. Europe

Altick, Richard David. 1978. *The Shows of London*. Cambridge, Mass.: Harvard University Press

Bancel, Nicolas. 2002. *Zoos humains: XIXe et XXe siècles*. Paris: La Découverte

Bostock, E.H. 1926. *Menageries, Circuses and Theatres*. London: Chapman and Hall

Burke, Thomas. 1941. *English Night-life: From Norman Curfew to Present Black-out*. London: B.T. Batsford

Coogan, Tim Pat. 1991. *Michael Collins: A Biography*. London: Arrow Books (1st edn,

Hutchinson, 1990)

Disher, Maurice Willson. 1938. *Winkles and Champagne: Comedies and Tragedies of the Music Hall*. London: B.T. Batsford

Disher, Maurice Willson. 1942. *Fairs, Circuses and Music Halls*. London: William Collins

Engelman, Todd M. 1990. *Radical Assimilation in English Jewish History 1656–1945*. Bloomington and Indianapolis: Indiana University Press

Ensor, R.C.K. 1936. *England 1870–1914*. Oxford: Clarendon Press (Oxford History of England, 14)

Gerzina, G., ed. 2003. *Black Victorians/Black Victoriana*. New Brunswick, NJ, and London: Rutgers University Press

Green, Benny. 1986. *The Last Empires: A Music Hall Companion*. London: Pavilion Books/ Michael Joseph

Hewison, Robert. 1983. *Footlights: A Hundred Years of Cambridge Comedy*. London: Methuen

Horrall, Andrew. 2001. *Popular Culture in London c.1800–1918: The Transformation of Entertainment*. Manchester: Manchester University Press; and New York: Palgrave

Hyman, Louis. 1972. *The Jews of Ireland from Earliest Times to the Year 1910*. London: Jewish Historical Society of England; and Jerusalem: Israel Universities Press

Lentz, John. 1977. 'The revolt of the freaks'. *Bandwagon*, 21 (5, September–October): 26–9

Lindfors, Bernth. 1983a. 'The Hottentot Venus and other African attractions in nineteenth-century England'. *Australian Drama Studies*, 1 (2, April): 82–104

Lindfors, Bernth. 1985. 'Courting the Hottentot Venus'. *Africa* (Rome), 40: 133–48

Low, Rachel. 1950. *The History of the British Film*, [III] *1914–1918*. London: George Allen and Unwin

Lownie, Andrew. 1995. *John Buchan: The Presbyterian Cavalier*. London: Constable

Mackenzie, J.M., ed. 1986. *Imperialism and Popular Culture*. Manchester: Manchester University Press

Mander, Raymond, and Joe Mitchenson. 1974. *British Music Hall*. London: Gentry Books [1st edn, 1965]

Merriman-Labor, A.B.C. n.d. *Britons through Negro Spectacles: or, A Negro on Britons with a Description of London*. Brixton, London: Imperial and Foreign Co.

O'Donnell, Charles James and Brendan Clifford. 1992. *Ireland in the Great War: The Irish Insurrection of 1916 Set in Its Context of the World War*. Belfast: Athol Books

Pertwee, Bill. 1979. *Pertwee's Promenades and Pierrots: One Hundred Years of Seaside Entertainment*. Newton Abbot, Devon: David and Charles; and North Pomfret, Vermont: Westbridge Books

Parsons, Q.N. 1969. 'The sad story of Klikko'. *Kutlwano* (Gaborone), 7 (2, February): 2–3

Prunty, Jacinta. 1999. *Dublin Slums, 1800–1925: A Study in Urban Geography*. Dublin and Portland, Oregon: Irish Academic Press

Rose, Jonathan. 2001. *The Intellectual Life of the British Working Class*. New Haven: Yale University Press

Russell, Dave. 1987. *Popular Music in England, 1840–1914: A Social History*. Kingston and Montreal: McGill-Queen's University Press

Samuels, Andrew. 1995. Letter re Carl Jung. *London Review of Books*, 17 (10, 25 May): 4–5

Scott, Harold. 1946. *The Early Doors: Origins of the Music-Hall*. London: Nicholson and Watson

Shephard, Ben. 1986. 'Showbiz imperialism: the case of Peter Lobengula', in Mackenzie (1986), pp. 94–112

Shephard, Ben. 2003. *Kitty and the Prince.* Johannesburg: Jonathan Ball

Strickland, Debra Higgs. 2000. 'Monsters and Christian enemies'. *History Today,* 50 (2, February 2000): 45–51

Strother, Z.S. 1999. 'Display of the body Hottentot' in Lindfors (1999), pp. 1-61

Taylor, A.J.P. 1965. *English History 1914–1945.* Oxford: Clarendon Press (Oxford History of England, 15)

Tyrwhitt-Drake, Garrard. 1946. *The English Circus and Fair Ground.* London: Methuen

Waites, Bernard, Tony Bennett and Graham Martin, comps. 1982. *Popular Culture: Past and Present.* London: Croom Helm/Open University Press (reprint from *Literature and History*, 1, 1975)

Walvin, James. 1978. *Leisure and Society 1830–1950.* London: Longman (Themes in British History, ed. J. Stevenson),

Zangwill, Shirley. 2001. 'Onward the toothbrush brigade: George Cunningham, pioneer of preventive dentistry'. History of Dentistry Research Group <www.rcpsg.ac.uk/ hdrg/2001Oct7.htm, accessed 3 August 2007

6E. America

Adams, Bluford. 1997. *E Pluribus Barnum: The Great Showman and the Making of U.S. Popular Culture.* Minneapolis: University of Minnesota Press

Adams, Rachel. 2001. *Sideshow U.S.A.: Freaks and the American Cultural Imagination.* Chicago: University of Chicago Press

Bakner, Andrew J. 1973. 'Side show attractions'. *Bandwagon*, 17 (6, November–December): 35–8

Blume, Harvey. 1999. 'Ota Benga and the Barnum perplex', in Lindfors (1999), pp. 188–202

Bogdan, Robert. 1988. *Freak Show: Presenting Human Oddities for Amusement and Profit.* Chicago: University of Chicago Press

Braathen, Sverre O. and Faye O. 1973. 'They made it click' [i.e. 20th century railroad circus bosses]. *Bandwagon*, 17 (2, March–April): 20–8

Bradbury, Joseph T. 1975. 'The Gumpertz era of Ringling Bros. and Barnum & Bailey 1933–37'. *The White Tops* (Circus Fans Association of America), (January–February): 27–8

Bradford, Phillips Verner and Harvey Blume. 1993. *Ota Benga the Pygmy in the Zoo: An African Odyssey in Savage Turn-of-the-Century America.* New York: Dell Publishing (Delta Book) (1st edn, New York: St Martin's Press, 1992)

Bradna, Fred, with Hartzell Spence. 1952. *The Big Top: My Forty Years with The Greatest Show on Earth, including A Circus Hall of Fame.* New York: Simon and Schuster

Chindahl, George L. 1959. *A History of the Circus in America.* Caldwell, Idaho: Caxton Printers

Cook, James W. 1996. 'Of men, missing links, and nondescripts: the strange career of P.T. Barnum's "What Is It?" exhibition', in Thompson (1996), pp. 139–57

Davis, Janet. 2001. 'The life of Tiny Kline and the evolution of twentieth-century American mass culture'. *Bandwagon*, 45 (23, May–June): 4–8

Davis, Janet. 2002. *The Circus Age: Culture and Society under the American Big Top.* Chapel Hill, NC: University of North Carolina Press

Drimmer, Frederick. 1973. *Very Special People: The Struggles, Loves and Triumphs of Human Oddities.* New York: Amjon Publishers

Dulles, Foster Rhea. 1952. *America Learns to Play: A History of Popular Recreation 1607–1940.* New York: Peter Smith

Durant, John and Alice. 1957. *Pictorial History of the American Circus.* New York: A.S. Barnes

Fiedler, Leslie. 1978. *Freaks: Myths and Images of the Secret Self.* New York: Simon and Schuster

Gilbert, Douglas. 1963. *American Vaudeville: Its Life and Times.* New York: Dover Publications; and London: Constable

Hammarstrom, David Lewis. 1992. *Big Top Boss: John Ringling North and the Circus.* Urbana, Illinois, and Chicago: University of Illinois Press

Harris, Neil. 1973. *Humbug: The Art of P.T. Barnum.* Chicago: University of Chicago Press

Hasson, Robert. 1980. 'A very turbulent season, 1938'. *Bandwagon*, 24 (5, September): 22–34

Hilliar, W.J. 1918. 'The circus side show'. *Billboard, the Show World Encyclopedia*, 30 (5, 23 March): 18 and 166

Hoffman, Malvina. 1936. *Heads and Tales.* New York: Charles Scribner's Sons

Hoffman, Malvina. 1965. *Yesterday is Tomorrow: A Personal History.* New York: Crown Publishers

Hynd, Alan. 1945. 'Smythe of the side show'. *Coronet* (Chicago: Esquire), 17 (4, February): 46–7 and 78

Jando, Dominique. 1991. 'Lillian Leitzel and Dolly Jacobs: two queens of the air, forty-five years apart'. *Bandwagon*, 35 (5, September–October): 18–23

Johnston, Alva. 1934. 'Side-show people: III'. *New Yorker*, 28 April

Kasson, John F. 1978. *Amusing the Million: Coney Island at the Turn of the Century.* New York: Hill and Wang (American Century series)

Lentz, John. 1988. 'Merle Evans: his final interview'. *Bandwagon*, 32 (1, January–February): 21–3

Lewiston, Harry, comp. Jerry Holtman. 1968. *Freak Show Man: The Autobiography of Harry Lewiston as Told to Jerry Holtman.* Los Angeles: Holloway House Publishing

Lindfors, Bernth. 1983b. 'Circus Africans'. *Journal of American Culture*, 6 (2): 9–14

Lott, Eric. 1995. *Love and Theft: Blackface Minstrelsy and the American Working Class.* New York: Oxford University Press

McCulloch, Edo. 2000. *Good Old Coney Island: A Sentimental Journey into the Past.* New York: Fordham University Press [1st edn, 1957]

McKennon, Joe. 1979. *Horse Dung Trail: Saga of the American Circus.* Sarasota, Florida: Carnival Publishers, with supplementary *Index (and A Few Remarks)* 1979

May, Earl Chaplin. 1963. *The Circus from Rome to Ringling.* New York: Dover Publications; and London: Constable [1st edn, Duffield and Green, 1932]

Morden, Ethan. 1978. *That Jazz! An Idiosyncratic Social History of the American Twenties.* New York: G.P. Putnam's Sons

North, Henry Ringling and Alden Hatch. 1960. *The Circus Kings: Our Ringling Family Story.* Garden City, New York: Doubleday

Peacock, Shane. 1990. 'Farini the Great'. *Bandwagon*, 34 (5, September–October 1990), 13–20

Peacock, Shane. 1995. *The Great Farini: The High-Wire Life of William Hunt.* Toronto: Viking

Pfening, Fred D., Jnr. 1972. 'Masters of the steel arena'. *Bandwagon*, 16 (3, May–June): 4–17

Pfening, Fred D., Jnr. 1985. 'Side shows and banner lines'. *Bandwagon*, 29 (2, March–April): 16–22

Plowden, Gene. 1967. *Those Amazing Ringlings and Their Circus*. New York: Bonanza Books and Crown Publishers

Plowden, Gene. 1971. *Merle Evans: Maestro of the Circus*. Miami: E.A. Seemann Publishing

Rydell, Robert W. 1984. *All the World's a Fair: Visions of Empire at American International Expositions, 1876–1916*. Chicago: University of Chicago Press

Rydell, Robert W. 1999. 'African shows at America's World's Fairs, 1893–1940', in Lindfors (1999), pp. 135–55

Rydell, Robert W., John E. Findling and Kimberly D. Pelle. 2000. *Fair America: World's Fairs in the United States*. Washington, DC: Smithsonian Institution Press

St Leon, Mark. 1990. 'An unbelievable lady bareback rider: May Wirth'. *Bandwagon*, 34 (3, May–June): 4–13

Saxon, Arthur H. 1989. *P.T. Barnum: The Legend and the Man*. New York: Columbia University Press

Sonnenberg, C.A. 'Red'. 2002. 'Old time circus fixers: legal adjusters'. *Bandwagon*, 46 (5, September–October 2002): 14–16

Taylor, Robert Lewis. 1956. *Center Ring: The People and the Circus*. Garden City, New York: Doubleday

Thayer, Stuart. 1972. 'A note on the decline of the [American railroad] circus'. *Bandwagon*, 16 (4): 17

Truzzi, Marcello. 1968. 'The decline of the American circus: the shrinkage of an institution', in Marcello Truzzi, *Sociology in Everyday Life*. Englewood Cliffs, NJ: Prentice-Hall

Twitchell, James B. 1992. *Carnival Culture: The Trashing of Taste in America*. New York: Columbia University Press

Waterman, Guy. 1959. 'Ragtime', in Nat Hentoff and Albert J. McCarthy, eds. 1959. *Jazz: New Perspectives on the History of Jazz by Twelve of the World's Foremost Jazz Critics and Scholars*. New York: Holt, Rinehart and Winston/Da Capo Press, pp. 53–7

Weeks, David C. 1993 *Ringling: The Florida Years, 1911–1936* [i.e. life of John Ringling]. Gainesville, Florida: University Press of Florida

6F. Reference Works

Alumni Cantabrigiensis: A Biographical Listing of All Known Students ... to 1900, ed. J.A. Venn. 1947. Cambridge: Cambridge University Press, part 2, vol. 2

Chambers Biographical Dictionary, ed. Melanie Parry. 1997. Edinburgh: Chambers Harrap

Defense Intelligence Agency. 1992. *Gazetteer of South Africa, Volume 4 (S–Z)*. Washington DC: Defense Mapping Agency, 2nd edn [copy in South African Public Library, Cape Town]

Evans, Ivor H. 1981. *Brewer's Dictionary of Phrase and Fable*. London: Cassell

Kilgarriff, Michael. 1998. *Grace, Beauty and Banjos: Peculiar Lives and Stage Times of Musical Hall and Variety Artistes*. London: Oberon Books

Mayer, Frank J., comp. 1936. *Ringling Bros. Barnum and Bailey Combined Circus Route Book for the Season 1936*. Joseph Mayer Publisher [copy in Circus World Museum, Baraboo: Route Books #67]

Nienaber, G.S. and P.E. Raper, comps. 1983. *Hottentot (Khoekhoen) Place Names*. Durban:

Butterworth Publishers; and Pretoria: Human Sciences Research Council, Onomastic Research Centre (Southern African Place Names 1)

Ogden, Tom, comp. 1993. *Two Hundred Years of the American Circus: From Aba-Daba to Zoppa-Zavata Troupe.* New York: Facts on File

The [Oxford] Dictionary of National Biography 1951–1956, eds. E.T. Williams and Helen M. Palmer. 1971. London: Oxford University Press

Raper, Peter E., comp. 1987. *Dictionary of Southern African Place Names.* Johannesburg: Lowry Publishers

Slide, Anthony, comp. 1994. *The Encyclopedia of Vaudeville.* Westport, Conn.: Greenwood Press

South African Almanack and Reference Book 1911–1912. 1911. Cape Town: Argus Printing and Publishing

Toole-Stott, R., comp. 1958–62. *Circus and Allied Arts: A World Bibliography 1500–1962.* Derby, England: Harpur and Sons (vol. 1, 1958; vol. 2, 1960; vol. 3, 1962)

ACKNOWLEDGEMENTS

THIS BOOK WOULD not have been possible without the generosity of Barbara Cook de Romain, and her mother, the late Evelyn Joyce Cook, who lived with Franz Taibosh for a decade and provided me with memories and copies of documents and photographs. Robert K. Hitchcock and Bernth Lindfors pushed me into extending my research into a book. My original inspiration came from two great teachers, George Shepperson and the late Christopher Fyfe at the University of Edinburgh. I also wish to acknowledge scholarly and personal debts: in *Africa*, to Frikkie Aucamp, Fiona Barbour, Henry Bredekamp, Liesel Hubbard, Pete Kallaway, Martin Legassick, Carl and Emlitia Loock, Susie Newton-King, Sven Ouzman, Nigel Penn, C.W. Roberts, Karim Sadr, Garth Sampson, Judy Seidman, Alinah Segobye, Dibora Taaibos, Anthony Traill, Lance van Sittert and Kate Angier; in *Europe*, John and Charlotte Aldridge, the late Paul Edwards, Jan-Bart and Gertie Gewald, Jeffery Green, Hugh Macmillan, Shula Marks, the late Isaac Schapera, Ben Shephard, Kevin and Pippa Shillington, the late Laurens van der Post, and Lucia van der Post; in *Australia*, Robin and Marguerite Derricourt, Norman and Peggy Etherington, Cherry Gertzel, the late Marilyn and Wayne Levy, Mark St Leon, John and Sue Taylor, and Richard Waterhouse; in *America*, Fred Dahlinger Jnr., Jim and Josi Denbow, Rob Gordon, Gay and Heinz Klug, Paul Landau and his student Roger Levine, Katha and Tom Levenson, Phil Steenkamp Junior.

For research facilities, I wish to acknowledge the help of staff at many institutions around the world. In *Africa*, the Cape Town Land Deeds Office, the Johannesburg Public Library (Africana Library), the Killie Campbell Africana Library in Durban, Kimberley Public Library, the McGregor Memorial Museum (library) in Kimberley, the National Library of South Africa in Cape Town, the South African Museum (library) in Cape Town, the South African National Archives (Cape Town Archives Repository and Pretoria Main Depot), the University of Botswana Library, the University of Cape Town Administration Archives and (Jagger) African

Studies Library, the University of Pretoria Library, and the University of the Witwatersrand (Cullen) Library. In *Asia and Australia*, the Singapore National Library, the Australian National Library in Canberra, the Performing Arts Museum and the Victoria State Library at Melbourne, the Western Australia State Library in Perth. In *Europe*, the Bibliothèque Nationale in Paris (consulted by Barbara Cook de Romain), the British Newspaper Library at Colindale, the Duckworth Laboratory (Department of Biological Anthropology) at Cambridge, Emmanuel College Library at Cambridge (assistant archivist: Janet Morris), the Institute of Commonwealth Studies Library in London, the National Archives of Ireland in Dublin, the Public Record Office (National Archives of England and Wales) at Kew, the Registrar of Births and Deaths in Dublin, the General Registry for Births Deaths and Marriages (England and Wales) in London, Rhodes House Library at Oxford, the School of Oriental and African Studies Library in London, the Theatre Museum Library at Covent Garden, the University of Edinburgh Library and Centre of African Studies, the University of London (Senate House) Library. In *North America*, the American Museum of Natural History (Anthropology Division: archivist Belinda Kaye, anthropologists Thomas R. Miller and Enid Schildkraut) in New York City, the British Columbia Provincial Archives in Victoria, the Circus Museum World Library at Baraboo, the Field Natural History Museum at Chicago, the Harvard University (Peabody) Library in Cambridge, the Hertzberg Circus Collection (then) at the San Antonio Public Library, the Library of Congress and the Smithsonian Institution Archives and Special Collections (National Anthropological Archives) in Washington, DC, the Nebraska State Historical Society Library at Lincoln, the John and Mable Ringling Museum Library at Sarasota, the University of California at Berkeley Library, the University of Texas (Harry Ransome) Library at Austin, the University of Wisconsin (Music) Library and the Wisconsin State Historical Society Library at Madison.

I am grateful to the University of Botswana for sending me, and to the University of California at Berkeley, the Institute of Commonwealth Studies in London, and the Research School of Humanities at the Australian National University, for receiving me on sabbatical leave. I must also thank seminars at the University of Edinburgh, the School of Oriental and African Studies in London, and the African Studies Centre at Leiden.

Finally, my sincerest thanks go to Russell Martin and Maggie Davey at Jacana Media for everything they have done in commissioning and originating this book. For assistance in locating and copying illustrations I thank the staffs of the Aldridge Press in London, the American Museum of Natural History in New York, the Circus World Museum at Baraboo, the Duckworth Laboratory at Cambridge, the Field

Museum at Chicago, and the Harry Ransom Library at Austin, as well as Barbara Cook de Romain, Bernth Lindfors and Robert Gordon for providing privately owned illustrations.

London & Gaborone, January 2009

Scattering red earth from Africa on the grave of Franz Taibosh.
(Prof. Robert J. Gordon)

INDEX